Sojourners and Settlers

The presence of Islam in America
is symbolized by the open hand (*khamsa*),
which represents the five precepts of Islam
and offers defense against evil in the Arab world,
and in the Yemeni community of
South Dearborn, Michigan.
Jonathan Friedlander.

Sojourners and Settlers

THE YEMENI IMMIGRANT EXPERIENCE

Edited by

Jonathan Friedlander

Ron Kelley, Associate Editor
Sheila Pinkel, Photo Editor

University of Utah Press
Salt Lake City

G. E. von Grunebaum Center for Near Eastern Studies
University of California at Los Angeles

Jonathan Friedlander, Project Director
Ron Kelley, Associate Editor
Jon Swanson, Consultant
Sheila Pinkel, Photo Editor

Library of Congress Cataloging-in-Publication Data

Sojourners and settlers.

Based on a traveling photograph exhibit held at the
Salt Lake Art Center and other locations.
Bibliography: p.
1. Yemenite Americans—Exhibitions. 2. Immigrants—
United States—Exhibitions. 3. Yemen—Emigration and
immigration—Exhibitions. 4. United States—
Emigration and immigration—Exhibitions. I. Friedlander,
Jonathan. II. Salt Lake Art Center.
E184.Y44S64   1988   973′.049275332   88-14377
ISBN 0-87480-292-X

Photo essays by:
Tony Maine, Detroit, Michigan, 1982–83
Milton Rogovin, Lackawanna, New York, 1977

Photo documentation by:
Jonathan Friedlander, Detroit, Michigan, 1979
Nikki R. Keddie, San°a, Central Highlands, Yemen, 1983
Ron Kelley, San Joaquin Valley, California, 1982–87
Shalom Staub, Atlantic Avenue, Brooklyn, New York, 1981
Thomas B. Stevenson, °Amran, Yemen, 1979, 1986–87
Jon C. Swanson, South Central Yemen, 1984
Manfred W. Wenner, North West Yemen, 1982, 1984

Snapshots taken by Yemeni workers in the San Joaquin
Valley, California, were given to Ron Kelley for inclusion.

Dedicated to my parents
Aryeh and Shoshana Friedlander

This publication is based on a traveling exhibition of photographs by Ron Kelley, Milton Rogovin, Tony Maine, Jon Swanson, and Nikki Keddie. To date, the photos have been on display at the Salt Lake Art Center, Minnesota Museum of Art, Detroit Public Library, Photo Center Gallery (New York), Ripley Center-Smithsonian Institution (Washington, D.C.), Nexus Contemporary Art Center (Atlanta), Lowie Museum (Berkeley), and the University of California, Los Angeles, Museum of Cultural History. The collection is scheduled to be exhibited at the Center for Creative Photography (Tucson), in Austin and Miami, and in Europe and the Middle East.

Contents

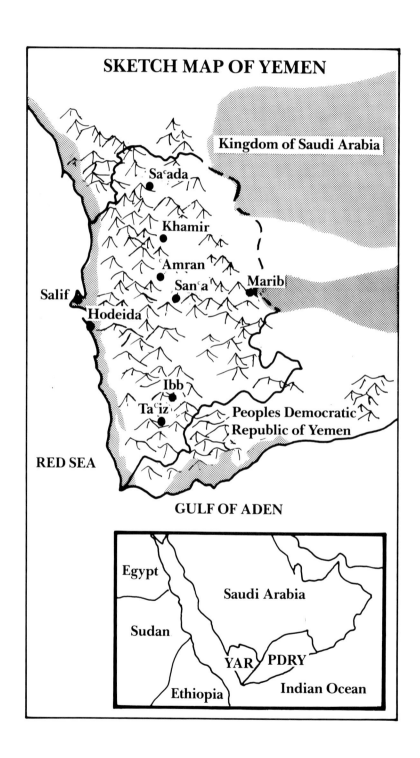

SKETCH MAP OF YEMEN

Kingdom of Saudi Arabia

Saʿada

Khamir

Amran

Sanʿa

Marib

Salif

Hodeida

RED SEA

Ibb

Taʿiz

Peoples Democratic
Republic of Yemen

GULF OF ADEN

Egypt

Sudan

Saudi Arabia

Ethiopia

YAR   PDRY

Indian Ocean

Introduction

I first became aware of Yemenis and the labor migration phenomenon during research travels to Detroit and California's San Joaquin Valley. Although visual artists, literary figures, and scholars have been documenting and analyzing these industrial and agricultural environments for more than half a century, the presence of Yemeni workers and Arab culture set against the awesome sight of the River Rouge automobile complex, or the endless rows of vineyards, fruit trees, and asparagus fields, still demands explication and elaboration. The necessity of seeking work abroad has extended to the remotest villages in Yemen and the Arab world. On the receiving end, the United States has employed immigrant labor to develop its economy since the mid-nineteenth century, absorbing the influx of mostly European nationals. The Yemenis are relative newcomers to America. After a millennium of isolation, they have suddenly been swept up by the tide of regional and international migration, which has transformed the character and history of Yemeni society and culture.

The strategy based on remittances channeled back to the mother country continues to be at the heart of the labor-intensive migration, for Yemenis and other Middle Easterners. Political, military, and cultural variables have also figured into the economic equation. In the case of Egypt, its sojourn workers in Libya may be victimized in the event of hostilities. Conflict in the Persian Gulf gave impetus to the migration of Egyptians to Iraq, where many work in agriculture and on infrastructure projects, replacing Iraqi men mobilized in the war against Iran. Ethnic and intracultural tensions, complicated by economic competition and distrust, underscore the presence of West Bank and Gaza Strip Palestinian day laborers in Israeli cities. Similarly, the large communities of North African and Turkish workers permanently settled in France and Germany have often felt the brunt of economic recession, ethnocentrism, and overt racism in their host countries

The case of Yemeni migration is extreme owing to its magnitude, estimated at one-fourth of Yemen's adult male population. Many scholars have pointed to the dangers inherent in the heavy reliance on remittances, which account for one-third of Yemen's Gross National Product. The eventual depletion or any sizable reduction of such funds may send Yemen into an economic downslide, which could be averted only by long-term development of indigenous industries and crafts, arduous and costly efforts to tap Yemen's newly discovered petroleum reserves, and most likely, by massive infusions of foreign aid. The effects of the enormous drain of manpower over the past twenty years may already have caused considerable damage to Yemen's fragile agriculture and created a chronic dependency on imports, even for basic sustenance. These conditions alone should give cause for serious concern to Yemen's political hierarchy and to Yemeni citizens at home and abroad.

Signs of economic vulnerability are already evident in the United States, where large numbers of Yemenis and other workers have lost their jobs in the automobile and steel factories. The size of the Yemeni farmworker community in California has also dwindled, as many Yemeni villagers cannot afford or find it unprofitable to travel 10,000 miles in search of employment. In considering the earlier prevalence of sojourning and the current phase, which has witnessed many workers returning to Yemen or settling in the United States, it is important to pose the following queries: What is the manner of adaptation of returning migrants to development, social change, and the new economic realities in Yemen? Conversely, how do Yemeni cultural traditions and Islamic religious values fare in this secular society, where emphasis on individualism, materialism, career, and financial success define and categorize all levels of social relations and interaction? Indeed, how do Yemenis, and many other Americans for that matter, reconcile their expectations of a "share of the pie" in the face of limited technological skills and education? This collection attempts to address some of these issues by presenting a synthesis of work by social scientists, humanities scholars, photographers, and critics. For the first time, the migratory experience can also be viewed from the vantage point of the Yemeni workers themselves, through candid interviews and their own snapshots.

The visual component has been an integral part of this project from the outset, when the initial photography began in California's San Joaquin Valley. The coverage was extended to Detroit, Buffalo, and New York City, and, simultaneously, to the Yemen Arab Republic. Together with the resultant photography—by most of the contributors to this volume—the collection of writings has emerged as a distinct methodological study of immigration, encompassing historical narrative, quantitative and political analyses, anthropological interpretation of ritual and behavior, folklore and the oral tradition, and social and photographic criticism. It should be noted, however, that the study focuses exclusively on the Yemeni and American rural and urban environments that have been at the core of the migration over the last three decades. It is neither a comprehensive portrait of the Yemen Arab Republic nor does it address the experiences of Yemenis not directly engaged in labor migration.

This collection was not intended as a supplement to the traveling photographic exhibit of the same name but will accompany it for the remaining part of its extensive American and international tour. It is hoped that beyond the span of the exhibition program the publication will remain as a permanent textual and visual record of a historic phenomenon which has affected millions of Yemeni and other Arab and Muslim workers, along with laborers from the Balkans and Southern Europe, Latin America, Asia and Oceana, Africa, and the Caribbean. The social, economic, and political forces unleashed by such immense displacement of people worldwide have yet to be felt fully by the individual societies and the international community.

The present volume owes much to Ron Kelley, my associate in this endeavor, for his contributions as photographer, writer, consultant, and facilitator. His commitment and resolution in the face of numerous obstacles and much frustration have inspired the creation of a rich body of work on agricultural migrant labor. Jon Swanson was a critical link to Yemen and the South Dearborn Arab community. His advice and expert fieldwork helped formulate and strengthen the project objectives and their implementation. The writers and photographers who were kind enough to share their work and knowledge deserve much credit for enriching this volume. I am indebted to our Yemeni friends in the United States and Yemen for allowing us to make their acquaintance in the spirit of honesty and friendship. In particular, I want to thank Mohamed Abdullah, foreman at the Delano camp and expert grape cultivator, as well as Marko Zaninovich Incorporated, for making it possible to conduct the photography in California. I also wish to express my gratitude to the staffs of the Yemen Center for Research and Studies (Sanᶜa) and the American Institute for Yemeni Studies for their assistance and support.

The work leading to the publication of *Sojourners and Settlers* was sponsored by the G. E. von Grunebaum Center for Near Eastern Studies, University of California, Los Angeles, with support from the California Council for the Humanities, the Mobil Corporation, the ARCO Foundation, and the UCLA Office of International Studies and Overseas Programs, under the leadership of John Hawkins. I also want to acknowledge Sheila Pinkel, who shaped the multitude of images into a cohesive and powerful visual statement; Kathleen Lewis for her careful copyediting of the manuscript; Marina Preussner and Anita Colby for editorial assistance; Rodger Reynolds for production and layout management; and Norma Mikkelsen for her encouragement, patience, and foresight. Most of all, I am grateful to Carolisa for her love and understanding that sustained me over the years.

Jonathan Friedlander

The Yemen Arab Republic (North Yemen): History and Society

NIKKI R. KEDDIE
Department of History
University of California, Los Angeles

GENERAL FEATURES OF YEMENI SOCIETY

Even more than many other parts of the Arabian Peninsula, North Yemen kept relatively isolated from Western influences until its republican revolution of 1962. Beneath the surface, to be sure, Yemen interacted with the West, beginning in ancient times, with the growth of Yemeni coffee trade before 1500, reviving and continuing through two periods of Ottoman Turkish rule and Yemeni independence under the Zaidi imams. The Ottomans brought in some modern arms and military organization, while European powers entered into trade in the Red Sea and beyond. In the twentieth century, such influences accelerated, despite the attempts of Yemen's rulers, the imams (leaders of the Zaidi sect of Shiʿi Islam), to isolate Yemen as much as possible. For all the impact of the West, and the earlier changes in Yemeni society since the rise of Islam in the early seventh century and its dominance in Yemen soon thereafter, certain general features of Yemeni society reappear in all, or virtually all, periods since the seventh century A.D.

In pre-Islamic and even very ancient times, Yemeni social structure may have been rather different, and we know that there was important irrigation agriculture and even major dams in areas that are now virtual desert. It appears likely that both nat-

ural and human factors—such as salination of irrigated soil, deforestation, lack of maintenance, silting up, and overgrazing—led to the decline in settled agriculture. Well before the rise of Islam, Yemen had changed into a country where agriculture was no longer carried out in the mainly eastern desert region, but in part in the lowland Tihama, the hot region bordering the Red Sea, and especially in the inland highlands concentrated to the north. These highlands and mountains required labor-intensive terracing and care and also, by their difficulty of access, discouraged strong central government and encouraged the persistence of a form of social organization usually called tribal, although tribes also existed in the east and in the Tihama. "Tribal" is used herein to mean a form of political organization based on real or fictive genealogical ties and lacking the bureaucratic structure of a state. In much of the Middle East, tribes are mainly pastoral nomads, but in Yemen they are mainly settled farmers; indeed, to some Yemenis the word qabili (tribal) means little more than a settled farmer, though the armed tribespeople concentrated in the north might deny this name to unarmed farmers in the south. In Yemen, therefore, tribal organization has no necessary relation to a pastoral nomadic mode of production, but relates rather to a kinship organization that claims significant autonomy, includ-

1. Dufur is typical of the highland Yemeni villages whose economies rely heavily on labor migration to Saudi Arabia, Western Europe, and the United States. *Manfred Wenner.*

ing an independent fighting role and a respect in practice for tribal customary legal systems that may be in conflict with the Islamic Shariᶜa.

The major role of tribes, and notably warlike tribes, in Yemen until 1962, and in some cases even today, is related both to the difficulty of centralizing Yemen—and hence the need for an alternative mode of local organization and protection—and to the relative lack of modernization in the country until very recently. Modernizing rulers in the third world, especially since the early nineteenth century, have concentrated on building centralized armies and bureaucracies in order to gain political and financial control over their countries. This is a process that is not yet complete in Yemen, so that the tribes are still armed and sometimes fight the central government—at times in the name of a political cause (more often of the right than of the left) that they share with nontribal peoples.

In addition to the prominence of tribal structures and fighting, observers have often noted in Yemen a system of endogamous classes or "castes" that seems at variance with the theoretically egalitarian structure of Islam. Although different Yemeni regions rank Yemen's largely endogamous hierarchies in various ways, it seems clear that at or near the top are two religious groups, the sayyids, or descendants of the Prophet Muhammad, and the qadis, a word that elsewhere means religious judges, but in Yemen normally means those from certain religiously educated families. Tribal leaders also have high status. Below these groups are various townspeople and peasants, with some crafts and trades having low status; at the bottom is a group known as *akhdam*, or servants, who undertake various forms of menial work and entertainment and appear to be at least partially of African origin. While the republic discourages such distinctions, they are not dead. Although some ranked endogamous or occupational groups have been found in other Arab Muslim societies, they have been more pervasive in North and South Yemen than in other Arab countries.

While this system of ranked endogamous groups is losing its importance, especially as some men of middling origin occupy important government posts, it continues to play a role in choosing marriage partners and in some social relations. The origins of this system are unclear, though pre-Islamic, Indian, and African influences are sometimes adduced. Like tribalism, caste-like forms of organization seem to flourish in societies where centralization is rare and difficult; in the absence of a central government and generally recognized legal system, it may be easiest to

organize society by keeping people in their clear economic and social places as defined by birth. Even in many noncaste societies, occupation has tended to be inherited, but the lack of centralized government and institutions may encourage a customary ordering of relations between occupational groups that in part replaces a legal statement of these relations. As in the case of India, the structure in Yemen was more rigid in theory than in practice, and one anthropologist has noted theoretically high-ranking sayyids who are in fact poor townsmen or farmers.[1]

Since the coming of the republic in 1962, both tribalism and endogamous ranking have declined in the face of demographic mobility, new socioeconomic structures, a growing national army, bureaucracy, communications, and national educational and legal systems, but neither of these older forms of organization has died out. Tribalism in particular, especially in areas with grievances where the tribes have military strength, has continued to be a counterforce to the centralizing republic, and tribes have mounted various armed struggles, in addition to their role, mainly on the conservative Saudi-backed side, in the civil war of the 1960s. The receipt by northern tribal leaders of money and arms from the Saudis and from Yemeni factions seems to have led to an increase in their power in the years after the 1962 revolution.

HISTORY

Pre-Islamic Yemen was noted not only for its complex irrigation systems and ancient empires but also for its role on the trade routes from the ancient Mediterranean to the Far East. Yemen supplied myrrh and frankincense, and was an intermediary for Eastern goods. Once the Romans discovered how to use the monsoon winds to sail to India, however, and found that many of the goods they got from Yemen originated further east, the importance of what the Romans called "Arabia Felix" or "Happy Arabia" declined. Nevertheless, Yemen remains today the most fertile and populous part of the Arabian Peninsula.

To Yemen has been ascribed a key role in the domestication of the camel, which was of central importance in the overland caravan trade in many of the arid areas of the world. Christians, Zoroastrians, and Jews were numerous in Yemen before the rise of Islam. The Jews remained until their mass exodus in 1948–49. They were largely craftspeople, though also farmers, and were responsible for some of Yemen's best metalwork as well as more utilitarian crafts.

Shortly before the rise of Islam, Yemen was invaded by Ethiopia, and then it became a satrapy of

2. The ancient city of Barakish once stood on the spice and incense route which linked Yemen to India, East Africa, northern Arabia, the Mediterranean basin, and Europe. Recollections of Yemen's history (Noah's ark is said to have rested in mountainous San꞉a) and of Yemen's important role in the rise of Islam form a repertoire that connects workers abroad to their ancestral homeland. *Jon Swanson.*

the Persian (Sasanian) Empire. The last Persian satrap converted to Islam during the life of Muhammad. After Muhammad's death in 632, Yemen was among the areas that had seen its allegiance to him as personal and had to be brought back to Islam by the so-called wars of apostasy.

After Muhammad's death there developed the "party" or Shi꞉a of Ali, which said that Ali, Muhammad's cousin and son-in-law, should succeed to the caliphate, or leadership of the Muslim community. In time, three different branches of the Shi꞉a developed, similar mainly in saying that the rightful leader of the Muslim community, whom they called the imam, must be a descendant of Ali. Those who today form the great majority are called Twelvers or imamis, found especially in Iran, Iraq, Lebanon, South Asia, and the Gulf. Twelvers were never important in Yemen. Significant in Yemen have been, first, the Zaidis or Fivers, the most moderate group of Shi꞉is, whose law is very close to Sunni law, and who are named after their fifth imam, Zaid. This group says that the imam should be elected from among the sayyids descended from Ali and Fatima, based on his high qualifications in specified areas. While this theory may seem reasonable and "protodemocratic," in practice it encouraged, especially in Yemen, continual

disputes over the Imamate. The other Shi꞉i group prominent in medieval Yemen and still found there in small numbers are the Ismailis or Seveners, in medieval times considered to be the most radical of Shi꞉i groups, though they were in Yemen mostly representatives of the nonradical Fatimid dynasty that ruled Egypt after 969 A.D.

Some followers of Zaid, the fifth imam, came from among those who fled to East Africa after Zaid was killed in rebellion. More important was the coming in the late ninth century of the Imam Yahya, known as al-Hadi ila al-Haqq, who established the Zaidi Imamate in Yemen, which continued, though often with little power, until 1962. Al-Hadi came in from the Hijaz at the invitation of a tribe. According to an Arabian custom going back to pre-Islamic times, a leading member of a holy lineage was eligible to mediate tribal and local disputes (it was for such mediation that Muhammad was called to Medina in 622 A.D.). Al-Hadi's leadership came to be accepted by other tribes, and he set up the Rassid dynasty, which in some sense lasted until 1962 with the last imam, Badr, who was the 111th of the dynasty. This continuity often masked powerlessness, however (as with many Abbasid caliphs or Japanese emperors). Many local tribes continued to rule themselves or to form autonomous federations, and they might also have arrangements called Hijra (somewhat like Muhammad's Hijra to Medina in 622) with other holy men from among the sayyids, who might run small theocracies. In Yemen, unlike some other tribal areas, the sayyids were armed and often fought in battles, so their role was not purely one of law and mediation.

But the Rassid imams spread neither their sect nor their rule to all Yemen. The south during most of the Islamic period was dominated by the Shafi‘i legal school of majority (Sunni) Islam, and the Zaidi-Shafi‘i distinction (spoken of in Yemen in those terms, and not as Shi‘i-Sunni) remains the crucial one in Yemen today. Also, Ismaili Shi‘is came to Yemen and made converts and conquests at the same time as the Zaidi imams. The Ismailis in Yemen also got tribal support and were for a time stronger than the Zaidis. They underwent sectarian splits over the centuries, and the remaining Ismailis have some doctrines not shared by the major Ismaili groups elsewhere.

Members of the first Ismaili dynasty in Yemen were called the Sulayhids, and in the eleventh century A.D. they eclipsed the Zaidis and united Yemen, with a commitment to the Egyptian Fatimid imams. The Ismailis were reputed to be more egalitarian toward women than were Zaidis or Sunnis, and this is reflected in the long rule of the Sulayhid Queen Arwa, the wife and widow of a paralyzed head of state. She refused to deal with a new husband, became revered as a peaceable ruler, and died at age ninety-two in 1137 A.D. The locally based economy and tribalism were, as usual, forces leading to a decline of the centralized state. The Ismaili Fatimids made no strong efforts at conversion to their sect.

The Zaidi Imamate, which ruled concurrently in the northern highlands and had been brought in by the tribes, remained dependent on them. The tribes who called in al-Hadi had wanted a prestigious mediator, but al-Hadi tried to impose on them as well as on townspeople a rigid code of Islamic behavior. Al-Hadi's biographer tells how he used to tour the marketplace to insure that this code, including veiling, was enforced.[2] He tried to tax tribespeople and to recruit them in holy war against non-Zaidis. Over time, however, tribesmen came to accept at least the theoretical sovereignty of imams and the aristocracy of the sayyids. But it was several centuries before the Zaidi rulers became the decisive political force in Yemen.

After the Sulayhid-Ismaili decline, much of Yemen was ruled by dynasties that also came from Egypt or from north of Arabia, notably the Egyptian Ayyubids and then the Rasulids, who ruled most of Yemen for over two centuries, becoming the most durable Sunni regime in south Arabia. Under them there was a revival of Gulf and Red Sea trade, and agriculture was encouraged. The Rasulid period set up structures that continued to be important, especially the division between Shafi‘i nontribal southern Yemen and the Zaidi tribal north, where the Zaidi imams continued, isolated from the trade and prosperity of the south. With the decline of the Rasulids, the imams spread over all of today's Yemen Arab Republic; but in the period 1539–1635, the Ottomans conquered and ruled Yemen. After their expulsion, Yemen was left on its own until the nineteenth century, when there was first an Egyptian invasion and then an Ottoman occupation beginning in 1848 and moving to the highlands from 1879 to 1919.

The British took Aden in 1839 and spread their influence to Aden's hinterland thereafter. Today's division between the People's Democratic Republic (South Yemen) and the Yemen Arab Republic (North Yemen) reflects the line of demarcation between the British in the south and the Ottomans in the north. There is much all-Yemeni national feeling, even though the entire area of Yemen was never a single state.

Under the second Ottoman rule, there were minor steps toward modern education, communications, and public order, and the gap with modern countries was smaller than under later imams. But Ottoman rule was generally harsh and taxes high. The northern tribes opposed any kind of centralized rule, while many loyal Zaidis wanted the imams restored to power.

Imam Yahya of the so-called Hamid ad-Din line succeeded to the Imamate in 1904 and began guerrilla attacks on the Ottomans. Some intellectual leaders, influenced by Muslim modernists, began to argue that injustice and the weakness of the Muslims as compared to the Christian powers were due to departures from the Shari‘a, and this argument was used to defend fighting for the imam and against the Ottomans. In 1911, the Ottoman sultan had to sign a peace making major concessions to the imam in the Zaidi highlands, which the imam virtually ruled, while keeping Ottoman control in the Tihama and in the highlands south of ‘Amran. Yahya kept some of the Turks who remained in his territory to run a military academy, but generally let modern reforms lapse and worked to keep out Westerners. Through tribal alliances and shrewd policies, he succeeded in extending territory and central control.

Yahya came closer than any of his forbears to

3. Bayt Souhouba, Riyashiyah district, Yemen. Sojourners usually make trips back to Yemen every few years. Here, a Yemeni restaurant worker recently returned from Connecticut is visiting his village. *Jon Swanson.*

building a unified state, but local order remained in the hands of the tribes or religious scholars. Imams were unable to supplant tribal law with the Shariᶜa. Yahya, like earlier imams, was theoretically responsible for justice as well as for fighting and ruling. He gave much time to justice in his majlis, succeeding more than most of his predecessors in this form of direct justice, which did not pass through the hands of the ulama. The struggle between the imam and local ulama and particularly tribal leaders was one between different sectors of the elite, not of the middle or popular classes against the elite.

Yahya was one of the few Zaidi imams who was able to take control of Shafiᶜi areas, including the Tihama and the south, which he did by means of fighting in the 1920s. His attempts at absolutism were opposed by both conservatives and modernists, however, and he made few concessions to Shafiᶜi sensibilities or interests. He modernized his army leadership by sending cadets to Baghdad in the 1930s; but there they saw different ways, as well as military coups. Yahya withdrew the mission and instead brought in Iraqis to instruct Yemenis. One of them, Jamal Jamil, stayed on and became a prominent modernist; he was involved in the 1948 assassination of Imam Yahya and was executed. Other modernists were also involved in this assassination, which aimed at change via a new

line of imams, but was abortive; the old line of imams retained power and there was no basic change in policies.

The Hamid ad-Din imams tried to secure succession for their sons, flouting the tradition according to which imams were elected by their peers. In 1948, the Imamate passed briefly, as desired by the reformers, to another family, but then Yahya's eldest son, Ahmad, conquered Sanᶜa and the throne and continued his father's policy of isolating Yemen from the outside world. In an age of modern communication this proved impossible, however, and both modern ideas and dissatisfaction grew. The popular classes suffered increasingly from abuses in taxes and land tenure.

Growing numbers of people were forced into emigration for economic or political reasons, with first Aden and then Egypt being key points for discontented émigrés. Some studied or did business abroad, and among the large number of emigrants there was agitation against the old regime. The Organization of Free Yemenis, formed in Aden at the end of World War II, was even joined by one of Imam Yahya's sons. Internally dissatisfaction grew even among the Zaidi tribes, especially after Imam Ahmad had two tribal leaders executed. Within Yemen new secular and liberal ideas spread, and military officers became a focus of opposition. Many Shafiᶜis were among the modernizing emigrants and became members of the opposition. Shafiᶜi merchants also opposed the Imamate. Relations with Nasser's Egypt and the Soviet Union opened Yemen to new influences. The imam even declared an abortive union with Egypt, partly to disarm the Nasserite opposition.

The 1948 assassination of Yahya was partly the result of opposition plotting, but disagreements among the conspirators prevented real change and the new imam backed by the plotters lasted only weeks. But after this, dissatisfaction grew and became more focused and organized. Imam Ahmad died in 1962 and was succeeded by his chosen son, Badr, but the change in ruler was taken as an opportunity to launch a successful revolution, led by the younger generation of mostly Egyptian- and Syrian-trained army officers, with considerable popular support and important financial support from Shafiᶜi merchants. The sayyids, who under the modern imams had monopolized high civil posts, were ousted and sometimes executed. The revolution was, however, followed by a seven-year civil war, with the Saudi Arabian regime backing Badr along with some northern tribes, and Egypt (and the Soviet Union) backing the republic. The defeat of Egypt in the 1967 war with Israel made its money and troop support to the already unpopular Yemeni war untenable; as a tacit condition for a Saudi subsidy, Nasser agreed to withdraw his troops from Yemen. When Saudi Arabia was still unable to win for Imam Badr, it encouraged negotiations between Yemen's royalists and republicans; a republican state of conservative reconciliation, including royalist ministers, resulted. Egypt's unpopularity and defeat and Saudi financial power, along with internal divisions, brought a resurgence of old elites in the republic.

The civil war increased localist and tribal power and also instability, so it is not surprising that Yemen had much difficulty in agreeing on a constitution, while its first two presidents were forced into exile after coups, and its next two were assassinated. A purge of hard-line royalists and especially of radical republicans led to a reconciliation of the remaining ex-royalist and conservative republicans, with Saudi blessing and aid, in 1970. The 1971 constitution restored much power to sayyids and qadis by making the Shariᶜa the only source of law (a slightly flexible formula) and Shariᶜa scholars the only judges and jurists. The elected consultative assembly came to be dominated by traditionalists and tribal shaikhs, and the more modernist Shafiᶜi middle class, which had contributed much to the revolution, occupied few positions in the government. The northern tribes had

been strengthened in the civil war by getting money for their aid, and some tribal uprisings, disruptions, and refusal to recognize the center continued. The 1962 revolution had become both conservatized and fractionalized. Also, Saudi Arabia and the newly formed (1967) People's Democratic Republic of Yemen (PDRY) continued to back their respective supporters within Yemen, so that both internal and external factionalism made it difficult for the government to carry out significant programs.

Many of the projects that have been carried out since 1967 have owed much to foreign aid or input, and Yemen is open to aid from both Western and Eastern sources. The major highways are Chinese- and Russian-built, and both Eastern and Western countries, including the United States, have carried out a variety of educational, infrastructural, industrial, agricultural, and health projects. The Arab Gulf states' Gulf Cooperation Council has also been a large donor. Some have questioned whether Yemen is really a good country for aid investment—the galloping inflation caused by remittances from Yemenis in oil-rich countries makes projects far more expensive than in many more needy countries, while Yemen's confidence that it can call on a variety of foreign aid sources seems to discourage it from effective planning or from real taxation of remittances. But foreign countries, heavily involved in military aid, are tempted to give economic aid for strategic reasons.

Fighting between the Yemen Arab Republic and the People's Democratic Republic of Yemen occurred from 1967 until 1972, when it ended with an agreement calling for the unity of the two Yemens, which remains the official position today. In June 1978, however, North Yemen's President Ghashmi received the self-proclaimed envoy of Ali, the pragmatic leader of the PDRY, who assassinated Ghashmi. The story credited by most experts is that South Yemeni hard-liners wished to discredit Ali, who was in fact tried and executed. The incident clearly hurt relations between the two Yemens, which fought a war in 1979, but relations are now restored. Unity with the south is a popular idea in North Yemen and serves to temper the overwhelming influence and pressure of Saudi Arabia.

While the state has not centralized, liberalized, or modernized as much as many Yemenis hoped, there has been some change in elites, with a decline in the sayyids and the old religious and court elite and a rise in army officers, who have been the chief leaders of the republic, and of technocrats, who comprise most of the ministers. Sayyids continue to be important as rural judges; and while the technocrats include many

4. Plowing near Gayhlan, ᶜAmmar district, Yemen. Yemen's agriculture is dependent on maximizing rainfall through elaborate stone terraces. These have fallen into disrepair because of the chronic labor shortage brought about by the migration of able-bodied men. *Jon Swanson.*

Shafiᶜis with modern education, they are outweighed by the ruling army, which is mainly Zaidi. The army still has a large tribal component, and many tribal shaikhs remain powerful. The qadi class has retained much power and is often identified more with public service than with the old regime.

The republic early abolished the holding of tribal hostages (traditionally used to control the tribes). It declared Yemen neutral and part of the Arab nation. Yemen is still one of the least economically modernized countries in the world, however, and has been held back not only by the policy of the imams and by weakness in the republic but by its very rugged terrain and pattern of small isolated settlements. In the 1970s, 95 percent of Yemen's over 52,000 settlements had fewer than 250 inhabitants. In 1975, 86 percent of the population lived in settlements with fewer than 1,000 persons.[3] Most Yemenis depend on subsistence agriculture on marginal land with low rainfall and a high labor input. The modest economic growth experienced in the 1970s came mainly from foreign and external capital and occurred in the modern sector, while traditional agriculture and trade stagnated or declined. The drain of labor emigration abroad has brought a decline in agriculture, while food consumption is rising, paid for by foreign remittances.

The government's development budget gets almost nothing from remittances and depends on foreign aid. Government tax revenue is small and comes mostly from customs duties, which encourages smuggling. The government has, however, made attempts at development with some success. In 1972, a Central Planning Organization was set up, and the three- and five-year plans that followed brought some improvements, owing largely to foreign financial and technical aid. In addition, Local Development Associations (LDAs) with some autonomy were set up in two hundred localities, and they have constructed roads and schools and provided health care and water. The elected quality of these LDAs has often meant domination by tribal shaikhs.

Despite these advances, Yemen still has great problems of development and instability. Unlike the oil countries that receive oil revenues directly into government coffers, which strengthens the center and enables it to spend freely on development projects, Yemen receives money indirectly into the economy through remittances, which do not reach the government and have little effect on productive investment or planned development. Remittances contribute to high inflation rates via investment in land and houses and spending on consumer imports. The discovery of

5, 6. Taᶜizz, Yemen. The new building on the right (top), with intersecting block construction and ancient design motifs, illustrates the growth which sojourning affords—often through arduous labor abroad and years of family separation. The Chinese-built hospital in the background and the increased use of motorized vehicles, evident in both photographs, signify improvements in health care and transportation that foreign aid and remittances have made possible. *Jon Swanson*.

oil in the mid-1980s should provide the government with more direct revenue, however.

The central government is still not in real control of some tribal areas, although this problem seems to be decreasing. In the Shafiᶜi areas, a leftist National Democratic Front has put forth demands for land reform and an end to landlord-oriented oppression that voice some popular grievances. The Saudis generally try, in great measure successfully, to keep the government from becoming too strong, and they also encourage socioeconomic and cultural conservatism.

As the Arabian Peninsula's most populous country, Yemen has a potential importance that it has not yet realized because of its lack of oil income and its relative instability and decentralization. While development of business, trade, communications, and especially consumer goods imports is impressive as compared to the prerepublican period, and health and education are improving, Yemen still ranks very low in such quality-of-life indices as health, education, life expectancy, and child mortality. Increasing numbers of Yemenis, however, are concerned about these matters; what they see on both right and left, whether in South Yemen or Saudi Arabia or simply on their television screens, is making them more aware than ever of the gaps between their society and others both near and far. It seems likely that pressures for change will continue to grow.

SOCIETY

Some comments about social structure have been made above, and here a few additional points are stressed. One concerns the position of women, which has recently been studied in several books and articles.[4] As elsewhere, women's position, past and present, varies according to social class and work activity. Regarding the most visible point, veiling and seclusion, these are most strictly observed in Zaidi towns, less in small towns and the countryside, while in the Shafiᶜi south there are groups of women, especially those who engage in trade, who are completely unveiled. One community near the southern city of Taᶜizz is known for its generally wealthy trading women who do not veil, carry out all their own business activity, and are highly respected. At the other extreme, there still exist Zaidi religious families in northern cities that do not let their women out of the house except, say, for one weekly visit to relatives.

As young girls have begun to be educated, they talk more to their peers and less to the older women, who no longer share their knowledge and interests. More dramatic is the fact that highly educated women, like highly educated men, at least among the Zaidis, tend to come from sayyid or qadi families. Since we are talking of *secularly* educated women, who often go abroad for their final education, this may seem strange — it might be supposed that religious leaders would oppose Western-style education for their daughters, and possibly for their sons. In fact, however, what distinguishes these religious men or ulama in relation to their own societies is learning, and many of them have been quick to see that the old learning is insufficient for the modern world, which requires new knowledge if their country and their children are to advance. Hence, a girl growing up in an atmosphere in which study and books are respected is likely to want to pursue them, while her father, though sometimes reluctant, ends up being less conservative in these matters than many a tribal chief. In fact, every Zaidi woman I met with a good modern education and a job based on it came from an ulama family — among Shafiᶜis, with their history of trading and traveling abroad, she might come from a merchant family.[5]

In the countryside, as in most societies, women have always worked hard, particularly in harvest and planting seasons, and especially with the tasks that center more on subsistence agriculture and are closer to home. In the past decades, women's work has increased as more and more able-bodied men are spending most of the year working abroad, so that in many cases all, or nearly all, of the agricultural tasks devolve on women, old men, and children. Sometimes this has been a factor in agricultural decline — the women are simply unable to keep up the terraces, say, and also to do all the other jobs that they must.

In Yemen, as in much of the Middle East until fairly recently, top-to-toe veiling on the street is considered a sign of respectability. Since the revolution the unfitted, colorfully printed *sitara* has been increasingly replaced by the all-black, more fitted and tailored *sharshaf*, which was apparently introduced by the Ottomans and then reserved for the imam's family until the revolution. The rapid spread of the *sharshaf* thereafter has led to its ironic dubbing as "the Flag of the Republic." Some lower-class women may unveil even in Sanᶜa, but the reverse process of less all-covering dress for the upper or educated groups, found in much of the Middle East, has just begun in Yemen. There it takes the form of the *balto* (ultimately Fr. *paletot*, which becomes *pal'to/palto* in Russian and Persian, *balto* in Egypt). Its local version is a raincoat of ankle length, generally worn over jeans with high-heeled shoes, and a head scarf either tied behind the head or wrapped around the neck. This is worn even inside when working with men. Such dress might seem Islamic revivalist in another country, but in Yemen it is a step *away* from veiling. As in many countries, at the same time that strict veiling begins to give way in the cities, it is spreading in parts of the countryside, so its class significance is no longer unidirectional.

Many observers have noted the moral and physical strength of Yemeni women, the ways they have to undermine male dominance, and even the proclivity of some to mock men and their values in their social gatherings, either in their own conversations or via playlets or hired entertainers who make fun of men.[6] (Similar things exist in Iran and elsewhere.) A common traditional practice is for a dissatisfied wife to leave her husband and go to the home of a relative, after which the husband, unless he wants a divorce, must make concessions to get her back.

The combination of easy cash owing to migration, too much work for many women, especially those with absent husbands, and a lack of basic health education combined with a faith in Western consumer goods has led to a new problem, the rapid spread of bottle feeding, using powdered milk and formula. Few areas in Yemen have clean water supplies or adequate resources to sterilize bottles and nipples; indeed, if women felt they had to do all these things they probably would not use powdered milk—it would be more trouble than breast feeding. As it is, however, bottle feeding has become widespread and has added to infant illness and mortality. Government and foreign efforts have slowed, but not stopped, the spread of bottle feeding.

Both men and women have their own social subsocieties, organized mainly by visiting patterns, which center around afternoon parties where, especially among men, the stimulant qat is chewed. In the highlands particularly, many urban men and some women stop their work around 1 P.M. and go to qat parties that last all afternoon. The government has been ineffectual in its attempts to reduce qat chewing, which it considers harmful to health and to productive labor. Rather, improved communications have meant that qat can be more widely grown and still rushed into town (it is supposed to be chewed within a day after picking), and higher incomes and remittances bring higher qat consumption.

Until recently, and to some degree even now, male dress and adornment were an even clearer sign of social or class status than female dress. Sayyids and qadis wore special long robes and distinctive headdress, as befits their status in religion and learning; and they were also entitled to wear the curved dagger,

or *janbiyya*, as befits their fighting role. Leading tribesmen also wore the dagger, turned a different way to indicate their status. City craftsmen and the lower endogamous classes were forbidden to wear the *janbiyya*. Most men wore (and wear) a skirtlike garment, which some say was brought by Yemeni traders to Indonesia (though it is unclear on what evidence beyond long contact between South Yemen and Indonesia). Today *janbiyyas* are still widely worn, but they are no longer limited to sayyids and tribesmen. Western clothing is worn by some men, but by a smaller proportion than elsewhere in the Middle East. The great majority tend to wear a headdress made from a large square of print cloth, wrapped around the head in a special manner.

As in most Middle Eastern countries, marriages are usually arranged by the parents, and there is a theoretical, and in part real, preference for a man to marry his paternal cousin. Girls, and sometimes boys, may marry quite young, and there is a bride-price, as in most Muslim countries. In recent years, with inflation and rising living standards, bride-prices have become very high, and the government has tried to limit them with little success. Despite theoretical traditional or Islamic norms and urban veiling, Yemeni women are sometimes surprisingly independent in such areas as their attitudes toward extramarital relations and their desire to have fewer children than their husbands might like.

Yemen's multistory stone or stone and mud brick buildings and open street patterns are very different from those in most Middle Eastern countries and go back to pre-Islamic times. This building pattern is handsome and sturdy, but it rarely provides the open courtyards where women can move freely that are found in the low courtyard-centered style of Mediterranean architecture.

A serious understanding of Yemeni social history will require study of Yemen's interaction with non-Arab societies from Africa to Indonesia, as well as with Arab ones, and most such research remains to be done. As an area with a long history of maritime trade directed at distant regions, Greater Yemen shows signs of a great variety of cultural and economic influences and interactions.

SOCIOECONOMIC STRUCTURES

The great majority of Yemenis are still engaged in agriculture, but this agriculture is now far from supporting or fully feeding them, and food imports, ultimately paid for by remittances, grow every year. It appears that coffee and some other crops have been

7. San͑a, Yemen. *Nikki Keddie.*

8. Village in Jabal Rayma district, Yemen. *Nikki Keddie.*

9. Jabal Rayma district, Yemen. The prolonged absence of Yemeni men has redefined the role of women in the rural sector, where they have taken on more responsibility for agricultural work, substituting for their sojourning husbands and other male family members in all tasks except plowing. *Nikki Keddie*.

10. Alley in San^ca, Yemen. Increased acreage has been devoted to the cultivation of qat, a mildly stimulating, leafy plant chewed by men and women. The preoccupation with this major cash crop has permeated all walks of Yemeni life (see photographs 11, 27, 28). Here, qat is transported in bundles for sale in the market. *Nikki Keddie*.

11. Television singer chewing qat, San^{c}a, Yemen. The widespread popularity of TVs and VCRs has enabled many women to gain greater public exposure and visibility. *Nikki Keddie*.

12. Advertisement for powdered milk, San^{c}a, Yemen. *Nikki Keddie*.

13. Street in San^{c}a, Yemen. *Nikki Keddie.*

14. Family portrait, Yemen. *Sojourner snapshot.*

displaced by qat, which does not require very good soil or rainfall and is highly profitable (and expensive to the consumer). Ultimately the qat-centered agriculture is also supported by emigration and remittances, since if Yemen did not have the foreign exchange to overcome its large food deficit, it would have to grow its own food, as it once did. Clearly, remittances have led to a generally higher living standard, but it is a standard in which large sums go to large houses built by emigrants, land purchase, qat, televisions, VCRs, cars, and other often expensive consumer goods, while comparatively little goes yet to health, hygiene, education, or productive investments or technical improvements. This creates a situation of growing dependence on the outside world, and little prospect for withstanding the shocks that might come if and when Yemeni temporary emigrants abroad either are forced by their host countries to go home for good or have their pay greatly lowered. Saudi Arabia has some awareness of this problem and has not sent Yemenis home or cut them off completely as Saudi oil production declined, but, just as oil will not last forever in Arabia, so Yemen's secondhand profits from oil cannot last. Even the recent discovery of oil will not necessarily cover Yemen's growing economic needs, although if profits are used for productive investment it could help.

It thus seems to be necessary to build up a more self-sufficient society and economy in Yemen as rapidly as possible. It seems unlikely that this can be done mainly by increasing foreign advisers and aid, which may do some good things but also foster the illusion that such aid will always be there to count on. Rather, it seems that foreign advisers can only be adjuncts to new Yemeni initiatives that demonstrate a determination to meet some minimum goals: to create greater equality in landownership and income; to provide productive work and investment opportunities for men and women within Yemen; greatly to accelerate educational and health programs; and to mobilize remittance income for productive goals. While Yemen has gone far since 1962, it still has much further to go.[7]

NOTES

1. Tomas Gerholm, *Market, Mosque and Mafraj: Social Inequality in a Yemen Town* (Stockholm: Department of Social Anthropology, Stockholm University, 1977), 125–30. "Caste" is discussed in several anthropological and other works on both Yemens. See especially Joseph Chelhold, et al., *L'Arabie du Sud* (Paris: G.-P. Maisonneuve et Larose, 1985), vol. 3, chapter 1.

2. R. B. Serjeant and Ronald Leacock, eds., *San'a: An Arabian Islamic City* (London: World of Islam Festival Trust, 1983), has two translations of this passage from al-Hadi's biography; that by Martha Mundy is clearer regarding different kinds of veiling demanded of premenopausal (strict) and postmenopausal women.

3. Hans Steffen, *A Contribution to the Population Geography of the Yemen Arab Republic: The Major Findings of the Population and Housing Census of February 1975. . . .* (Wiesbaden: Reichert, 1979).

4. Carla Makhlouf, *Changing Veils: Women and Modernization in North Yemen* (Austin: University of Texas Press, 1979); Cynthia Myntti, *Women and Development in Yemen Arab Republic* (Eschborn: GTZ [Agency for Technical Cooperation], 1979); Susan Dorsky, *Women of 'Amran: A Middle Eastern Ethnographic Study* (Salt Lake City: University of Utah Press, 1986); and Martha Mundy, "Women's Inheritance of Land in Highland Yemen," *Arabian Studies* 5 (1979): 161–91.

5. From extensive interviews, Yemen, summer of 1983.

6. See especially Claudie Fayein, *Une française médecin au Yémen* (Paris: René Julliard, 1955).

7. Other useful general works on North Yemen include Robin Bidwell, *The Two Yemens* (Boulder: Westview Press, 1983); Sheila Carapico and Richard Tutwiler, *Yemeni Agriculture and Economic Change* (San'a: AIYS, 1981); J. E. Peterson, *Yemen: The Search for a Modern State* (London: Croom Helm, 1982); Robert W. Stookey, *Yemen: The Politics of the Yemen Arab Republic* (Boulder: Westview Press, 1978); and Thomas B. Stevenson, *Social Change in a Yemeni Highlands Town* (Salt Lake City: University of Utah Press, 1985).

The Political Consequences of Yemeni Migration

MANFRED W. WENNER
Department of Political Science
Northern Illinois University

Migration—for whatever combination of reasons—is surely one of the most widespread socioeconomic and political phenomena of the modern world. This study looks at one limited aspect of this phenomenon: the sociopolitical consequences for the sending country. In the past, much of the literature presumed numerous advantages with only minimal disadvantages. More recently, social scientists and economists have raised serious questions about the economic value of large-scale migration. Here, I am more specifically interested in the potential political impact of such migration, and I suggest some avenues that ought to be researched if we are to answer those questions. I point out that there are indirect consequences, which should be of interest to social scientists as well as practicing political leaders, for countries that export their population (even though all the relevant materials in this instance are drawn from the Yemeni case).

Many previous studies have not distinguished clearly among the impacts, effects, and characteristics of emigration at the individual level and the same kinds of issues at the national or regional level. Although emigration as a social, economic, or political phenomenon may well have its major impact at the regional or national level, it is usually far more easily analyzed at the individual level, since it is, after all, an individual activity. In this essay, more emphasis is placed on the national impact of such mass activity, as well as on regional impacts in the Yemeni context.

INDIVIDUAL ISSUES

There are at least a dozen factors that one could investigate at the individual level, and the following list represents those most readily apparent:

Age (among Yemenis, from as low as twelve to as high as sixty)
Sex (almost exclusively male)
Social status (*qabili? nuqqas?*)
Occupation (of the individual as well as the family)
Educational level (literate? any formal schooling?)
Religion (Zaidi/Shafi'i/Ismaili)
Religiosity (level of commitment/activism)
Regional origins
Landowner? Type?
Purpose of emigration
Ethnic characteristics (skin color? Arab? Somali? Ethiopian?)
Experience in recipient country (presence of ethnic/regional/familial cohorts? previous employment?)

Those familiar with Yemen know that many of these categories are highly correlated with each other;

15. Imported goods, Ta'izz market, Yemen. The large-scale migration of Yemeni men has resulted in agricultural decline and increased reliance on foreign products including foodstuffs. The items in this photograph come from China, France, England, and the United States. *Jon Swanson.*

even so, we do not know with any certainty which may be of greatest importance with respect to the decision to emigrate or return and with respect to the characteristics of the migrant upon his return to Yemen.

Information on many of these matters is difficult if not impossible to obtain. Some are sensitive in the Yemeni context; even outside of Yemen, there is often a reluctance to provide information about them (for example, among the migrants in California). In part, at least, this is due to a lack of experience with social scientists and their methods and goals; in part, however, it is due to the general sense of alienation and perhaps fear in the American social system and economy.[1]

Although we may surmise about single explanations for the original decision to leave, it is likely to be for complex reasons. For example, aside from the obvious demographic/situational variables that might warrant investigation, is there some sort of anticipatory socialization that takes place in the specific circumstances of the individual, in the family unit, or in the village? Are there sets of social and economic parameters in the family or village that predispose certain individuals or families to leave, and others to remain behind? Consider the consequences of primo-

geniture for the careers and expectations of second sons in the British system.

Of course, for many, the most obvious starting point might be in the economic circumstances of the family. For example, does the family own spring-fed agricultural land of high value or is it essentially landless or restricted to poor-quality land?

For others, seasonal, recurrent, or permanent emigration might be related to other demographic, economic, or even political factors. Consider in this instance the impact on emigration of the domestic policies of Imam Ahmad during the 1950s.

Another approach would be to look at the specific attributes and concerns of the individual: what is the migrant's view of the value of the migration? Is it to overcome local problems with which the current system has not coped effectively? Is it solely to produce income to increase the individual's income for purposes of marriage, land acquisition, or rising in the Yemeni social system? Is the migrant leaving for personal reasons or perhaps for wider family or clan interests? The widespread perception that the Yemeni social system is more permeable than ever before is probably quite significant in this context.

These questions are complemented by those surrounding the experience of the emigrant in the foreign environment. For example: how selective are the migrants in the host environment? Do they tend to retain the social and structural relationships of their origins in the new location? For example, do those from the ᶜAmran region tend to congregate? Do those from the Hujjariyya district similarly stick together? Or does their joint Yemeniness overcome these regional, religious, and ethnic differences? The evidence from contemporary studies is not entirely clear.[2] It is, of course, logical and likely that the size of the Yemeni emigrant community will be an important factor, since increasing size will make such selective associations more possible, but it would be interesting to know how important new associations and relationships are and whether they are retained upon return.

Social scientists do not, as yet, have the answers to these and many related questions; we are only beginning to get some information from studies of the past few years. At the same time, we are also getting studies among returnees, done by American and other anthropologists and ethnologists, and in time we may have clearer answers.[3]

It is probably precisely because of the difficulty in obtaining data on individuals that most analyses have been made of aggregate behavior. In other words, lacking precise information on individuals, social scientists have imputed to the individuals who have emigrated certain characteristics of the aggregate — origins, behavior patterns, and, perhaps most important, specific reactions to the socioeconomic and sociopolitical characteristics of contemporary Yemeni society upon their return.[4]

COLLECTIVE ISSUES

At the national level, some previous studies have suggested that there are relatively clear and frequent (generally beneficial) effects for the labor-exporting country. The following list, while not exhaustive, provides the major categories into which such presumed benefits have been grouped:

The remittances that are sent back are (or at least can be) a source of investment capital, which can be used to develop and/or promote local resources and industries, thereby raising both personal and national living standards.

The migrants will acquire at least a modicum of skills and work experience that, upon repatriation, will contribute to the human and productive resources and capabilities of the country.

The emigrants, by their departure, lessen the pressure on local food, land, and other resources and facilities (especially on the usually rudimentary social and welfare services), thereby making them more capable of dealing with the remainder of the population. Their departure is depicted as taking the "population pressure" off the limited infrastructure that exists in countries labeled as "developing."

The foreign work experience is likely to lead to an increase in labor productivity, as more sophisticated and demanding employers instill new values and orientations (for example, the value of time, cooperation, and so on) that assist in the development of a modern economy, modern industries, and modern employment patterns (with all of the attendant benefits and responsibilities).

These experiences are, in sum, likely to promote heightened ambition, increased expectations, and changed values concerning such traditional behaviors as marriage, nutrition, housing, the family, employment, and entrepreneurship. By indirection, this is assumed to cover such related values as social organization, political cooperation, and political action (of all types).

While it may be argued that this list of benefits is intuitively sensible, and that there are places and times where these features have been demonstrated, the evidence from some case studies, including the Yemeni one, raises legitimate doubts and questions concerning the "universal" nature of these effects.[5]

It is, then, of value to consider the evidence from the Yemeni example concerning the assumed benefits.

There is little evidence to indicate that the remittances are channeled into what Western economists would consider productive investment. In fact, most remittance money (in some years in excess of $1 billion) is spent on a rather limited list of items: land, insofar as it is available; imported consumer goods, such as cars, VCRs, and similar durables; inflated bride-prices (which the government has sought, unsuccessfully, to regulate); construction, usually for improvements or additions to existing single-family dwellings, or for new homes for relatives; and imported foodstuffs of all types (that is, necessities as well as luxuries).

Very little, therefore, has been available for the development of local industry or the development of import-substitution activities. Although this is due in part to the lack of any effective method whereby the government could tax the remittances and/or channel them into desirable investments, it also clearly reflects the desire of the Yemenis to acquire goods and services that were either forbidden or unavailable until the 1970s, and therefore represents pent-up

16. Shireh, ᶜAmmar district, Yemen. Cutting stones for new dwellings. *Jon Swanson*.

17. Talib, Central Highlands, Yemen. A major portion of the capital remitted by the workers is used to finance the building of new, larger homes, seen on the right. *Jon Swanson*.

18. Migrants returning home with goods purchased in Saudi Arabia, on the road between San⁽c⁾a and Ta⁽c⁾izz. *Jon Swanson.*

demands that no Yemeni government can afford to ignore or resist. It shows the priorities of the Yemenis and may eventually prove to be socially and politically, if not always economically, the most advantageous course of action.[6]

Similarly, there is little evidence that skill acquisition is a widespread phenomenon, especially skills that are useful or relevant to contemporary Yemeni society and economic conditions. Of course, some diesel mechanics have been trained; but in general, the overlap between learned skills and their effective contribution to economic development is relatively small. In part, of course, this is due to the fact that migrant labor in all countries is usually engaged in unskilled work (for example, the Yemeni asparagus and grape harvesters in the San Joaquin Valley in California). Although some Western European countries established training institutes for migrant labor (in the era prior to the recessions of the 1970s and the associated political opposition to programs benefiting migrant labor), the skills imparted were almost completely irrelevant to the Yemeni environment—for example, assembly-line work in Wolfsburg or in the automobile plants in the Detroit area.

Furthermore, many of the recipient countries turn to other sources of supply when more highly skilled labor is required. For example, the Western European Economic Community member states give first priority to EEC nationals in all instances. In such oil exporters as Saudi Arabia, there are a combination of factors, including labor costs (South Koreans are cheaper than Yemenis), political concerns (Yemenis are perceived as constituting a potential internal security threat, particularly after some were implicated in the 1979 attack on Mecca), or the inclination to invest in capital projects that have been contracted to "turnkey" contractors such as Bechtel Corporation or Morrison-Knudsen, which use other sources of labor (Koreans, Thais, Filipinos, etc.). In the case of California, the Yemenis are so different in culture and behavior that they make the more numerous Mexicans appear to be fully integrated.

With respect to the presumed positive impact on services, the picture in Yemen is also not what conventional theory suggests. Although emigration has surely reduced the pressure on the limited services that exist, this "gain" appears to have been offset by the necessity of importing foreign manual labor for both public and private construction projects and a substantial growth in the domestic population, especially in the fifteen-and-under age group, which has produced a heightened demand for schools, health-care facilities, municipal water systems, and roads—demands that the government cannot satisfy even with the extensive set of foreign donors and donor programs.

There is also little evidence that emigration, directly or indirectly, has contributed significantly to either increased productivity or innovation, with certain exceptions. In fact, in the most important sector, rural agriculture, production has declined rather substantially in nearly all commodities and in almost all regions. The exceptions are the successful truck farms for the major urban agglomerations, and the increased qat acreage (this increase in availability and consumption can be attributed to the increased personal disposable income levels). However, these exceptions are just that, since the balance of payments deficit continues to grow; the amount and percentage devoted to foreign foodstuffs replacing the more expensive domestic equivalent continue to increase as well.[7]

Of more immediate interest for the purposes of this essay (that is, the political consequences) is a review of some of the actual changes of the so-called decade of affluence (1974–84), since they are most likely to have had an impact upon the attitudes that are an important component of the long-term political effects.

An important change is the development of significant domestic inflation, which is probably most visible in the major domestic outlet for investment: land. The opportunity to become a landowner, or to expand one's current holdings, has clearly affected the class (social) system in Yemen. In one sense, of course, it has markedly improved the opportunities for individuals in the lower classes (under the old system) to achieve social mobility. So, although the traditional classes and categories (for example, the sayyids and the qadis) have not lost all their relevance, most of the "upper" ranks are now more permeable than ever before. This, one may surmise, is seen as a positive development by the majority of the population and is one of the reasons for the republic's positive image and the support it enjoys.

The increased purchasing power made possible by the remittance flow has resulted in very high levels of personal consumption; typically, as indicated above, the demand is for consumer and luxury goods (most of which require electricity, thus spurring the government's rural electrification program, which in itself will doubtless have far-reaching impacts in the future). The problem lies in the fact that most of these goods are imported; thus, the only domestic industry that has benefited directly is the class of importers, traders, and financial institutions that fund the imports. Depending upon one's location in the coun-

try, the types of expenditures and the commodities purchased are likely to have an impact on governmental development priorities and construction programs. (In other words, widespread purchases of certain goods, for example, motor vehicles, will influence the government's priorities as far as road building is concerned, as well as the kinds of demands made upon the government and others for ancillary services.)

In addition, the consumption patterns for a variety of goods and services have been significantly altered. For example, there is now a growing preference for imported wheat and rice, rather than the traditional (and locally produced) millet and sorghum. This has surfaced in the preference for soft white breads (often as an indicator of status) as opposed to the far more nutritious traditional breads. This, in turn, has affected agricultural production patterns and is likely to have some effect upon the socioeconomic relationships and patterns that were part of the old system of production and priorities — not to mention its impact upon income levels among the growers, shippers, and merchants involved in the various alternatives.

Probably one of the more interesting and potentially important consequences of recent events is the depletion of the local labor market. The most obvious and immediate impact was a sharp rise in the cost of domestic labor in almost all fields. The most fascinating aspect, however, is the effect on the role of women in Yemeni society. Generalizations for the whole of Yemen are notoriously difficult, and this certainly applies to the role of women and how it has changed as a result of the "decade of affluence." Traditionally, rural women have experienced greater freedom and participated more actively in wide areas of agriculture and the economy than their urban counterparts. It has, however, been suggested that recent developments in mechanization and in the labor supply, as well as emigration, have markedly affected the role of women in the economy. Among the changes that have been noted as having the greatest impact are the tendency to restrict the freedom of — and the range of roles assigned to — women as the level of income goes up and the pressures upon the Yemeni government from the Saudis with respect to women's roles (for example, threats to decrease the subsidy if the Yemenis continue to permit coeducation at the University of San'a, etc.).[8]

The "brain drain" phenomenon — the loss of trained personnel with essential technical and administrative skills because of higher pay and better working conditions elsewhere — is generally not a problem for the vast majority of Yemenis employed in the

19, 20. Nadirah, ᶜAmmar district, Yemen (above) and Kawkaban, Central Highlands, Yemen (below). Electricity and telecommunication are spreading rapidly throughout the Yemeni countryside. *Jon Swanson*.

United States and Western Europe; in a very limited fashion, it applies to some of the other Arab states. Its relevance is far more important within Yemen itself: it has proven extremely difficult to retain skilled and trained personnel in the more remote areas of Yemen; the lure of the capital and the other larger urban centers for medical, administrative, and similarly trained personnel is very great. This has required that the government employ foreign donor personnel to fill many of these positions, several of which are highly important because of their symbolic role in demonstrating the commitment of the central government to expanding the number and range of services to the rural areas. Foreign donor personnel chafe under the same conditions and often fail adequately to understand local social and political conditions, thereby engendering friction with the foreign donor, as well as promoting disenchantment with the central government, its policies, and its agencies.[9]

There are some indications that subtle but potentially important shifts in the relative importance of different districts and regions in the balance of Yemeni domestic politics may be taking place. For example, the National Democratic Front, the major domestic opposition movement, had its greatest success in an area with the highest rates of emigration. Emigration and remittances have changed the politico-economic characteristics of regions in the sense that they have weakened the power of traditional shaikhs and helped to break down old relationships, as well as the old landholding patterns. Unfortunately, we do not know the extent of the change that has taken place in landholding patterns in contemporary Yemen (since no cadastral survey has ever been undertaken). It is, of course, pure speculation, but in view of the fact that the traditional elite was associated with landholding, it does not seem unlikely that knowing more about landownership patterns would tell us something about the bases of political and economic influence in Yemen.

The wave of emigration of the 1970s does not seem to have accomplished very much with respect to Yemen's endemic population pressures.[10] In fact, there may be more pressures and demands for a wider range of governmental services than was the case prior to emigration. The increased income levels seem to have combined with growing expectations of many of the returnees to produce a demand for services and facilities that never previously existed. (Of course, this is in part related to the end of the isolation of the past and the access of contemporary Yemenis to goods and services never before thought possible.) In fact, the government would be hard-pressed at present to pro-

vide adequate primary health care facilities in all of the rural areas, greater access to education (the value of which is undoubtedly one of the important lessons learned by those who wind up taking only menial and unskilled jobs), improved sanitation (including piped drinking water), better transportation, governmental outreach and assistance programs, and a host of other services and facilities that are likely to have been encountered (if not used) in the United States as well as the other states of the Arabian Peninsula.

For those whose experience with Yemen extends over the past decade, another phenomenon is striking: the increased emphasis upon public displays of religiosity. Its most obvious manifestation to the occasional visitor is the increased incidence of urban veiling, especially the replacement of the traditional colorful *sitara* by the all-black *sharshaf* in the major urban agglomerations.

Although there is widespread agreement that, in part, it is the influence of Saudi Arabia that has contributed to the change, this probably does not suffice as an explanation if one takes into account the widespread resentment and dislike of the Saudis. I think that at least two factors are at work here and may be linked to the experiences of the migrants. First, religion, especially in such non-Islamic states as the United States, becomes a vehicle for preserving one's identity in stressful situations — a development that is, of course, unique neither to Islam nor to Yemenis. (In fact, many social analysts would argue that this is an almost predictable consequence of the overwhelming onslaught of Western goods, ideas, methods, and mores on Yemen and the Yemenis in the past fifteen years.) Since Islam has traditionally provided the moral, social, economic, and even political "cement" that characterizes Muslim states, individual Yemenis tend to cling to their Muslim beliefs and mores in the foreign environment as the key link that binds them together, as well as to their home. It is not surprising that few abandon their Islamic principles.

Second, and probably more important, is the fact that religiosity becomes an indicator of greater education and wealth (or at least greater disposable income and the ability to purchase a variety of labor-saving devices from the West). These make it possible for women to gain more leisure time (as they are freed from many of the more menial and time-consuming tasks of women in traditional Yemeni society). This time can be spent in women's meetings (including qat sessions), as well as activities that involve public movement, which, of course, require veiling in the major urban centers. And I think that the increase in veiling that is evident in San ͨa and other major towns is being used as an indicator of increased wealth.[11]

If this is true, it is still difficult to assess what the long-term effects might be, although there are signs of an increased politicization of Islam (in the activities of the various Islamic religio-political organizations that now operate in Yemen, including various factions of the Muslim Brotherhood).

Although there is a reluctance to discuss the issue in Yemen, it seems clear that the total number of migrants and the level of remittances have both declined (though not precipitously, yet). One result is that some of the returnees are superfluous to the economy, which has, of course, significantly changed over the years. Few have marketable skills, and many of their traditional functions have been taken over by machinery (especially in the rural areas). As a result, at least some observers have suggested that the traditional breakdown of employment categories is inapplicable in societies such as Yemen's—what has developed as a consequence of the "decade of affluence" is a large "informal sector." They posit an economy that is no longer growing and is unable to provide the level of employment and activity that was possible in the heyday of high remittances; therefore, some of the former migrants move to the major urban centers and participate in business ventures that are largely of a marginal nature in order to gain at least some income. In other words, an internal rather than external migration takes place.[12]

Finally, it would be interesting to know if the Yemenis perceive the social and economic distance between the traditional categories of the social structure as greater or smaller today than they were in the past. To the outside observer, it occasionally appears that the gross displays of wealth that are possible today were inconceivable in the past (that is, the imamic period), and one cannot help but wonder if the gulf between the groups, for all the heightened social mobility, is now perceived as greater. If so, this would seem to be a danger sign for the long term.

If one accepts this as a reasonably accurate description of the changes that have taken place, it is time to return to the suggestion that the experiences of the migrants may promote significant changes in their values, their social orientation, and eventually their political orientation. In other words, if we accept that the experience of the emigrants will change their economic position, as well as their values, how will these affect the domestic political situation in Yemen?

Some of the effects are likely to be immediate; others are likely to be subtle and long-term in their impact, rather than abrupt and of immediate concern to the authorities. For example, as long as significant numbers of Yemeni males find employment abroad and continue to remit enough to provide an engine for domestic employment and the continued consumption of imported goods to which many have grown accustomed, there is likely to be little political change. At the same time, there would continue to be some progress in the development of a modern infrastructure and the provision of services to an increasing percentage of the rural population. In fact, it is quite likely that Yemen's domestic stability is closely tied to the ability of the population to continue the slow but steady improvement in its living standard and access to goods and services.

Conversely, it is difficult to conceive of continued domestic stability if the remittance flow were to decline drastically and the range of gifts, loans, grants, and similar financial devices that donors have provided to develop the economy (and eventually the domestic market) underwent a similar decline.

The key problem is what will happen if there is a substantial reduction in the number of migrants able to find remunerative employment abroad (and therefore choose to return home), or if there is a substantial decline in the amount of remittances as well as capital from abroad, or both.

These possibilities, intricately related, can be treated in two ways: the effect on Yemen's foreign policy and the effect on domestic policy.

FOREIGN POLICY ISSUES

One result of the "decade of affluence" is that Yemen has become far more closely tied to the rest of the world than was previously the case—economically as well as politically. In essence, it may be argued that the current standard of living, the current way of life that many Yemenis enjoy, was bought, rather than produced, in the sense that it was Yemeni labor abroad that enabled Yemen to afford the range of goods and services it is now possible to find at home.

It has, therefore, been suggested at various times that Yemen is dependent upon the countries that employ its emigrant labor force. (It is worth noting that in the heyday of Yemeni emigration, it was sometimes suggested that the countries in which the Yemenis were providing the labor, for example, Saudi Arabia, were dependent upon Yemen.)[13] Although this dependency relationship is usually alleged to exist most clearly with Saudi Arabia and the Gulf states, it applies as well (but in less significant ways) to the other communities in which Yemenis have become numerous, such as Lackawanna, Dearborn, and the

21. Auto parts dealer, ᶜAmran, Yemen. *Thomas Stevenson*.

22. Suq (market), Yemeni highlands. *Jon Swanson*.

In addition to consumer goods available in the central market (bottom), there has been a proliferation of new shops (top) specializing in car parts, pharmaceuticals, cameras, watches, sound and video equipment, and other imported items.

San Joaquin Valley in the United States. This "dependency," of course, refers to the continued flow of external funding, as well as the soaking up of the Yemeni population "surplus."

The extent of the dependency relationship is often illustrated — by Yemenis and foreigners alike — by Yemen's current inability to provide itself with more than a fraction of its food requirements. Although too much could be (and sometimes is) made of the fact that Yemen is now so dependent upon the rest of the world for its foodstuffs (compared to the near-autarky with respect to food that is widely perceived to have existed under the Imamate), it is indicative of a real change in the relationship between Yemen and the remainder of the world.

It is, of course, the conclusion that both many Yemenis and interested observers draw from these developments that is of greatest interest: Yemen's current living standard is at the very least heavily dependent upon the goodwill of those states that employ its emigrants and permit them to remit their earnings. In the past few years, especially since 1983, however, some of the Peninsula states have, first of all, elected to have their economies developed with expatriate labor from the Far East and Southeast Asia; second, more recently, they have seen their oil earnings decrease, leading to an overall decline in construction and infrastructure-developing industrial labor demand. The consequences of this development if continued for many years would be profound, most especially for Yemen. It is, therefore, of some interest that the Peninsula states have not repatriated all of the Yemeni labor force, nor indeed made any overt and significant effort to have its numbers decrease (beyond perhaps natural attrition), probably because they understand the political and economic consequences for Yemen, and the Peninsula, were they to do so.

Inevitably, comments such as these require some attention to the relationship between North and South Yemen. Since neither of the two is, at the moment, economically self-sufficient (and does not seem likely to become so in the immediate future, despite the rosy hopes raised by the discovery of oil in exportable quantities in the north), there is really little point in associating with one another more closely. Such an affiliation would eliminate the financial assistance that North Yemen receives from Saudi Arabia, the Gulf states, and a host of Western states, and what South Yemen receives from its Soviet bloc suppliers and allies. There does not seem to be any reason to see a significant change in Yemen's international position, associations, and policy orientation if conditions remain essentially as they are at the present.

DOMESTIC POLICY ISSUES

Although the above implies that a large number of disparate factors are relevant to contemporary policy questions, some issues seem to be more important.

If, as a result of limits on migration, a drop in the remittance flow to the general populace (the private sector) or a progressive closing off of the current permeability and flexibility of the existing social system were to take place, the outlook for the future would become pessimistic. What Yemen has experienced in the last fifteen years is, as indicated above, the release of years of pent-up frustration with respect to many of the characteristics and benefits of the modern world and a significant relaxation of the very rigid set of class and social distinctions that characterized the *ancien régime*. If current social patterns and conditions were to become frozen as a result of some of the possibilities discussed above, the political consequences would probably be very serious. Critical to the current arrangements is a continued outflow of migrants as well as continued repatriation of a significant amount of foreign exchange.

The export of oil in significant quantities would, of course, affect the situation markedly; it would not, however, eliminate some of the basic problems. Furthermore, such a development would have other, perhaps equally serious, sociopolitical consequences. For the moment, however, even the most optimistic observers do not expect that Yemen's oil exports will do much more than cover about one-third of its requirements (for capital and budgetary funding).

There is a belief in a large part of the Yemeni population that the future will take care of itself and no long-range planning or preparation for the future is necessary. This is the result of a belief that their country is the linchpin of the area and that, whatever happens, someone will step in to correct the situation in the interest of Yemen and the Yemenis. One observer, who is unquestionably guilty of overstatement, suggests that the Yemenis have begun to take a very transitory view of their own country, since "with the exception of children and old men, practically every male in Yemen is either preparing for his first emigration, or merely visiting between two stints abroad. Surely one cannot expect these people to have a sense of belonging to, or the ability to participate in, a national project of development."[14]

It would, of course, be a serious distortion to believe that significant efforts have not been made to develop long-term solutions to some of Yemen's contemporary economic problems. For one thing, there are the various governmental ministries and agencies that have tried to coordinate the various foreign donor programs in an attempt to see that there is some logic and equity in the allocation of these new resources. For another, attempts that have been made in the private sector have attracted a great deal of attention. The first of these was the so-called LDAs—associations that sought to raise money and coordinate available resources for the projects that had the highest local priority (usually roads, schools, water supply, and clinics). Soon amalgamated into a national movement, the Confederation of Yemeni Development Associations (CYDA), their goals, leadership, and methods became heavily influenced by national leaders and goals, although they have continued to provide an important source of planning and implementation.[15]

The second, and more recent, domestic effort to cope with the economic conditions in contemporary Yemen is the Specialized Cooperative Associations (SCAs). Beginning in the early 1980s, these bodies were founded to coordinate the efforts of individual entrepreneurs in a number of areas; by far the most numerous grouping was in the field of agriculture (more than 80 percent of the roughly 100), with others in the areas of handicrafts, fishing, and even consumer goods. The basis for the SCAs is a mutual economic interest and membership in a specific economic activity group. Capital is raised from among the shareholding members, for the purpose, of course, of promoting increased production, more effective marketing, and new services. The government understands their value, as it did the value of the LDAs, and supports their activities with tax exemptions and incentives.[16]

One should not be too quick to assume that the existence of the LDAs and the SCAs proves there is a widespread cooperative ethic in rural Yemen that could tap the remittances for local development projects. In the first place, the years of imamic rule conditioned most Yemenis to a fierce independence in economic matters, and it is this independence that has fueled much of the initiative that the private sector has demonstrated in the past twenty years. Cooperation is likely to be found in only limited kinds of activities and is, furthermore, likely to be closely linked to local relationships and concerns.

In the second place, this is better used to illustrate the level of independence Yemenis are likely to demonstrate when they attempt to invest their capital in the local economy. In fact, what occurs is the founding of dozens of small firms all engaged in the same line of activity, making them all marginal.

It is, of course, possible that Yemenis who return after years of working abroad, particularly in the United States or Western Europe, where they earned the right to a pension (for example, social security), are interested in investing in some local enterprise or are willing to assist other family members (perhaps even close friends) in developing a local business that would provide a reliable source of revenue now that they can no longer emigrate. We have little information on such activities, though some scholars are willing to speculate on where such cooperation and investment are most likely to take place.

Perhaps most damaging in the long run is the remittance income, and the technological "progress" it has engendered and encouraged, which has also changed the orientation of many Yemenis with respect to the environment (in the broadest sense of that word). For all the emphasis among Yemenis upon the grandeurs of their country and their evident love of its features (effectively symbolized by the very high rate of return among those who go), as well as their desire to purchase *baladi* (locally produced) goods whenever possible even though they cost more, behaviors and circumstances have developed that are rapidly undermining the resources of the country (most especially land and water) and its ecology. The most obvious examples are the unrestricted use of groundwater supplies (through diesel-powered tube wells), the completely unregulated application of all types of toxic materials to the soil in an effort to increase productivity, the decline and even collapse of many of the traditional irrigation and cultivation systems (often if not always more appropriate to Yemeni conditions and microclimates than the imported ones), the almost total lack of concern with sewage and garbage management, and other activities that, in total, show a nearly complete lack of concern with the future consequences of current living and consumption patterns. It does not seem unreasonable to fear that this particular consequence of the "decade of affluence" may have a more important and far-reaching impact upon the economy and the society than some of the others—once they are forced upon the public consciousness, as they are likely to be in the near future.

CONCLUSIONS

In view of the difficulty of gathering appropriate data on many of these matters, definite conclusions are impossible. In fact, there are now many scholars and analysts collecting materials on precisely these matters, and we should be able in the near future to be

23. Yemen Bank for Reconstruction and Development, San͏ᶜa Branch. The Yemeni government has attempted to strengthen the domestic economy by investing in commercial and infrastructural projects, many of which have contributed to social development. Ironically, with Yemeni labor employed abroad, the government has been forced to import foreign labor for its own development programs, as seen by the crew of Chinese workers assembled in front of the bank. *Manfred Wenner*.

24. Along the road to Rida^c, Yemen. This once-productive field is now a dump for urban refuse—the by-product of the growth of consumerism in the 1970's "era of affluence." *Manfred Wenner.*

a good deal more precise on both the domestic and foreign policy impacts of the "decade of affluence" and its aftermath (the current retrenchment in the Yemeni economy). One significant problem, however, is that some of this research is directed at the most sensitive of all questions—both to the government and to the general population. Furthermore, it will be a long time, if ever, before we can lay out a clear causal relationship between the experience of a migrant Yemeni laborer in the Imperial and San Joaquin valleys of California and his inclination to support a particular political movement or leader in Yemen or to invest his surplus capital in a budding SCA.

On the other hand, it seems both fair and accurate to suggest that even if the migrants associate with religious and regional cohorts abroad, try to remain committed to the traditional values and behavior patterns, and attempt to retain a life-style they perceive as distinctively Yemeni, it is inevitable that they will return with some values changed, some new values gained, and some of their orientations (toward the material as well as the spiritual world) altered. Furthermore, the cultural artifacts they purchase and accumulate will also contribute to the slow but inevitable change in attitudes and behavior. Again, difficult though it may be to prove, it would appear that the development of the National Democratic Front in

the Hujjariyya region provides rough support for the contention that there is a link between emigration and one's political orientation (and inclination to engage in appropriate action to promote it).[17]

Of course, all these assertions have achieved the status of clichés; like other clichés, however, they often contain a grain of truth (if not more). What is clear is that the very act of emigrating and then returning is corrosive to the traditional belief systems—social, economic, and political—and the current instance is definitely not the first example thereof. It should not be necessary to recount in detail the rise of the Free Yemeni Movement and similar activities during the reign of Imam Ahmad to make the point more forcefully. We may, therefore, be confident in asserting that we have only begun to see the consequences of the latest wave of emigration from Yemen.[18]

NOTES

1. Ron Kelley, "Yemeni Farmworkers in California," (this volume); Juan Sanchez and Saul Solache, "Yemeni Agricultural Workers in California: Migration Impact," *Journal of Ethnic Studies* 8 (1980): 85–94.

2. Cf. Pat McDonnell, "Yemenis in California," *Middle East* 2 (January 1984): 30–31; Sanchez and Solache, "Yemeni Agricultural Workers."

3. Earlier relevant studies, besides those listed in notes 1 and 2, include S. Abraham and N. Abraham, eds., *Arabs in the New*

World (Detroit: Wayne State University Press, 1983); Mary Bisharat, "Yemeni Farmworkers in America," *MERIP Reports* (January 1975): 22–26; Ahmed al-Kasir, "The Impact of Emigration on Social Structure in the Yemen Arab Republic," in *Economy, Society and Culture in Contemporary Yemen*, ed. B. Pridham (London: Croom Helm, 1985); the works of Günter Meyer, especially "Labour Emigration and Internal Migration in the YAR," in *Economy, Society and Culture*, ed. Pridham; Thomas B. Stevenson, *Social Change in a Yemeni Highlands Town* (Salt Lake City: University of Utah Press, 1985); Susan Dorsky, *Women of ʿAmran: A Middle Eastern Ethnographic Study* (Salt Lake City: University of Utah Press, 1986).

4. J. A. Socknat and C. Sinclair, *Migration for Employment Abroad and Its Impact on Development in the Yemen Arab Republic* (Durham: Durham University Press, 1978); Nader Fergany, "The Impact of Emigration on National Development in the Arab Region: The Case of the Yemen Arab Republic," *International Migration Review* 16 (1982): 757–80; J. S. Birks, C. A. Sinclair, and J. A. Socknat, "Aspects of Labour Migration from North Yemen," *Middle Eastern Studies* 17 (1981): 49–63; as well as others.

5. The best survey of the literature on the presumed and alleged effects of migration is found in Jon Swanson, *The Consequences of Emigration for Economic Development: A Review of the Literature*, Papers in Anthropology, no. 20 (Santa Fe: Museum of New Mexico, 1979), 39–56; a different version is found in Swanson, *Emigration and Economic Development: The Case of the Yemen Arab Republic* (Boulder: Westview Press, 1979), 1–21.

6. It is, despite the protestations of the economists, perfectly rational for the Yemenis to spend on personal consumption. As many of the writers on the subject have pointed out, there is no financial-institutional infrastructure, there are no systemic opportunities for collective investing, there is no efficient institutional vehicle for saving, and last, but not least, there was no opportunity to buy these commodities until the 1970s; consequently, a pent-up demand had to be (and was going to be) fulfilled no matter what financial and government authorities might have wished. See on this subject Swanson, *Emigration and Economic Development*; Birks, Sinclair, and Socknat, "Labour Migration from North Yemen"; and many others.

7. The Yemeni government has provided exceptionally good statistical data on these and other matters covered in this essay in its annual *Statistical Yearbook*, published in Sanʿa.

8. On the changes in the role of women, a considerable literature has appeared in the past few years. It is best to begin with the works of Cynthia Myntti, especially her *Women and Development in Yemen Arab Republic* (Eschborn: GTZ [Agency for Technical Cooperation], 1979). See also Carla Makhlouf, *Changing Veils: Women and Modernization in North Yemen* (Austin: University of Texas Press, 1979). A more recent addition to the literature is Dorsky's *Women of ʿAmran*.

9. Two of the best-known examples were projects begun by U.S. AID: the Integrated Rural Development Project in Mahwit, and the Local Resources for Development Project in Hajja (both in the 1970s).

10. It has been suggested by many writers, including T. H. Lawrence, that Yemen has suffered multiple periods of overpopulation and has often experienced the phenomenon of mass emigration — as a result of either internal conflict or the attraction of other areas as places of alternative employment (the Red Sea basin, Southeast Asia, Western Europe, etc.).

11. See the works cited in note 8 above; although there is agreement among many regular observers of Yemen concerning the increase in veiling, the data on the subject are wholly impressionistic (at least at the present time).

12. On the process of internal migration, see the works of Günter Meyer ("Labour Emigration and Internal Migration" and the essential *Arbeitsemigration, Binnenwanderung und Wirtschaftsentwicklung in der Arabischen Republik Jemen* [Wiesbaden: Reichert]).

On the "informal sector," see J. S. Birks and C. A. Sinclair, "Employment and Development in Six Poor Arab States: Syria, Jordan, Sudan, South Yemen, Egypt, and North Yemen," *International Journal of Middle East Studies* 14 (1982): 45ff. On the decline in numbers of emigrants, in remittance flows, and the consequences for the Yemeni economy, see the publications of the International Monetary Fund as well as Yemen's *Statistical Yearbooks*.

13. A number of foreign (specifically American) aid experts who undertook analyses for U.S. AID and other organizations espoused this point of view in the period 1977–79.

14. Fergany, "Impact of Emigration," 775.

15. The literature on the LDAs is now nothing less than staggering in its size, though much of it is repetitive. Although somewhat overly optimistic in its assessment, the work by John Cohen et al., "Development from Below: Local Development Associations in the Yemen Arab Republic," *World Development* 9 (1981): 1039–61, is a good starting point. See also Sheila Carapico, *The Cooperative Framework for Local Development in Hajja and Hodeida Governorates* (Sanʿa: U.S. AID, 1980); and Richard Tutwiler, "Taʿawon Mahweet: Development and Social and Economic Change in a Yemeni Community," *Dirasat Yamaniyyah* 2 (1979): 3–14.

16. Edward Hogan et al., *Agricultural Sector Assessment: Yemen Arab Republic* (Washington, D.C.: U.S. AID, 1982).

17. On the National Democratic Front, see Ursula Braun, "Prospects for Yemeni Unity," in *Contemporary Yemen: Politics and Historical Background*, ed. B. Pridham (London: Croom Helm, 1984); J. E. Peterson, *Yemen: The Search for a Modern State* (London: Croom Helm, 1982), especially chapter 4; and Stephen Page, *The Soviet Union and the Yemens* (New York: Praeger Publishers, 1985), as a starting point. More details on the events of 1979–81 are to be found in an extensive literature that cannot be adequately covered here.

18. On the Free Yemeni Movement, see Manfred Wenner, *Modern Yemen, 1918–1966* (Baltimore: Johns Hopkins University Press, 1967); and more recently Leigh Douglas, "The Free Yemeni Movement: 1935–1961," in *Contemporary Yemen*, ed. Pridham.

SELECTED BIBLIOGRAPHY

Abraham, Nabeel
    1977   "Detroit's Yemeni Workers." *MERIP Reports* (May): 3–9, 13.

Abraham, Sameer, and Nabeel Abraham, eds.
    1981   *The Arab World and Arab Americans*. Detroit: Wayne State University Press.
    1983   *Arabs in the New World*. Detroit: Wayne State University Press.

Birks, J. S., and C. A. Sinclair
    1982   "Employment and Development in Six Poor Arab States." *International Journal of Middle East Studies* 14: 35–51.

Birks, J. S., C. A. Sinclair, and J. Socknat
    1981   "Aspects of Labor Migration from North Yemen." *Middle Eastern Studies* 17:49–63.

Bisharat, Mary
    1975   "Yemeni Farmworkers in California." *MERIP Reports* (January): 22–26.

Carapico, Sheila
    1980   *The Cooperative Framework for Local Development in Hajja and Hodeida Governorates*. Sanʿa: U.S. AID, 1980.

Chandavarkar, Anand G.
    1980   "Use of Migrants' Remittances in Labor-Exporting Countries." *Finance and Development* 12:36–39.

Cohen, John, et al.
  1981   "Development from Below: Local Development
           Associations in the Yemen Arab Republic." *World
           Development* 9: 1039-61.

Dorsky, Susan
  1986   *Women of ᶜAmran: A Middle Eastern Ethnographic Study.*
           Salt Lake City: University of Utah Press.

Fergany, Nader
  1982   "The Impact of Emigration on National Develop-
           ment in the Arab Region: The Case of the Yemen
           Arab Republic." *International Migration Review* 16:
           757-80.

Gerholm, Tomas
  1977   *Market, Mosque and Mafraj: Social Inequality in a Yemen
           Town.* Stockholm: Department of Social Anthro-
           pology, Stockholm University.

Halliday, Fred
  1984   "Labor Migration in the Arab World." *MERIP
           Reports* (May): 3-10, 30.

Hogan, Edward, et al.
  1982   *Agricultural Sector Assessment: Yemen Arab Republic.*
           Washington, D.C.: U.S. AID.

Lackner, Helen
  1978   *A House Built on Sand.* London: Ithaca Press.

McClelland, Donald
  1978   "Yemeni Worker Emigration and Remittances."
           Unpublished paper prepared for U.S. AID,
           Yemen.

McDonnell, Pat
  1984   "Yemenis in California." *Middle East* 2 (January):
           30-31.

Makhlouf, Carla
  1979   *Changing Veils: Women and Modernization in North
           Yemen.* Austin: University of Texas Press.

Meyer, Günter
  1986   *Arbeitsemigration, Binnenwanderung und Wirtschaftsent-
           wicklung in der Arabischen Republik Jemen.* Jemen-
           Studien, no. 2. Wiesbaden: Reichert.

Myntti, Cynthia
  1979   *Women and Development in Yemen Arab Republic.*
           Eschborn: GTZ (Agency for Technical Coopera-
           tion).
  1984   "Yemeni Workers Abroad: The Impact on
           Women." *MERIP Reports* (June): 11-16.

Niblock, Tim, ed.
  1982   *Society and Economy in Saudi Arabia.* London: Croom
           Helm.

Page, Stephen
  1986   *The Soviet Union and the Yemens.* New York: Praeger
           Publishers.

Pridham, Brian, ed.
  1984   *Contemporary Yemen: Politics and Historical Background.*
           London: Croom Helm.
  1985   *Economy, Society and Culture in Contemporary Yemen.*
           London: Croom Helm.

Richards, Alan, and Philip Martin
  1983   "The Laissez-Faire Approach to International
           Labor Migration: The Case of the Arab Middle
           East." *Economic Development and Cultural Change* 31
           (April): 455-74.

Ross, Lee Ann
  1977   "Yemen Migration—Blessing or Curse?" Unpub-
           lished paper prepared for U.S. AID, Sanᶜa.

Sanchez, Juan, and Saul Solache
  1980   "Yemeni Agricultural Workers in California:
           Migration Impact." *Journal of Ethnic Studies* 8:
           85-93.

Seragaldin, I., J. Socknat, J. Birks, and C. Sinclair
  1984   "Some Issues Related to Labor Migration in the
           Middle East and North Africa." *Middle East Journal*
           38: 615-42.

Shaw, R. Paul
  1983   *Mobilizing Human Resources in the Arab World.* Lon-
           don: Kegan Paul.

Socknat, J., and C. Sinclair
  1978   *Migration for Employment Abroad and Its Impact on
           Development in the Yemen Arab Republic.* Durham:
           Durham University Press.

Swanson, Jon
  1979a   *The Consequences of Emigration for Economic Develop-
           ment: A Review of the Literature.* Papers in Anthropol-
           ogy, no. 20. Santa Fe: Museum of New Mexico.
  1979b   *Emigration and Economic Development: The Case of the
           Yemen Republic.* Boulder: Westview Press.

Tutwiler, Richard
  1979   "Taᶜawon Mahweet: Development and Social and
           Economic Change in a Yemeni Community."
           Dirasat Yamaniyyah. 2: 3-14.

Wenner, Manfred
  1967   *Modern Yemen, 1918-1966.* Baltimore: Johns Hop-
           kins University Press.

Migration as a Rite of Passage in a Highland Yemeni Town

THOMAS B. STEVENSON
Middle East Center
Ohio State University

INTRODUCTION

The Yemen Arab Republic (Yemen) has a long history of labor emigration dating from the mid-1800s. The first emigrants were subsistence peasants from the southern highlands who sought work in the British colony in Aden. Although long famous for agriculture, Yemen's production has been robust only in comparison to that of its neighbors. Swanson (1979:47–55) suggests that it was production declines brought on by climatic and rainfall fluctuations that forced men to seek new, more stable economic activities. Myntti (1984:13) points out that in addition to the impetus provided by unpredictable, often sub par harvests, men left to avoid conscription into the army of Yemen's ruler, the imam. Also, Islamic inheritance rules and large families fragmented landholdings, often into unproductive parcels; sharecropping contracts awarded landlords from 25 percent to 75 percent of harvests; and, particularly in the years before the 1962 revolution, excessive government taxation undercut the incentive to produce (Halliday 1974:85–87).

Until the late 1960s, most emigrants continued to be from the southern region. Following in the paths of their kinsmen or fellow villagers, Yemeni men emigrated to a variety of overseas locations ranging from

Vietnam and Indonesia to Great Britain and the United States. The majority of these emigrants probably returned after a few years, but many men remained abroad permanently. The Yemeni communities in Cardiff, U.K., and Detroit and Buffalo, U.S.A., are only a few examples.

In the late 1960s and early 1970s, the range of travel narrowed, but the number of emigrants increased. The development projects that accompanied the growth of the oil industry in Saudi Arabia and the Persian Gulf states created a tremendous continuing demand for workers. Since the Saudi Arabian government lifted immigration restrictions in the early 1970s (Weir 1985:20), there has been a constant flow of Yemeni laborers across the border. In this period, emigration became an important economic outlet for men from Yemen's traditionally conservative northern tribal areas. Like their counterparts from the southern highlands, emigrants from the north were driven by the desire to escape a depressed, stagnant economy at home and to find an economic niche that enabled them to amass savings.

Emigration became so common that in most areas of the country there were few families that had not had men abroad. Estimates of the number of emigrants vary, but the "official" Swiss census conducted in 1975–76 put the number of long- and short-term

25. ᶜAmran, Yemen. *Thomas Stevenson.*

emigrants at 635,000, or 13.5 percent of the population. This means that 30 percent of homes had an absent male (Central Planning Organization 1978: I/73). Fergany (1982:761) concludes that in 1975 about 25 percent of the male labor force was abroad. Labor had become Yemen's primary export.

Work in the oil states became an important part of Yemeni men's lives. Although primarily an individual economic activity, the emigration experience has had broader personal and collective significance. All emigrants regard expatriate work as a means to acquire a new or enhanced status. In that sense, the emigration process is analogous to the rituals of status change described by van Gennep (1909) and Turner (1967, 1969). Drawing on data from 1978–79, this paper examines how and why emigration became an integral part of life in a town in Yemen's northern tribal highlands. First, applying van Gennep's and Turner's ideas, I show that emigration has the stages and symbolic components of a rite of passage. Second, I offer several explanations for this transition becoming an important—and, judging from 1986–87 data, a temporary—element of social life. Finally, I suggest that this rite has been both an individual and societal transformation in response to rapid social change. While the focus is on emigration to Saudi Arabia, the ritual processes and their implications do not differ significantly from those associated with emigration to the United States.

SETTING AND BACKGROUND

ᶜAmran is a market town in the central tribal highlands about an hour's drive north of the capital, Sanᶜa. In 1979, its population numbered around 6,000, of whom about half were traditional residents. Most of the roughly 3,000 newcomers settled during the period of rapid economic expansion that followed the 1962 revolution and the conclusion of the ensuing civil war (1962–69) that replaced Yemen's theocratic ruler, the imam, with a republican form of government.

Situated at the southern end of a large, fertile valley, ᶜAmran's prerevolutionary economy was based on subsistence agriculture. The town was the site of a weekly market, the local seat of the imam's government, and the center of ᶜAmran tribal territory. Government officials, religious experts, tribal leaders, merchants, tribesmen-peasants, and service providers all were ᶜAmran residents. The traditional social structure divided the population into three endogamous strata, each associated with ascribed occupations and personal attributes. In the ideal, tribesmen

were self-sufficient small-scale farmers and warriors responsible for protecting their tribal territory and its nontribal residents, the sayyids and the merchants and marketeers. Sayyids, the descendants of the Prophet Muhammad, were equated with religious expertise and honorable behavior. As members of the same elite stratum from which the imam was selected, sayyids often held important administrative and overseer positions. Merchants and service providers—marketeers whose professions ranged from butcher, barber, and innkeeper to praise singer and bleeder—were seen as deficient because their occupations were stigmatized.

These criteria were far from absolute. There were often too many men "assigned by birth" to an occupational category for the available work. Despite ascribed occupations, the economy was largely undiversified and land was distributed unequally. Tribesmen identified themselves as the landowning group. Yet in addition to tribesmen and their leaders, government agents, wealthy merchants, and the ruling imam all had land and many had large holdings. A few estates were as large as 3,000 to 5,000 *libna* (30 to 50 acres), but typical holdings were in the range of 20 to 300 *libna* (0.2 to 3 acres). Some of these parcels were poorly located and produced little; others had been repeatedly divided by inheritance and were too small to be productive. To pay taxes, to repay debts, or to compensate for poor yields, some farmers borrowed against their lands and eventually lost ownership of all or parts of their holdings. Small landowners supplemented their production through sharecropping contracts that paid landlords rents of up to 50 percent of harvests. For all but the largest property owners, it was impossible to accumulate savings. Since wealthy landowners invested their profits primarily in new rental properties, either shops or additional lands, and sometimes did so in Sanᶜa or elsewhere, the local economy remained undiversified and stagnant.

There were many adaptations to the formal ascriptive system. While some tribesmen sharecropped, others either worked for the government, as middlemen, or at nonstigmatized crafts that brought them into close contact with the marketplace. Many merchants and service providers farmed their own or sharecropped others' lands. Only a few sayyids had either religious or administrative expertise; most were small-scale farmers or craftsmen. Despite the apparent rigidity of the formal structure, some deviations were acceptable. But no sayyid or tribesman would risk censure and status loss by engaging in those commercial or service activities ascribed to the merchant or marketeer stratum.

Differences in wealth and resources produced intrastratum inequalities. The strata were ranked — sayyid, tribespeople, marketeers — and each was internally stratified. Thus, there were sayyids, who were poor and held fewer economic assets than the lowliest marketeers.

In the prerevolutionary era, some men emigrated to Ethiopia, Saudi Arabia, and elsewhere to escape from these harsh economic conditions. Probably a much larger number migrated to urban areas in Yemen. Some of these men returned to ᶜAmran; others have been forgotten.

The republican regime that replaced the sayyid-dominated theocracy in 1962 was not able to effect wide-ranging changes. Other than confiscating the lands of the imam and his close followers, the revolution did not change the patterns of landownership or otherwise alter the distribution of wealth.[1] The government declared an end to ascribed status, but this did not erase centuries of practice; nor did it remove the stigma attached to certain individuals and categories of work.

In the first years of republican rule, economic development projects were concentrated in the southern areas of Yemen where the population had been most supportive of the revolution. In the north, tribal conservatism and lack of government initiatives forced development to proceed at a much slower pace. Despite the change in government, economic progress remained limited. Thus, when Saudi Arabia's burgeoning economy created a huge demand for labor in the late 1960s and early 1970s, some ᶜAmranis saw this as a chance to start anew and emigrated. In addition to the prospect of amassing savings, these early emigrants sought to free themselves from the grip of a stagnant economy and to escape from the uncertainties of a lingering civil war.

During the 1970s, ᶜAmran became a boom town. Men returned from the oil states with savings and invested in new businesses. Money repatriated by emigrants stimulated the rapid expansion of the commercial sector at the expense of agriculture. The number of shops in ᶜAmran increased twentyfold, and productive topsoil was sold for landfill.

Returned emigrants were at the forefront of this economic change. Having abandoned agriculture to work in the oil states, often having only limited lands to return to, and reluctant to resume the arduous peasant life, returnees tried to create new economic niches for themselves. The emigrants' success in establishing commercial ventures spurred the town's expansion both by encouraging others to follow their lead and emigrate and by stimulating an influx of new settlers from adjoining villages and more distant regions. Most of the new settlers were returned emigrants who, like native ᶜAmranis, sought a place to invest their savings.

Not every returnee was able to set up a business. Although the economy was booming, growth was limited to only a few types of enterprise. While by 1978–79 there was a surfeit of establishments in a few basic categories, particularly small retail shops and taxis, there was insufficient demand to support the development or expansion of peripheral service activities such as automobile parts sales, freezer repair, automobile mechanics, or dry cleaners or laundries. With limited investment possibilities, many returnees demonstrated their break from the past by using savings to build modern single-story houses in areas outside the town's walls. Also, imported consumer goods, such as sewing machines and televisions,[2] became the major purchases for all returnees. These forms of conspicuous consumption were symbols of modernity and success for ᶜAmranis.

Along with economic growth stimulated by the large sums of money repatriated by emigrants, Yemen also experienced the oil states' high inflation rates. In order to maintain one's social position and standard of living, expatriate labor became essential. Work in the oil states was the only way a man and his family could keep up with other ᶜAmranis. It was also the easiest means of accumulating the capital necessary to participate in the town's rapid commercial expansion and of saving money to arrange a marriage. For those ᶜAmranis content with agriculture or reluctant or too poor to emigrate, the town's economic growth was disadvantageous. Those men who did not go abroad neither accumulated the savings nor acquired the skills gained by emigrants; they risked status loss.

Emigration seems to have begun as an escape for tribesmen and sayyids with modest landholdings; the smallest proportion of emigrants appears to have come from the marketeer and merchant stratum. But, by the mid-1970s, there were few households in ᶜAmran that had not had a father, son, or brother absent.[3] With so many men having worked abroad, emigration was a normal and expected event.

RITES OF PASSAGE

Although prerevolutionary ᶜAmran was a kinship-based society with a subsistence economy in which celebrations of status change might be expected, there were few rituals or ceremonies.[4] ᶜAmran was part of

26. ᶜAmran, Yemen. Traditional wedding procession. *Thomas Stevenson.*

and dominated by a theocratic state apparatus. Islamic doctrine stresses the equality of all believers. In local terms, the collective celebration of status change, such as entry into adulthood, might diminish or obscure the status differences ascribed in the formal hierarchy.

Aside from marriage, which usually occurred in the mid-teenage years, there were no male adolescent rites of passage in ᶜAmran society. The transition to adult status was casual, beginning with the uncelebrated wearing of the dagger, *janbiyya*, and culminating with the marriage ceremony. This gradual process coincided with sons moving toward greater participation in managing the household's agricultural or other economic pursuits and was a logical extension of the strong patriarchal principles that dominate family life.

Whereas marriage had formally designated adulthood, in the 1970s the town's economic growth forced men to delay getting married (Central Planning Organization 1978:I/93). Inflation increased bride-prices and it took longer to accumulate the money to arrange a marriage. During this period some young men began to break away from the traditional occupations of their fathers, but their search for new livelihoods was often difficult. As conditions

changed, entry into adulthood began to be defined by new criteria, particularly completion of secondary or military school or enlistment in the armed forces.

It was in this context that emigration functioned as a new rite of passage. Most emigrants have been young men between seventeen and twenty-five years old; the remainder of the discussion focuses upon this group.[5] For them, emigration served as an initiation since it provided the training, capital, and other intangible assets necessary to establish a new status. Often emigration preceded marriage and was the primary means of accumulating the money for a bride-price. As a rite of passage, the emigration process has many structural parallels to the marriage celebration.

Arnold van Gennep (1909) has demonstrated that important changes in status are marked by rites of passage and that these life crisis rituals have three identifiable stages: rites of separation, rites of transition, and rites of incorporation. Although in different ceremonies there may be variation in the importance or emphasis attached to each stage, all rites of passage must have these phases. Victor Turner has expanded on van Gennep's model.[6] In describing the stages he states that separation involves "symbolic behavior signifying the detachment of the individual" from his position in the social system (Turner 1967:94). In the transition or liminal phase, the passenger is placed in an ambiguous position, one that may have few of the qualities of either the former or future state. Often individual statuses and relationships may be inverted during the liminal phase (Turner 1969:106). In the final phase, incorporation, the passenger returns to a stable state, one signified by the assumption of clearly defined rights and obligations. Turner views this process as transformative, taking the neophyte and redefining his relationship in society.

In the cases described by van Gennep and Turner, the rite of passage is clearly circumscribed. Although the emphasis placed on each stage may vary, the entire rite is fixed in time and has a clear group or class of participants. Emigration does not have such sharply defined characteristics. For the individual, each phase and the entire rite are discrete, but there are no well-defined groups that pass through the stages together, nor is the rite an annual or periodic event. For the society, the rite is constantly in process: only the neophytes change and at any time there are passengers entering and exiting each phase. Finally, and in contrast to some rites of passage, this transition has at its core an overtly economic objective.

THE EMIGRATION PATTERN

Van Gennep and Turner have identified elements characteristic of each rite of passage stage. In the following sections, these criteria are presented with data typical of the emigration pattern as it was observed in ^cAmran during 1978–79.

Separation

Rites of separation set the stage for the liminal or transitional phase by physically or symbolically removing the neophyte from society and establishing some of the conditions under which he will make the transition. Individuals divest themselves of their status in and sever their ties to society. This places neophytes in an ambiguous status, one that is sometimes marked by their loss of gender symbols.

In ^cAmran, separation is the least precisely circumscribed stage. Since an emigrant's departure may be postponed for a variety of reasons, this phase may be brief or extremely drawn out. Still, there are clear indicators of separation.

While it is generally common knowledge that a man intends to go to Saudi Arabia or the Gulf states, the neophyte's intentions may also be signified by his

behavior. If he has been working—often at temporary day-labor positions or on family-owned or share-cropped lands—he stops and begins to "hang out" in the market. For many ^cAmranis, especially young men, "hanging out" has come to symbolize their separation from both the traditional and the emerging social system. Men may continue in this disconnected, ambiguous category for a protracted period until they decide on a course of action. Not all those youths who "hang out" will emigrate. For those men opting to go abroad there are often delays while arranging for transportation or, as in the late 1970s, the necessary travel documents. The neophyte signals the approach of his departure by his temporary absences in the capital while completing arrangements.

In the days prior to departure, some neophytes appear to enter a state of semiseclusion that is analogous to the physical separation or isolation adopted by the groom in the weeks preceding his wedding. Although he may continue to work, the groom avoids lingering in public. The neophyte also is not seen "hanging out" and, like the groom, may receive a few guests in his home for daily qat chews.[7]

The separation stage is completed when, without ado, the emigrant departs, leaving behind his dagger and guns, symbols of his status and, sometimes, wealth. These are also male symbols, and thus the neophyte enters the liminal phase, as is the case in many rituals (Turner 1967:96–98), without gender markers.

Transition

The transition stage is the most protracted and places the passenger in an ambiguous position. Turner (1967:95–101) views the liminal period as the center of the transformation. During this phase, the neophyte's invisibility to members of his society makes him unclassifiable in normal terms; he has no social reality. The liminal period is unstructured; the neophyte's status is inverted. The relationships characteristic of the liminal period are the antithesis of those that represent the neophytes' lives before and after the transition. Using binary oppositions Turner (1969:106–7) defines typical inversions found in the liminal phase. Among those applicable to the emigration case are (normal state/liminal state): inequality/equality; property/absence of property; status/absence of status; dress distinctions/uniform dress; wealth distinctions/no wealth distinctions; avoidance of hardships/hardships; and autonomy/domination (Turner 1969:106–7). Finally, in addition to not having appropriate gender markers, the neophyte is sometimes polluted and polluting because of his association with ambiguous or contradictory states or statuses.

Usually emigrants are abroad for two years or more; some men may spend ten years or more in intermittent emigration. The length of the absence depends on many factors. These include the amount of money a man feels he must save, his type of employment and wage rate, and whether the work is permanent, temporary, or seasonal. These factors notwithstanding, the rite is open-ended; it is the emigrant who decides when the transition is completed.

Generally, the emigrant maintains only indirect contact with his family and friends during the transition. In addition to money sent with friends or through agents, sometimes specific messages and occasionally cassette tapes are carried by men going to or returning from the oil states.[8] More often returnees pass along formal greetings attributed to the emigrant and report on his well-being. Infrequently, men come home for short visits of up to thirty days. These occur irregularly and are not made by all emigrants. In such cases, although the returnee is treated and feted as if he had completed the transition, all are aware that he will reenter the liminal phase. The time between return visits is at least one year.

As the rite is unbounded, there are always other emigrants further along in the transition. New emigrants tend to follow in the paths of fellow ᶜAmranis, often heading directly to a local contact in the oil states who will assume responsibility for them until they are settled. Although they are also neophytes, these guides or instructors introduce newcomers to the transition phase. For example, they explain the conduct expected of emigrants in Saudi Arabia and confirm or correct accounts the new emigrant has heard from returnees. The guides may provide initial temporary housing and help arrange for employment. Once they are settled and informed of local norms, the newcomers are on their own. Since the formal objective is capital accumulation, the balance of the liminal phase may be conducted without additional instruction from these guides.

Emigrants work long hours and live frugally. It is normal, and in order to meet their financial goals probably essential, for men to live in cramped conditions, ten to fifteen often sharing a house, with four or five men sleeping in the same room (cf. Ross 1981:3). Little money is spent except on necessities; making the *hajj* or pilgrimage to Mecca is the most common exception.

During the liminal period, emigrants are subject to a set of social rules and behaviors different from those expected at home. In ᶜAmran, many tribesmen and sayyids do not visit with merchants and marketers. In the oil states, where all emigrants, by virtue of experiencing the same conditions, have comparable status, interstratum socializing is not unusual. All emigrants tend to be on the same level or experience a sense of community.

Normal work patterns are sometimes inverted. In the oil states, some emigrants work at jobs, particularly those seen as service provision, that in Yemen are ascribed to low-status individuals. Although it is said that performing stigmatized or defiling tasks risks censure and status loss, this is true only if demeaning tasks are carried out in ᶜAmran. While some emigrants may work at "polluting" jobs, so long as the pollution is not brought home, the condition is temporary and not damaging. In the prerevolutionary era many men went to Sanᶜa and other cities in Yemen and worked in forbidden and demeaning jobs but retained their status upon returning to ᶜAmran.

Customarily ᶜAmranis work for themselves. Although it is often an overstatement, farmers and craftsmen are said to view themselves as their own bosses. Farmers, in particular, like to portray themselves as obtaining all their household food needs from their own fields. In fact, the low status of merchants and marketeers is sometimes attributed to their dependence on others for the products they sell or the services they provide (Gerholm 1977:130–32). During the transition, the situation is reversed; in the oil states, all ᶜAmranis become employees, learning to accept orders. Many positions are new and require training. All demand compliance with new work procedures, including punctuality and following directions.

The transition phase is completed when emigrants believe they have acquired the money and skills necessary to reenter ᶜAmran society and feel psychologically prepared to do so. Since men seek funds to establish a business and to arrange a marriage, they must estimate the necessary amounts. With high levels of inflation, the time necessary to acquire the requisites for a new status is variable.

Incorporation

Rites of incorporation serve to reintegrate the neophyte into society and his new status. Ceremonies surrounding this phase may include collective activities, such as communal feasts (van Gennep 1909:29). In ᶜAmran, these patterns are associated both with periodic visits and with the final return.

The emigrant's return is usually anticipated by messages or rumors, although the exact date of his

27. Bargaining for qat, outskirts of Taᶜizz, Yemen. The man on the left is a retired seaman from Michigan.
Jon Swanson.

28. Talib, Riyashiyah district, Yemen. The *takhzinah* or "qat chew" allows men and women, separately, to relax and exchange information in an informal setting. *Jon Swanson.*

reappearance is not known. The formal celebration of incorporation generally lasts between two weeks and a month, although it may be a much longer time before the returnee has established himself in ᶜAmran society. The returnee reassumes the symbols of his former state, particularly wearing the dagger, usually abandoning Saudi costume for Yemeni. Some men also display new weapons they have purchased.

During the first week, whenever the returnee is in public, he is accompanied by a close friend or relative. The escort reintroduces the neophyte to ᶜAmran society. He prompts the returnee, saying the names of approaching men in a low voice. All encounters require formal ceremonial greetings that include handshakes and kisses. These are very similar to the greetings that welcome a groom back into daily life following the postwedding period of seclusion.

When the emigrant returns to resettle, he receives well-wishers, particularly men in his age group and others from his family, in his home for the afternoon qat chewing parties. Every guest provides his own qat, and the returnee is expected to spend a fairly large sum on high-quality leaves for his own chewing.

This is the returnee's most common, and often most public, form of conspicuous consumption.

Qat parties have significance beyond the display of wealth. I agree with Varisco's (1986) contention that in Yemen's rapidly changing society, where traditional symbols and measures of status have become blurred, chewing qat has become a means of defining or emphasizing one's Yemeni identity. Qat consumption distinguishes Yemenis from other Arabs. Thus, in addition to displaying one's wealth, the daily qat parties emphasize a distinctively Yemeni activity and symbolize the returnees' incorporation into Yemeni society.

The emigrant is expected to give some portion of his earnings to his father and brothers. In addition, he must bring gifts of clothes, shoes, and appliances to members of the household and other close relatives and presents, ranging from wristwatches to mementos, to his friends.[9] These are signs of his success and a reaffirmation of his ties to his kin and friends. The gifts also demonstrate the emigrant's completion of the formal aspects of the rite of passage and, as in a potlatch, signify his claim of a new status. It may actually be some time before a man is able to solidify the acquisition of his improved status since this depends on his arranging a marriage and establishing a business.

THE IMPORTANCE OF EMIGRATION IN ^CAMRAN SOCIETY

This section examines how, during the late 1970s, emigration became an essential part of ^cAmran life and took on rites of passage attributes. In fact, the rite operated on several planes, some—but not all—of which were obvious to ^cAmranis. The following discussion of transformations begins with those aspects readily apparent to ^cAmranis, ones connected with establishing an adult status.

As we have seen, by 1978 ^cAmran's economy was based on commerce. For small-scale farmers to shift to a new means of production required capital. Most families had limited convertible assets. Apart from selling gold and silver jewelry, guns, or daggers, the usual means of raising capital was selling land or giving a daughter in marriage (discussed below). Throughout the post–civil war years, the price of land, even good agricultural plots, did not keep pace with inflation; in fact, except for plots immediately surrounding the town and desirable as building sites for houses or shops, land values remained at nearly prerevolutionary levels—a reflection of the almost total abandonment of agriculture during this period. This rejection of farming is emphasized by the sales of productive topsoil for landfill.

Without adequate convertible assets, emigration became the primary means of acquiring the funds to enter the commercial sector.[10] The amount of money repatriated varied, but it was common for men to report savings over two years of 50,000 to 80,000 Yemeni riyals ($11,100 to $17,800; in 1978–79, $1 U.S. was worth 4.5 Yemeni riyals). Many returnees' reported earnings exceeded these figures.[11] By providing a ready source of capital, emigration enabled a man to abandon one economic activity and start another.

In addition to being a source of savings, work in the oil states was a form of training. Emigrants emphasize the importance of acquiring a skill they could employ in ^cAmran. ^cAmranis, like virtually all Yemenis, entered the oil states as unskilled workers, and their range of job opportunities was limited. Although they received training, this was usually sufficient only to meet the standards for unskilled work.[12] Construction techniques, machinery operation and repair, driving a variety of vehicles, and

some basic forms of retail management were the most commonly acquired skills, but because Yemen's economic development lagged behind those of the oil states, these were valuable. In a broader sense, emigrants were immersed in a developing diversified economy and became aware of new economic possibilities, especially those of the retail trades.

Emigration also provided money for the bride-price. Fathers generally arrange marriages for their sons. Until the social and economic transformations of the 1970s, sons worked with their fathers, whose duty it was to provide all or most of the bride-price. Repatriated money and Yemen's economic growth led to a high inflation rate, and it was no longer possible for most fathers, particularly those in traditional occupations like subsistence farming, to meet escalating marriage expenses (cf. Stevenson 1985*a*, 1985*b*). Between 1976 and 1979, the amount of the bride-price jumped from 8,000–10,000 Yemeni riyals ($1,780 to $2,225) to 55,000–60,000 Yemeni riyals ($12,225 to $13,335).[13] Young men had to accumulate some or all of the money themselves by working abroad for several years. This dramatically increased men's age at marriage. Emigration became a form of bride service not only where a man demonstrated his ability to provide for a wife but where many of the funds he accumulated would be passed on to his father-in-law. In essence, fathers used their daughters' bride-prices to enter commerce or make an investment without having to work in the oil states.

Young men wish to be independent. In the past, they were expected to work for their fathers. Only as a youth matured, married, became a father, and established his own reputation did he achieve an identity apart from his father. Where independence once meant establishing self-sufficiency, today it means being free from many of the economic and social obligations of the past. Agriculture and traditional occupations represent the hard work of the past and being under the control of fathers who are often seen as out of touch with modernity. Young men want to have their own businesses and separate houses. For them, emigration has been a means of escaping from years of servitude to a patriarch and a way of propelling themselves, socially and financially, into the emerging socioeconomic system and sometimes onto an even plane with their elders.

These are the reasons ^cAmranis cited for emigration. Each is related to a young man's striving for a separate identity, one apart from that of his family. Emigration leads to the breakup of the extended family, itself a significant rite of passage, and facilitates this process by providing the wherewithal to sever

29. The spiraling inflation of recent years has caused bride-prices to rise so dramatically that many young men working in foreign countries can no longer afford to marry. *Sojourner snapshot, Yemen.*

30. Native *janbiyyas* and Soviet-made AK-47 assault rifles denote an owner's status. Returning migrants resume the display of these symbols of power once they are back home. *Sojourner snapshot, Yemen.*

some of the ties of former relationships. To ᶜAmranis, emigration allows for the formation of a new set of relationships. But these are only the most obvious expressions of emigration as an initiation. The rite of passage also facilitated changes in ᶜAmran's social system.

It was not only the emigrant who experienced dislocation. Male absence created a void in the household unit. Where families continued to farm, women, in addition to doing their share, often undertook the tasks and decision-making responsibilities of men. Myntti (1984:12–13) describes this in a village in the Hujjariyya district of Taᶜizz province in the south of Yemen, where the loss of labor was in part countered by emigrants sending home money that enabled fathers to make investments and "retire" from agriculture. For married couples who followed local custom and resided with the husband's family, long male absences also caused strains in the household. Women often have conflict with mothers-in-law and feel more

vulnerable without their husbands being present. It was not uncommon for ᶜAmran women to return to their fathers' homes for the duration of their husbands' absences, causing an additional labor loss. While it was the emigrant who experienced the most obvious hardship, his family also bore a heavy burden.[14]

In the post–civil war years and into the mid-1970s, tribesmen and sayyids continued to view commerce with disdain. Formerly, if men in these social strata engaged in commerce or service provision in ᶜAmran they would lose status. Yet the most common form of enterprise established by returnees, the majority of whom are of tribal descent, was a general goods shop selling imported foods and clothing. In 1979, ᶜAmranis owned eighty-seven shops of this type, and 54 percent of these were owned and operated by tribesmen. None had lost his traditional status; although occasionally the butt of jokes, this type of work had lost most of its stigma. Turner (1967:105) notes that during the liminal phase the passenger is forced or encouraged to think about the values of his society. ᶜAmranis usually say they learned in Saudi Arabia that it was acceptable to engage in commerce, a view suggesting a pronounced shift away from the traditional tribal attitudes toward mercantile activity.

As an expression of their new attitude toward some forms of commerce, ᶜAmranis used two terms to describe mercantile activity. "Merchant" is the word used to describe the traditional buyer and seller of local products or those born into this stigmatized stratum.[15] "Businessman" refers to those men engaged in those newly reclassified, acceptable forms of commerce based primarily on the sale of imported consumer goods, although the dividing line between the categories is not precisely drawn. Tribesmen became businessmen, not merchants. New occupations such as taxi driving, wholesaling consumer goods, or supplying building materials and skilled trades like modern carpentry, watch repair, welding, or concrete construction are novel categories that have no association with traditional low-status service provision.

The shift to new occupations, as Tutwiler (1985) has argued, created a different relationship to the means of production. In contrast to modernization theory, he contends that rather than leading to or emphasizing class differences,[16] the wealth repatriated by emigrants actually created a period, probably brief, in which the former class system is replaced by what is essentially an egalitarian society. This may be seen as a vestige of the classlessness typical of the liminal period. Having provided their own start-up capital, peasants were in control, owners of their own establishments. No longer were they subject to the stipulations, restraints, and exploitation of sharecropping contracts. Although their control was far from absolute,[17] all new operators entered the marketplace on an equal footing.

Viewed from a national perspective, emigration drew together all Yemenis. As is the case with age grade systems, the emigration-cum-initiation experience integrates all Yemenis. ᶜAmranis, like other Yemenis, are provincial. Under the imam, they had little contact with other Yemenis or the outside world. In the oil states, while still preferring to live and socialize with others from their town or from nearby villages, ᶜAmranis also had a wide variety of contacts with fellow Yemenis, other Arabs, and foreigners. Often their fellow workers have been from different areas of Yemen or other countries. This cosmopolitan atmosphere is a sharp inversion of patterns at home, where non-ᶜAmranis are viewed with suspicion. Emigration lowered social barriers and may have contrib-

uted to a sense of unity among all Yemeni emigrants. Turner (1969:95–96) describes this feeling of community: "Among themselves, neophytes tend to develop an intense comradeship and egalitarianism. Secular distinctions of rank and status disappear or are homogenized."

THE CASE OF NONEMIGRANTS AND LOST INITIATES

Most accounts of initiations remark on the importance of proper decorum during the ceremony and the consequent loss of good standing that failure to behave properly ensures; there are even bleaker prospects for those who do not undertake the transition at all. As local or regional economies diversify and become connected to complex social systems, there may be an increase in the number of ways to achieve adult status. Each applies to a particular group; each individual need not pass through the same rite, although there may be some consequences if an individual does not complete the transition appropriate to his cohort. In the present context, status loss may result from not undergoing a ritual transformation, but this transition need not be emigration.

In ᶜAmran, emigration was not required of all young men. There seem to have been two, not mutually exclusive, high-status categories of nonemigrants. The first group includes the sons of men who, although affected by inflation, held sizable assets. This small group, including some young men from the shaikh's household, seems not to have needed the money or training that others sought in the oil states. Their adult status seemed to be based on traditional status scales or criteria.[18] The second group includes the graduates of secondary and military schools, who form an elite class of nonemigrants. For this group, most of whom will become high-ranking officers or bureaucrats, initiation was completed with the awarding of the diploma.

Enlisted military service is an option available to all young men. While it provides a career, in 1978–79 most youth regarded this as a poor choice, one with little prospect for the future.

Beyond these exceptions, emigration became nearly essential, and young men were under social pressure to fulfill their obligations to their families by going abroad. Those young men who neither emigrated nor fell into either of the high-status nonemigrant categories were on the periphery of ᶜAmran society. Some men who "hung out" in the marketplace were in this group. Some were too poor and apparently could not raise travel expenses; others seemed to lack the desire.

There were consequences for those who did not emigrate. First, lacking the financial resources to keep pace with social change, they inevitably faced status loss. This was of increasing significance since money and other assets were beginning to take precedence over ascribed status criteria. While returned emigrants might enjoy comparable standing and reenter society on a common footing, inflation widened the monetary gap between individuals. Differences in assets became more pronounced, especially between emigrants and nonemigrants. Second, nonemigrants who did not remain in traditional work usually could not find any but the most modest employment. This insured their status loss.

Additionally, nonemigrants were viewed as lacking status or, more appropriately, a place in ʿAmran society. This is perhaps the clearest indication of the importance of establishing an adult status. As one returnee, the owner of a general goods shop, remarked to me (Stevenson 1985b:106–7), "Men without a place wander about like children."

This same remark might have been made about those men who seem never to reenter ʿAmran society. There are a number of men who periodically returned from Saudi Arabia, spent excessively on qat, consumer goods, and sometimes whiskey, then—with little money left—departed. Either they had saved little and could not complete the transition or they could not identify a suitable position for themselves in the local economy. These men were also seen by ʿAmranis as not having status. With few new avenues opening, the size of this group of semipermanent emigrants seemed destined to increase. In 1978–79, for example, there was a surfeit of taxi drivers and general goods dealers, the most common enterprise taken up by returnees. For all the town's growth, the range of economic activities conducted in ʿAmran remained quite limited until the opening of a cement factory in 1982.

CONCLUSION

Labor emigration, at least to Saudi Arabia and the Persian Gulf states, has probably been a temporary phenomenon for ʿAmranis. The amount of available work is affected by the demand for oil, oil revenues, and the reinvestment of petrodollars in development projects and is, therefore, not limitless.[19] In 1978–79, there were indications that it was becoming more difficult for new Yemeni emigrants, who were generally paid higher wages than emigrants from Asia, to find positions in Saudi Arabia. Fergany's (1982:760–61) prediction of a decreasing

demand in the oil states for unskilled laborers, like most ʿAmrani and other Yemeni workers, has proven accurate. For example, many ʿAmranis began to return in the early 1980s; by late 1986, the number of emigrants declined to the point that informants could rarely give the names of more than a few dozen absentees, most of whom are now regarded, like their counterparts in America, as nearly permanent emigrants. When world oil prices dropped sharply in early 1986, public expenditures in the oil states were reduced, and many emigrants were forced to return to Yemen. In late 1986 and early 1987, it was common to see as many as ten vehicles per day, crammed full and piled high with consumer goods, passing through ʿAmran as emigrants returned to their villages farther south.

Most ʿAmranis regarded emigration as a way to acquire status in ʿAmran. They say they intended to remain abroad only until they were able to return and establish their own businesses. Despite rapid growth, ʿAmran's economy has boasted relatively few occupations. The nature of the local economy changed, but it continued to offer limited investment opportunities and remained largely undiversified. Emigrants experienced increasing difficulty in reinserting themselves into the economy, a factor that in part explains the strong attraction of the modest wages paid by a public sector cement factory that opened near ʿAmran in 1982. Were high-paying jobs to continue to be available, men would continue to emigrate with the hope of keeping up with the pace of change and being able to arrange marriages, but they would not be assured of being able to establish a commercial enterprise.

Recent events suggest the end of the current period of emigration, but they do not alter or weaken the former importance of the experience, nor do they diminish its rite of passage qualities. Emigration was, and for some still is, a process that integrated and initiated ʿAmranis and ʿAmran into Yemen's emerging social and economic systems. On an individual level, emigration provided the means—new ideas, skills, and funds—to acquire new statuses. From the societal point of view, emigration contributed to a transformation of the social system, easing traditional parochialism. Working abroad provided emigrants with a common experience that united all Yemenis and facilitated the development of a common national identity. The sense of community, although established abroad, was repatriated.

Ritual is sometimes regarded as a mechanism facilitating social change. Ceremonies provide a release from the tensions associated with alterations of the social system and contribute a structure that normalizes change. In ʿAmran, emigration has been an economic necessity. The ritual features that have crystallized around it served to place the transition in an appropriate, understandable social context, one that incorporated the process into ᶜAmran life.

NOTES

1. In ᶜAmran, most confiscated properties were acquired by prominent tribal families, especially those of the shaikh and his relatives.

2. By 1986, these included vehicles (cars and trucks), videotape players, washing machines, bottled gas cookers, and—in areas without electricity—diesel motors and electric generators.

3. I do not have actual figures to support this contention, but similar results can be reached through analysis of the 1975 census data. By eliminating roughly 50 percent of the population that may be regarded as new settlers, and returnees, and then calculating emigration rates, the rate among native ᶜAmranis becomes 6.7 percent or 12.8 percent of males.

4. There are no ceremonies comparable to the elaborate tribal celebration of circumcision described by Weir (1985: 139–40) in Razih in the far north of Yemen.

5. Although there are no statistics giving an age breakdown, emigrants are not merely from the seventeen- to twenty-five-year-old age group. This group is used as the focus because it best demonstrates the rite of passage aspect of emigration. There are older emigrants, the age range being roughly seventeen to forty. Some men do not emigrate because of prohibitive costs. Ross (1981:4) mentions initial expenses of 10,000 to 20,000 Yemeni riyals. Also when all young men in a household do not emigrate, it is often because one man has been sent as a "family representative."

6. Turner (1973) has described pilgrimages as liminal phenomena. While there are many similarities between emigration and pilgrimages, emigration lacks any sort of sacred aura.

7. Qat (*Catha edulis*) is a shrub, the leaves of which, when chewed, produce a mild euphoria. Yemeni chew qat daily, both for the effect and because it is an important social activity.

8. The installation of telephone service in ᶜAmran in 1983 does not seem to have increased the extent of contacts.

9. In some respects, emigration is analogous to men going off to war. Although ᶜAmran tribesmen have occasionally participated in armed conflicts, warfare has not been a major part of their history, but it remains an important part of their ethos. Young men may be absent for long periods in times of conflict and their rewards, the spoils, are comparable to the goods brought home by returnees.

10. Not everyone raises all the necessary capital in Saudi Arabia. Some men supplement their savings with funds borrowed from relatives and patrons. In this case, control of the means of production resembles that of sharecropping, with the notable difference that men can repay these loans if their business is profitable.

11. Various figures have been suggested as the sums individual emigrants repatriate. Ross (1981:4–5) offers amounts in the range of 20,000 to 25,000 Yemeni riyals annually. Weir (1985:20, 170) cites several sources, including Steffen and Blanc's (1982:103) estimate that in 1977–78 annual remittances averaged 12,575 Yemeni riyals ($2,800).

In 1978, informants in ᶜAmran were vague about the extent of their earnings, but some purchases suggested the figures were much higher. There were cases where men seem to have repatriated funds in excess of 100,000 Yemeni riyals (in 1978–79, $1 U.S. equaled 4.5 YR) over the full term of their expatriate work.

Some very preliminary results from a survey of returnees conducted in ᶜAmran in 1986 revealed they had been paid wages ranging from 1,500 to 5,000 Saudi riyals per month. (From 1975 to 1986, $1 U.S. equaled roughly 3.5 Saudi riyals.) A few workers had earned 7,000–8,000 SR per month. Emigrants spent as little as one year to as many as twenty-five years abroad.

12. Compared to other emigrants in the oil states, Yemenis are reportedly paid high wages for the types of work they perform (see Harvey [1985], for example). This largesse has to do with Saudi efforts to gain and maintain influence in the region (cf. El Azhary 1984).

13. In 1980 or 1981, a bride-price limit of 30,000 YR was established for the ᶜAmran region. This local policy corresponded, coincidentally, with the beginning of the end of unlimited job prospects in Saudi Arabia.

14. In 1986, returned emigrants were more likely than in 1978–79 to portray their years abroad as difficult. They often complained of poor or discriminatory treatment by Saudis. This may be viewed as another hardship of the transition period.

15. The term translated as "merchant" (*bayaᶜ*) has the additional important meaning of having accepted the authority of others. This is a reference to the protected status of members of this group (Stevenson 1985b:64).

16. Weir (1985) argues that emigration has produced wealth that allows everyone to display social equality through qat chewing. Qat parties are arenas for announcing news and reinforcing traditional social status.

17. The operations of these shops, including the pricing and supply of goods, are regulated by outside forces. The government sets the maximum prices that can be charged for many imported items. Thus, it is wholesalers who control profit margins and the range of wares stocked in a shop.

18. To avoid emigration, a family's assets must be diversified and produce a cash income. This excludes agricultural land, since this has not kept pace with inflation. Some young men from wealthy families have also emigrated. This may be because their cohorts are doing so, and there is a strong ideology of tribal equality, or because they have nothing to do at home.

19. There have been obvious declines in the number of emigrants. Still, according to preliminary 1986 census data (Central Planning Organization 1986) 17.3 percent of the male population was outside the country.

SELECTED BIBLIOGRAPHY

Central Planning Organization, Yemen Arab Republic
    1978   *Final Report of the Airphoto Interpretation Project of the Swiss Technical Co-operation Service.* Berne: Swiss Technical Co-operation Service.
    1986   "Preliminary Results of the Population and Housing Census, February 1986: Sanᶜa." Mimeograph, March 1986.

El Azhary, M. S.
    1984   "Aspects of North Yemen's Relations with Saudi Arabia." In *Contemporary Yemen: Politics and Historical Background*, ed. B. R Pridham, 195–207. London: Croom Helm.

Fergany, Nader
    1982   "The Impact of Emigration on National Development in the Arab Region: The Case of the Yemen Arab Republic." *International Migration Review* 16(4):757–80.

Gennep, Arnold van
    1909   *The Rites of Passage.* Translated by M. B. Vizedon and G. L. Caffee. Chicago: University of Chicago Press.

Gerholm, Tomas
    1977   *Market, Mosque and Mafraj: Social Inequality in a*

Yemeni Town. Stockholm: Department of Social Anthropology, Stockholm University.

Halliday, Fred
    1974   *Arabia without Sultans: A Political Survey of Instability in the Arab World*. New York: Vintage Books.

Harvey, Nigel
    1985   "Consumption in the Yemen Arab Republic." In *Economy, Society and Culture in Contemporary Yemen*, ed. B. Pridham, 102–6. London: Croom Helm.

Myntti, Cynthia
    1984   Yemeni Workers Abroad: The Impact on Women. *MERIP Reports* (June):11–16.

Ross, Lee Ann
    1981   "An Informal Banking System: The Remittance Agents of Yemen." Working Paper No. 12. Cornell University.

Steffen, Hans, and Olivier Blanc
    1982   "La démographie de la République Arabe du Yémen." In *La Péninsule arabique d' aujourd'hui*, ed. Paul Bonnenfant, vol. 2, 73–106. Aix en Provence: Centre d'Etudes et de Recherches sur l'Orient Arabe Contemporain.

Stevenson, Thomas B.
    1985*a*   "Inflated Bride-Prices Threaten Status Relationships: A Case from Yemen." Paper presented to the Central States Anthropological Society, Louisville.

    1985*b*   *Social Change in a Yemeni Highlands Town*. Salt Lake City: University of Utah Press.

Swanson, Jon
    1979   *Emigration and Economic Development: The Case of the Yemen Arab Republic*. Boulder: Westview Press.

Turner, Victor W.
    1967   *The Forest of Symbols: Aspects of Ndembu Ritual*. Ithaca: Cornell University Press.

    1969   *The Ritual Process: Structure and Anti-Structure*. Ithaca: Cornell University Press.

    1973   "The Center Out There: Pilgrim's Goal." *History of Religions* 12(3):191–230.

Tutwiler, Richard
    1985   "Capitalism and Rural Social Structure: Observations on Class Formation in Highland Yemen." Paper presented to the Middle East Studies Association of North America, New Orleans.

Varisco, Daniel Martin
    1986   "On the Meaning of Chewing: The Significance of *Qat* (Catha Edulis) in the Yemen Arab Republic." *International Journal of Middle East Studies* 18(1):1–13.

Weir, Shelagh
    1985   *Qat in Yemen: Consumption and Social Change*. London: British Museum Publications.

31. Hajj Nasser (left), from Maᶜazoub in the Riyashiyah district, Yemen, whose son and three brothers have emigrated to the United States, stands hand in hand with a migrant who owns a store in California's San Joaquin Valley. *Jon Swanson*.

Sojourners and Settlers in Yemen and America

JON C. SWANSON
School of Social Work
University of Michigan, Ann Arbor

America is a nation of common people from marginal environments. In spite of contemporary America's preoccupation with coats of arms, few of our ancestors were the children of privilege. Nor did they come from lush plains or fecund valleys. More often, it was the mountains and hill country they left behind where stony soils, forests, or harsh weather made farming difficult and made them willing to tear themselves from their families and take their chances in far-off America. They were Irish from Kerry and Donegal, Italians from Sicily and Abruzzo, Romanians from the mountains of Transylvania, and Swedes from the forests of Smaland and Dalarna.

Although they were poor, they were rarely subject. In fact, most owned their land, though these meager holdings were rarely enough to assure more than a bare subsistence to the families that depended on them (Scott 1968:3). Not surprisingly, exaggerated rumors of high wages, easy work, cheap land, and even gold in the streets made the United States an irresistible alternative for many such impoverished peasants.

Despite America's glittering promise, few abandoned their native lands without regret; in varying degrees, most continued to maintain ties to relatives and friends back home. Once in the New World, the hardships and humiliations of being strangers in a strange land sometimes reinforced these ties as immigrants came to cherish memories of what more and more seemed the carefree life of their native villages.

American life was seldom, if ever, adopted wholesale. Rather, each group by one means or another attempted to maintain Old World traditions, customs, and beliefs in this new land. In the end, they usually settled on a compromise and, recreating the world in their own image, became Polish Americans, German Americans, Chinese Americans, and so forth.

While many migrants were content to fabricate a synthetic culture, others, more conservative, continued to measure their achievements within the cultural and even geographical context of the village. These migrants nurtured the dream of returning home to build a large house and adopt the status and life-style of the local gentry. Some were successful in realizing this ambition. Of the estimated 40 million people who immigrated to the United States between 1830 and 1930, fully one-third returned home (Kraut 1982:17). Not infrequently, however, migrants returned to disappointment, finding that the serenity of their childhood recollections evaporated as responsibilities shifted to their adult shoulders and they were struck as never before by the inconvenience, isolation, and pettiness of village life. In short, they discovered that they had accepted, however imperfect, a new reality

32. Winnowing grain in Kawkaban, Central Highlands, Yemen. The traditional agriculture practiced in Yemen differs markedly from the mechanized, labor-intensive agribusiness in the United States. The emigrant's ties to the land, as owner and farmer in Yemen, change drastically when he assumes a job as migrant farmworker in California. *Jon Swanson.*

that had bewilderingly transformed the familiar into the alien.

Although relative newcomers to America, the Yemenis fall squarely into this tradition of independent peasant immigrants. They are pilgrims in the land of plenty; though, like their Lebanese Muslim predecessors (Haddad 1983:14; Naff 1983:66), most do not intend to stay in the United States, many will remain and they and their children will make their contribution to America's vast and eclectic tradition. In the process, they will suffer pains of adjustment, perhaps more than most, for they are Muslims from a remote land with a tradition markedly different from that of the West.

Yemen is the relatively verdant patch of mountains in the southwest corner of the Arabian Peninsula that includes the Yemen Arab Republic (YAR) in the north and the Marxist People's Democratic Republic of Yemen (PDRY) in the south.[1] Isolated by deserts to the east and north and by the Arabian and Red seas to the south and west, it conforms to its usual stereotype as a hot, dry desert only on its lowland fringes. Elsewhere rugged mountains that reach altitudes of eight to ten thousand feet contravene the effects of its tropical latitude and produce a moderate, nearly perfect, climate.

Still, "relative" is the key word to use in describing the region's rainfall, for while Yemen is green, it is by no means lush. Most parts of the country receive no more than twelve inches of rain annually, about the same as Albuquerque, New Mexico. The bulk of this precipitation falls in two summer maxima, March–April and July–August. Even this pattern is unreliable, however. Thus, in 1982 rainfall in the coastal Tihama was so abundant that land normally given over to desert was planted and the area became a sea of green. The following year, the same region suffered a severe drought. Similarly, in 1984 the monsoon was late in coming to the highlands. No rain fell until mid-May, and by that time livestock had begun to die because of a shortage of fodder on the treeless, now totally barren slopes. In the past, farmers countered the weather's vagaries by maintaining a two-year supply of grain, or at least this was the ideal. Today, most peasants insure against famine with remittances from relatives working abroad. With this money they can buy American, Australian, or Canadian wheat and Dutch, Danish, or Austrian powdered milk.

The traditional subsistence pattern of Yemen centers around sorghum-millet and cattle with milk and grains providing the bulk of the diet. Sheep and goats

33, 34. Threshing wheat (above) and stacking grain for storage (below), ᶜAmran, Yemen. *Thomas Stevenson*.

35. Ford River Rouge automobile complex, Dearborn, Michigan. Like eastern and southern European villagers before them, Arab immigrants, including Yemenis, live in the small multiethnic community of South Dearborn, commonly known as the "South End," situated on the edge of the mammoth industrial park. *Jonathan Friedlander.*

36. Asparagus harvest, winter, Richgrove area, San Joaquin Valley, California. *Ron Kelley.*

37. Yemeni autoworker in "the pit," Cadillac assembly line, Detroit. *Tony Maine.*

38. Yemeni steelworkers and their families have settled in the Buffalo area, where they have established permanent residence in the "First Ward" neighborhood of Lackawanna, N.Y. The portrait of Nasser in this photo, and of Yemen's president and other Yemeni and Arab political figures (see photographs 7, 21, 107, 116) illustrate nationalistic and pan-Arab sentiments. *Milton Rogovin.*

39. Cafe in San^ca, Yemen. The coffeehouse is an important social and cultural institution transposed to the Yemeni emigrant communities in the United States (see photographs 40, 41). *Nikki Keddie.*

were also husbanded, though one should not assume that meat was a regular or frequent element in the fare of most villagers. The most important cash crop was coffee, which together with hides accounted for the bulk of the nation's modest trade surplus.

With the exception of the highland plateaus and lowland periphery, most of these crops are produced on terraces supported by elaborately engineered stone walls. Such fields, which climb the steep mountain slopes like giant stairs, slow runoff, conserve soil, and permit the cultivation of land that in better-favored regions of the world would be left to grazing animals and feral species. Often such fields are not amenable to the introduction of modern machinery, so that livelihoods can be wrested from the unaccommodating environment only with massive investments of hand labor.

Nevertheless, as is so often the case in alpine regions, minimal subsistence and rugged terrain have combined to discourage would-be conquerors, thwart the evolution of strong central government, and promote fierce individualism.[2] Traditionally Yemenis have organized themselves around locally autonomous tribal segments. Occasionally such groupings coalesce for brief periods to repel outsiders or conquer new territory; however, for the most part, competition for scarce resources within a subregion has a centrifugal

effect on sociopolitical relations, which are characterized by truculence and pugnacity at every level.

Regional groupings maintain a similarly fragile standoff with the central authority, which has usually been willing to accept a minimal tribute in order to avoid the costs of an inevitably unrewarding military campaign. No conqueror has held Yemen for long, and few have controlled it in its entirety. North Yemen's most recent colonizers were the Turks, who garrisoned the cities but only sporadically ventured into the countryside, much of which they never brought under their hegemony. In the south, the British reluctantly extended their control outside of Aden only when outlying shaikhs and sultans threatened the port and coaling station. In general, they were content to ignore most of what is now the Yemen Arab Republic.

In the past decade, the independence of the tribes has been eroded somewhat by the development of a comprehensive network of roads and the adoption of modern weaponry. Still, the irrepressible tribesman with his *janbiyya* (dagger) at his belt and rifle over his shoulder remains an everyday feature of the countryside, at least in the north.

The same conditions that helped secure the region's autonomy also encouraged many Yemenis to seek their fortunes in less austere environments. South

40, 41. Yemeni club, Dix Avenue, South Dearborn, Michigan. *Tony Maine*.

Arabians have been going abroad for millennia, no doubt well in advance of the catastrophic collapse of the dam at Marib that Yemeni folklore insists marks the beginning of the exodus.[3] In pre-Islamic times, Yemenis settled Oman and followed the spice and incense routes north as both traders and migrants. With the advent of Islam, they joined the armies of the Prophet and his successors, and today many people in North Africa and the Levant recognize South Arabia as their original home.

Modern emigration from the region began about the same time the British established themselves at Aden (1839) and may be divided into two phases. The most recent phase was initiated by hikes in the world price of oil, which by the end of the October War of 1973 had left Saudi Arabia and its neighbors awash in petrodollars. The Yemen Arab Republic, which is the focus of the remainder of this discussion, had at that time no commercially exploitable oil resources and, therefore, was not included directly in this bonanza.[4] It did benefit indirectly, however; as the Saudis, Kuwaitis, and other nations on the Peninsula embarked on development schemes that created labor demands exceeding their domestic resources, Yemen was able to export its labor force at premium prices.

Although not as lucrative as in the past, intra-Peninsular migration continues to attract large numbers of workers. It is estimated that there are at least 500,000 Yemenis working in Saudi Arabia and the Gulf.[5] During the second half of the 1970s, migrants regularly sent home more than a billion dollars a year (Central Planning Organization 1983:186) and for a time the republic boasted a positive balance of payments. Increased consumption had swallowed this surplus by 1979, however, and it now appears that lower demand and growing competition in the foreign labor market have led to a decline in the level of remittances and a weakening of the Yemeni riyal against other currencies.

The migration boom came shortly after the end of the civil war that secured the republic and expelled the last imam from Yemen.[6] Together these two events ushered in an era of unprecedented prosperity. Consumption levels rose dramatically, as did wages and prices of some locally produced goods. Schools and clinics were built throughout the country and a network of rural roads was created, giving formerly remote villages access to hospitals, schools, and markets. In the countryside, automobiles became commonplace, as did diesel irrigation pumps and electric generators, which not only illuminated homes but powered television sets as well. Urban areas expanded at a dizzying pace as returning migrants sought to settle their families in the more convenient cities or cash in on the expanding commercial opportunities in the towns. Land prices soared everywhere as new houses were constructed in village, town, and city.

Of course, not all of the changes that have taken place are good. Increased labor costs and cheap imported grain have forced a decline in agriculture and an enormous amount of new wealth that might have been better used as productive capital has been dissipated on consumer goods and unimaginative, unprofitable investments. Diet has also changed; while more meat is eaten, children have begun to consume large quantities of soft drinks and cheap imported sweets to the detriment of their dental health. A more serious nutritional problem has been the replacement of breast milk with powdered baby formula by illiterate mothers unable to read the proper proportions of powder to water and ignorant of elementary sanitation requirements. In addition, town and country have become cluttered with plastic bags, bottles, tin cans, and other flotsam of the modern world. Having had no prior experience with affluence, Yemenis are incapable of dealing with its by-products. Moreover, in the frenzy to consume, the desecration of the environment is a secondary concern if it is perceived as a problem at all. Finally, increased prosperity has reduced the need for mutual aid, cooperation, and interdependence as social ties are weakened, income differentials widened, and traditional obligations ignored or superseded by new priorities. Still, in spite of occasional expressions of nostalgia, few people would return to the old days when flour was ground by hand, water raised by camel or donkey, and people died for want of antibiotics, transportation, and hospitals.[7]

While this recent phase of migration had the greatest and most uniform impact on the region as a whole, it was the earlier stage of the exodus that brought Yemenis to America. As the British coaling station at Aden developed from 1839 onward, the demand for labor in the colony increased steadily. At first the British employed Indians, but as time wore on more and more Yemenis found their way down the wadis or dry riverbeds that served as the main arteries of communication prior to the development of roads. As a consequence, this period of migration involved primarily the southern watershed of the Yemeni massif, including most of what is now the western portion of the People's Democratic Republic of Yemen and the provinces of Taʿizz, Ibb, and al-Bayda in the Yemen Arab Republic.

In 1862, twenty-three years after the British seizure of Aden, the French acquired an island across the Arabian Sea off the coast of Somalia. In 1884, they purchased the port at Djibouti, which was soon attracting Yemeni laborers just like its British counterpart. Indeed, these two factories rapidly became ports of entry into the Indian Ocean empires of both European powers. Soon Yemenis were working as stevedores, sailors, watchmen, and small-scale businessmen throughout East Africa, Madagascar, and Vietnam. Apparently it was not much later that they found their way to England, France, and the United States.

No one knows exactly when Yemenis first arrived in the United States. Mary Bisharat (1975:24) has suggested that they probably began to make their appearance on these shores shortly after the opening of the Suez Canal in 1869. Almost certainly, a handful had come by 1890, and a few acquired U.S. citizenship by fighting in World War I.[8] Yemenis continued to dribble into the United States throughout the 1920s, usually entering the country illegally.

Because there were no radios in those days and most of the population was illiterate, few people knew that there was a United States, let alone where it was located. As a consequence, going to America was not unlike traveling to the moon. Frequently a would-be migrant would board a ship in the harbor at Aden under the pretext of selling fruit, vegetables, or other items to the crew. When the sailors' attention was diverted elsewhere, he would stow away, emerging only after the ship was at sea. His strategy at that point was to ask for work and hope to make himself useful enough so that the captain would allow him to remain on board. Some, of course, were hired as legitimate sailors, but almost all of these pioneers arrived in the United States without papers, jumping ship in New York City and blending into the local Lebanese or Palestinian communities. One can only marvel at the tenacity, courage, and desperation of these uneducated peasants who were willing to fly headlong into the unknown in search of a chance to improve their conditions.

Once in America, many headed inland, where they accepted what were often the most backbreaking jobs. They worked as laborers on farms in California's San Joaquin Valley and in factories in Detroit, Buffalo, Canton, and Weirton. When the Depression struck in the 1930s, many of these men returned to Yemen to wait out the hard times. Others were rounded up by U.S. immigration authorities and deported. To this day, one meets old men in the villages south and east of Ibb who remember a smattering of the English they learned over fifty years ago in America. The few men who managed to remain in the United States through the Depression became assets during the labor shortage of World War II and were allowed to cross into Canada and return as legal immigrants.

Yemeni migration resumed after World War II, when the United States established a formal diplomatic relationship with the government of North Yemen. While most had relatives or acquaintances among the earlier migrants to the United States, many of this early postwar group did not migrate directly from Yemen but instead came by way of Vietnam, where they had worked as watchmen in warehouses and shops and on the docks. These men explain that by obtaining their visas in Vietnam they avoided the requirement that they be literate in their native tongue. At the same time, owing to the revolution against French colonialism, many of these men were anxious to escape the growing uncertainties in Southeast Asia. Typically, after establishing themselves in the United States, they sent for their relatives and friends, so that there was soon a steady trickle of Yemenis arriving in the United States every year. This flow increased sharply after 1965, when a new law abolished the quota system and gave Asians an equal opportunity to obtain entry to the United States.

Before 1970, almost all of the migrants who came to America were adult males. Some of these came from Aden or Yafaᶜ in South Yemen. Still others originated in the district of Hujjariyya near Taᶜizz. The majority, however, came from an area known as the Mantiqah al-Wustah or central region, which can be roughly circumscribed by drawing lines between the cities of Ridaᶜ, Qatabah, and Ibb. It includes the districts of al-ᶜArsh, Hajjaj, Juban, Morays, Riyashiyah, Hubashiyah, al-ᶜAwd, ᶜAmmar, Shaᶜar, and Baᶜadan and is recognized throughout Yemen as the migration center of the country.

A highland area 6,000–8,500 feet above sea level, the central region ranges from flat plateaus to steep terraced mountains and embraces both dry farms and irrigated gardens. It is for the most part a region of small independent landholders, neither rich nor poor, people Eric Wolf (1968) has characterized as "middle peasants." They are men who nurture the peasant's dream of more land and bigger houses—it was this vision that lured them to America. Some of the earlier migrants were fortunate enough to realize their ambition, acquiring new land or irrigating existing holdings, and their elaborate cut stone houses stand out in the villages like so many medieval castles. After 1970, however, it became more and more difficult to make this dream come true.

In America, the migrant divides his time among his home, his coffeehouse, and his job. Rarely is he without the company of his fellows in any of these situations; indeed, his life may be so insulated from the rest of American society that he can live for years in the heart of the city and gain no more than the most superficial understanding of the culture of which he is a part. One man told me that he had lived in the United States for eight years without ever really "tasting it." Nevertheless, the longer he stays in America, the more estranged he becomes from Yemen, so that in the end he is at ease neither in his adopted home nor in the world he left behind.

Home in America is, as often as not, a single furnished room or low-rent apartment shared with a number of other men from the same family, village, or district. If the men have especially low-paying jobs, they may even sleep in shifts so that two men can use a single bed. The rooming house or apartment is usually in a working-class or marginally poor neighborhood, often in an area of heavy industry and consequent pollution. Within the houses furnishings are spare and shabby, with the rooms frequently having an air of dingy utility. Invariably, the men living together cook together, and food is one area where they don't stint themselves, consuming huge quantities of lamb, steak, and freshly killed chickens.

The coffeehouse is not a Yemeni institution, but one adopted from the Lebanese and Palestinians. Like their sleeping rooms, it is austerely furnished, usually with worn Formica-topped tables and unmatched chairs. On the tobacco-stained walls are announcements of a concert of Arabic music, a benefit for Palestinian refugees, or an income tax service. There is a counter, a refrigerator for soda pop, and a range for brewing ginger-flavored coffee and sweet tea. At the coffeehouse, men play cards, usually *handrayman*, two-deck Russian rummy, and, less often, poker. Any given coffeehouse is frequented by men from the same or adjacent districts in Yemen. On weekends, when every table is occupied, the air is thick with cigarette smoke and filled with the buzz of conversation punctuated with laughter and occasional shouts as someone slams a winning card to the table. But the coffeehouse is more than a recreation center and club. It is an important clearinghouse for information about the local job market as well as political, personal, and economic conditions in Yemen. Someone has always just returned with mail or gossip from home or had a recent phone call from Ta⁺izz or San⁺a, so that any news over two weeks old is stale.

Yemenis today still hold many of the same kinds of jobs their grandfathers had in the 1920s. In California, they continue to work as farm laborers. In Detroit and Buffalo, they are fresh water sailors, steelworkers, auto workers, and restaurant employees. Whether in California, New York, or Michigan, Yemenis have in recent years gone into business for themselves. In concert with their brothers, cousins, or fellow villagers, men have purchased small grocery stores, newsstands, or candy stores. Often in the poorer, run-down sections of New York City, Buffalo, Detroit, or Oakland, these are labor-intensive businesses requiring twelve to fourteen hours of work a day. Such stores are not only time consuming, they are often dangerous — every year one or two Yemeni shopowners are killed in the course of an armed robbery. Just the same, men are willing to accept such risks in order to improve the economic circumstances of themselves and their families in Yemen.

Yemeni Americans' propensity for measuring their success not only according to Old Country values but within the physical context of Yemen itself has clearly had profound implications for their behavior in the United States. It is the desire to maximize savings for investment in land that leads the $25,000 a year auto worker to live in a cheap $60 a month rented room. To a certain extent, the migrant's previous experience in Yemen, where electricity, plumbing, and even roads were absent until recently, has preadapted him for such minimal conditions. Just as important, however, is the fact that Yemeni immigrants have tended to view America as a means rather than an end, a temporary stopping place rather than a permanent home.

Because of this, they draw a sharp, almost schizophrenic, distinction between their lives in America and their lives in Yemen. For example, Yemen's still traditional peasant society is divided into a system of occupational strata that do not intermarry.[9] Sweepers and servants fall at the very bottom of this social hierarchy; in Yemen, no self-respecting tribesman would ever consider performing either of these despised activities. Yet, in the United States, these same tribesmen will readily accept work as custodians, porters, and busboys with no consequent loss of face. Similarly, men who own liquor stores in America would never dream of selling alcohol in their Muslim homeland. Often even friendships forged between Yemenis in America are not transferred back to Yemen. The likelihood of such relationships being maintained appears to be inversely proportional to the distance between the men's villages. This would be easily understood, indeed obvious, if great distances were involved, but often it is a matter of only ten or twelve miles. Thus, men who have lived and worked together

42, 43. Workers' quarters, Coldwater, Michigan. Initially, most workers migrate without their families. In industrial Michigan, many rent apartments together and share domestic responsibilities that women would commonly perform in Yemen. Communal meals are an important part of their lives. *Tony Maine.*

44. Yemeni store, Bakersfield, California. Sometimes migrants pool their resources and purchase a small store as a stepping-stone to economic independence. The revenues are often sent back to Yemen as remittances, used to bring relatives to the United States or to help other sojourners get settled. *Ron Kelley*.

45. Outside Dix Avenue mosque, South Dearborn, Michigan. Selling clothes from a car trunk is a form of entrepreneurial activity for some Yemenis. *Tony Maine*.

for two or more decades have never visited one another's villages, even though they may be separated by less than ten miles. Common problems and shared hardships draw men together in America, while traditional rivalries and competition for scarce resources have a centrifugal effect in Yemen.

With the arrival of more and more families in the 1970s, this cultural segregation has become increasingly difficult to preserve. As families mature, the strains of convergence will almost certainly intensify and result in enormous pain for both children and their emigrant parents.

Whatever his occupation in America, the emigrant is an important person when he returns to his village after two, three, or five years abroad. He is never the same man who went away, though the level of change varies. If his adjustment to life in America was unsuccessful, he may be relieved to go back to his family and friends. Such men often return to Yemen permanently after one or two sojourns in the United States. Other men are disappointed. After dreaming nostalgically of their villages for several lonely years, they find that the reality does not live up to their inflated expectations. At the same time, their new attitudes and ideas may engender resentment among relatives and friends. Accustomed to higher standards of cleanliness and sanitation in America, they may arouse resentment by insisting that their homes be kept cleaner than those of their fellow villagers. Neighbors, jealous of the migrants' economic success, may resent their efforts to reintegrate themselves into the political and social life of the community. Even their families, who benefit most from their emigration, may feel angry at the long years of enforced absence. It is the tragedy of the emigrant that he leaves home for the sake of the family he rarely sees and that, after years of loneliness and hard work, he returns home to find his children strangers who are closer to his father or brother than they are to him.

For his part, the migrant may find the village petty and boring. This is particularly true of the younger migrants, who find the pace of village life agonizingly slow. They long to go to the cities or return to America; in fact, some men even go back early. Usually, however, the length of a migrant's stay is determined by the duration of his leave of absence from work and how long his money lasts.

The prestige enjoyed by the migrant during his stay in the village does not come cheap. He is expected to bring gifts and money to his family and lavishly entertain neighbors with food and qat.[10] He will also build a house, buy some land, finance a marriage, or make some other type of major investment while he is home. All of this creates the impression that money flows like water in the United States — the villagers, awed at the migrant's wealth, have no idea of the long hours he must work in factories and shops or on farms to foster this illusion. In any case, the dollars are spent quickly; usually, within three to six months, he is forced to borrow his air fare back to the United States. Fortunately, when he arrives in America, friends and acquaintances will stop by to catch up on the latest gossip from the district and collect the mail he has brought. Each will leave him with ten, twenty, or fifty dollars to tide him over until he gets back to work.

Although in the past the emigrant was fabulously wealthy by village standards, his relative economic position deteriorated steadily during the 1970s. This change, coupled with the persistence of an insurgency movement in the central region, contributed to fundamental changes in the immigration pattern and hence in the structure of the migrant community in the United States. Specifically, from about 1975 onward, there was a sharp increase in the number of families joining their husbands and fathers in America.

It would be misleading to imply that most Yemeni migrants have their families in America or even to suggest with certainty that most will ultimately bring wives and children to the United States. Like the Greek (Kraut 1982:17), the Yemeni migration stream may continue to include a large number if not a majority of adult males with strong commitments to their homeland. Alternatively, it may follow the Italian (Kraut 1982:17) and Lebanese (Naff 1985: 115–17) pattern wherein the early migrants were predominately male, with the sex ratio equalizing after two or three decades. Historically, Muslims have been somewhat more reluctant to bring their families (Naff 1985:90); indeed, Nabeel Abraham (1978:37) reports that even men who have brought their families to the United States "pay lip service to the notion of the 'return.'"

What is important, however, is that the number of Yemeni families arriving in the United States increased substantially in the mid-1970s. This in turn contributed to fundamental changes in the attitudes of Yemenis toward themselves and their role in American life and gave added stimulus to a growing Islamic conservatism as men struggled to preserve their families' cultural integrity in the midst of a secular materialist society.

Ironically, the guerrilla movement that convulsed the central region until 1982 was precipitated by the Republic of Yemen's central government during the siege of San^c a in 1968. Until that time, the largely republican southern governorates had been relatively untouched by the civil war, which was mainly fought in the north. Fearing royalist inroads but unable to divert troops from other parts of the country, citizen militias were created in these vulnerable areas. Arming the nationalist militias appears to have ignited long-standing rivalries over land and water. In other cases, the militias moved against local shaikhs who had taken advantage of the political vacuum in the countryside to expand their influence. When these shaikhs were of questionable loyalty to the republican cause or personal rivals of the local republican commander, the government was willing to turn a blind eye; however, it was soon clear that a Frankenstein's monster had been created. When the republicans sought to reassert their power, the *muqawamah* (resistance) fled south to the PDRY, where it acquired arms and the ideological trappings of a guerrilla movement.

The National Democratic Front (NDF) that finally emerged included a variety of Marxist and Arab nationalist elements. It continued to gain strength until forced into a tactical retreat by a 1973 government offensive. By 1974, the Front had regrouped; while the government continued to rule by day, the guerrillas ruled by night, planting mines on the roads and systematically assassinating local leaders who actively supported the San^c a government. Throughout the remainder of the 1970s, the government and the Front maneuvered for position, sometimes fighting, sometimes maintaining a tenuous status quo. The initiative, however, seems to have been with the Front, which is alleged to have obtained large-scale Libyan backing sometime in the late 1970s. In any case, it grew steadily, reaching a high-water mark in early 1981, when it spread as far north as Mahwit and Jabal Raymah. In 1982, the government launched a full-scale offensive against rebel strongholds throughout the country. At the same time it sought negotiations with the PDRY in the south. Aided by the defection of a large faction of the Front, the government was successful militarily and diplomatically in purging the nation of the NDF presence (Burrowes 1985). It has since maintained a strong military presence throughout the central area, with large troop concentrations on key strategic mountaintops and locally recruited garrisons in many villages. At the same time, it has launched an aggressive development program in the area that is providing clinics and schools to many villages. The strategy appears to be successful. Certainly the majority of the population is relieved to enjoy its first real peace in over fifteen years.

The role played by migration in this political drama is difficult to assess. It cannot be accidental, however, that the center of the resistance movement coincided with the region boasting the highest rates and most long-standing tradition of migration. It is true that the migrants' appetite for land inflated prices and tended to crystallize ownership patterns. This was bound to arouse resentment among those left out of the process. Still, emigration was hardly restricted to a limited elite. In many villages, over 50 percent of the adult male population had migrated to the United States, Saudi Arabia, or the Gulf states.

On the other hand, by providing a source of income outside what had been a more or less closed political economy, migration furnished people with the economic means to circumvent the power of the shaikhs. Indeed, by the 1960s, many migrant villages could no longer be said to have a shaikh. During the civil war, however, some of these elites tried to reassert their authority or expand their influence into villages without shaikhs. These moves were deeply resented, and the resistance provided a means for countering such actions.

The Front drew most of its support from young people who were impatient to achieve the rapid development of their country and disappointed at some of the compromises that the republican government had accepted in order to halt the civil war. Nor did the government help its cause in the early stages, with its heavy-handed policy of holding entire villages responsible for the actions of a few rebels. It is also worth noting that many young people were attracted less by ideology than by the glamor of carrying a Kalashnikov and being part of the "resistance."

As for the migrants in particular, most played a neutral role. A few joined the Front, and a few provided active support for the government. Most wanted simply to be left alone to enjoy the hard-won fruits of their labors. This was increasingly difficult to do, however, as they were condemned by the government for their passivity and labeled "bourgeois" by the Front.

The uncertainties of living in the countryside were not enough in themselves to promote the emigration of women and children to the United States. Indeed, many people simply moved their families to the growing urban centers of Ta^c izz or San^c a, where they built houses, usually with shops downstairs that could be rented out. In the end, it was economic factors that precipitated the exodus of families to America.

During the 1950s and 1960s, when the per capita income of Yemen was estimated by the United Nations to be only about $56 per year, the emigrant to America could return to his village and live like an oriental potentate. Land in the early 1960s was still only $25–$50 per *qasabah*, a unit 18.5 feet on a side. Agricultural labor was less than 25 cents per day. A house could be built for $5,000, and a man could get married by paying a bride-price of less than $1,000.

By the early 1970s, however, the economic picture had begun to alter. Agricultural land had jumped to $220 per *qasabah* and there was little available for sale. Labor was $1–$1.75 per day, and sharecroppers were not only demanding a larger share of the crop but refusing to farm all but the most productive fields. Nor did the situation improve with the onset of large-scale intra-Peninsular migration. Daily wages jumped to $7.50 in 1977 and then to $10 in 1980. By 1984, they had gone to $13 in some areas. Unfortunately, grain prices did not advance at the same rate, held in check by the importation of Canadian, Australian, and American wheat that was actually cheaper than locally produced sorghum.

Except for a few areas where pump irrigation could be introduced to initiate the cash cropping of qat, agriculture—the traditional investment of the emigrant—ceased to be viable. Unfortunately, the number of alternatives was limited; while a few Yemeni American returnees were able to cash in on the economic boom of the late 1970s, most found themselves helpless to counter the head-spinning erosion of their relative economic positions. Thus, the house that cost $5,000 in 1968 cost $50,000 or more in 1979. Bride-prices jumped from $1,000 to $20,000 and more. Almost overnight, the Yemeni American found himself reduced from being fabulously wealthy to being just a little better off than average.

As the peasant dream faded and it was no longer economically advantageous to maintain one's family in Yemen, men began to bring their families to the United States in ever-greater numbers. This step was not taken lightly; although the Yemeni migrant values America's wealth and respects its power, he also recognizes that it is a secular and not a Muslim society with attitudes, values, and customs that are fundamentally alien to his own.

One difference between the American ethos and the Yemeni ethos is in the attitude toward moral responsibility. Americans emphasize that the indi-

vidual is ultimately responsible for his own behavior. By contrast, Yemeni culture insists that it is the community that is responsible for evolving a social and political system that at once protects the individual from temptation and ensures his conformity to group values.

As single males, it was a simple matter for Yemeni Americans to insulate their families from the profane world of their migrant experience. In bringing their families to America, however, they have been forced to confront the problem of maintaining the sanctity of their Arab and Muslim traditions in an alien environment. More specifically, the challenge has been to create a social framework in America that will ensure that Yemeni children marry within their sectarian and ethnic backgrounds.

Like other ethnic groups before them, Yemenis have turned to religion as the principal vehicle for preserving their cultural integrity. This in itself has involved a break with tradition; unlike most churches, the mosque is a place of prayer and occasionally education but not a social institution. From its beginning, Islam emerged not merely as a system of belief and ritual but as a total design for living embracing belief, ritual, and law institutionalized in, and enforced by, the Islamic state. Recreating such an all-embracing system of behavior control is impossible in secular America. Still, some Yemenis, isolated in parochial communities, seem oblivious to the sociopolitical realities of their new home. Their efforts to maintain a "pure" Islam in this more restricted context have in some cases brought them into conflict with other American Arab Muslims with a longer tradition in the United States.

In Detroit, for example, the local mosque was largely a second-generation Lebanese phenomenon. However, Yemeni attendance increased sharply in 1975. This new participation created tensions for the Yemenis, who insisted on the practice of a more conservative brand of Islam and rejected as heretical many of the compromises the Lebanese had made with their adopted milieu. The Yemenis especially objected to the fact that the basement of the mosque, like that of most American churches, was used for social events, including wedding receptions. Although no liquor was permitted, the *dubkha*, a traditional Lebanese line dance, was occasionally performed.[11] In Yemeni eyes, this was a direct assault on the sanctity of the mosque and an affront to the faith. By 1976, dissension between the two groups reached a breaking point when the Yemenis together with a small group of Palestinian allies seized political con-

46. Men praying in Hamtramck mosque, Michigan. Spiritual activity is an important part of life for most migrants, regardless of where they settle. *Tony Maine.*

trol of the mosque and transformed it into a bastion of cultural and religious conservatism.[12]

This religious revival is not an isolated phenomenon, but parallels a similar trend in Yemen. There, religious fundamentalism has been fueled by anxieties arising from increased affluence, economic dualism, rapid urbanization, and disillusionment with Western secular and materialist ideologies. More recently, in both Yemen and America this shift toward Islamic fundamentalism has been given added impetus by economic reversals. Thus, after ten years of boom, the Yemeni economy shows signs of deterioration, evidenced by increased competition from South and East Asian workers in Saudi Arabia and the Gulf, a worsening balance of payments, and a weakening of the riyal.[13]

Yemeni Americans, especially those in the industrial Northeast, have also suffered economic setbacks. The near-collapse of the auto industry in the late 1970s and early 1980s resulted in large-scale layoffs of Yemeni workers, many of whom have never been called back to work. Indeed, because of robotization, a significant number of these men will probably never again be employed building cars and trucks. In Buffalo, reduced production and plant closings in the steel industry have hurt the Yemeni community. In both cities, freshwater sailors have suffered not only because of recession-related cutbacks in shipping, but also from the introduction of new boats that carry 50 percent more tonnage with one-third less crew. Some Yemeni sailors also charge that they have been inordinately affected by such layoffs because of alleged discriminatory practices on the part of the Seafarers International Union.

Besides increasing their religious commitment, Yemeni Americans have responded to the recession in a variety of other more immediately practical ways. As noted previously, many workers with sufficient capital have abandoned the factories and attempted to go into business for themselves. Men with less capital have left Detroit and Buffalo and migrated to the fields and orchards of California, often accepting pay cuts of more than 50 percent in the process. Still others, like their grandfathers before them, have drifted back to Yemen to wait out the hard times. In the spring of 1984, there were scores of Yemeni Americans in the central region who had after months, and even years, given up the search for work and gone home to their villages. Finally, as might be expected, the recession has temporarily slowed the immigration of women and children to the United States. However, neither a U.S. recession nor the improvement in the value of the dollar against the Yemeni riyal is likely to halt entirely the arrival of Yemeni families in

America. Even more remote is a significant reverse migration from America to Yemen.

In the midst of a bewildering and uncompromising economic milieu, first-generation Yemeni settlers and sojourners alike cling steadfastly, even desperately, to the symbols and meanings that define their tradition and comfort their spirits. Whether they will be successful in ensuring that their children sustain an equally intense degree of commitment remains to be seen. However, parental conviction alone is not likely to be enough to halt the process of acculturation.

Abner Cohen (1974:xxii) argues convincingly that economic incentives are necessary preconditions for the preservation of ethnicity past the first generation: "If in a dynamic contemporary complex society a group of second- or third-generation migrants preserve their distinctiveness and make extensive use of their endoculture, then the likelihood that within the contemporary situation they have become an [economic] interest group is strong." Barth (1969:14–15, 28) suggests that whether a person maintains his ethnic identity is an individual decision that rests on both the perceived advantages of membership in the ethnic group and ability to *perform* adequately his ethnic role.

For new migrants, ethnicity offers not only psychological and spiritual support, but economic benefits as well. At the same time, it is both easier and cheaper to maintain loyalty to traditional ethnic symbols than to adopt the signs and tokens of middle-class American life. Indeed, the migrant's ability to accumulate capital for investment in Yemen or America may rest on a rejection of the American consumer ethic. While future generations, educated and more familiar with American life, may continue to feel a sentimental attraction to traditional symbols, they will probably perceive fewer real economic benefits to be derived from exclusive identification with the group. At the same time, those attending public schools will face intense peer pressure to conform to the standards of the majority. This cohort will find it increasingly difficult to resist the attraction of the dominant society and is more likely to accept its symbols and values in part or in full.

The history of America's Muslim Lebanese provides a useful reference for understanding the present and future of the Yemeni American community. It suggests that the first-generation Yemenis' attempts to preserve their religious and cultural heritage intact are nearly certain to fail. Unfortunately, it is equally clear that the inevitable compromise with American attitudes and values will not be accomplished easily, probably not until the third generation. During the intervening years while this Americanization is taking place, families will become battlegrounds, with generation set against generation. As one astute second-generation Lebanese woman observed, "When the children [of Yemeni immigrants] start school they are forced to be Americans by day and Yemenis by night." The consequences of such conflicting expectations are often painful and sometimes tragic.

Like the Yemeni influx, Lebanese migration was initially dominated by males, most of whom were peasants who intended to accumulate "enough capital to build a house or start a business" (Haddad 1983:66).[14] Informants in Spruce River reported that many if not most of these men did in fact return to Lebanon. Others, however, chose to bring their wives and children to America. As the number of families grew through the 1920s, mosques were built and efforts were intensified to ensure that religious and cultural traditions were preserved according to the Old Country model. Special emphasis was placed on assuring intraethnic and intrasectarian marriages. Matches were arranged as in Lebanon, with minimum regard for the wishes of children, who after attending school with American peers often would have preferred to follow the American pattern of dating and marriage. Parents, however, would not permit dating, which they found culturally threatening and morally repugnant. Children faced an awful choice between the American values they shared with their schoolmates and the Old Country traditions cherished by their parents. If they followed American customs, they risked not only parental disapproval but, even more painful, outright rejection. Following the dictates of elders, on the other hand, often forced together two unwilling, uncommitted, and unhappy people who brought nothing to the relationship but fear, frustration, and hostility.

The result of these clashes between American and Lebanese traditions was frequently agonizing for everyone involved. Moreover, arranged marriages no longer served the same economic and political functions that they had in Lebanon, where they served as much to ally families as individuals. Gradually the Lebanese Muslim community began to compromise with American customs. Dating, if not encouraged, became an accepted part of adolescent behavior even while the pressure to marry within the group was maintained. Non-Muslim spouses were invited to the mosque and encouraged to convert to Islam, though attitudes toward mixed marriages were relaxed as well. The community also undertook to create social situations that would bring young people together. Youth groups were formed that met in the mosque and a national convention was initiated that brought together Muslim youth from all over North America. Many of these changes represented sharp breaks with Old Country ways. Still, they were accepted as a necessary means of preserving the group's heritage, if not intact at least in part.[15]

At present, most Yemeni Americans would vigorously deny that they will ever need to compromise their traditions with American life. However, as children mature in the context of American coeducational schools and in constant contact with television and other forms of mass communication, it will become increasingly clear that they are no longer Yemenis but Yemeni Americans. Ultimately, the pain of their denial will force them to make peace with the values and attitudes of their adopted country. It is likely that they will adopt many of the same compromises as their Lebanese predecessors.

SUMMARY

Like most immigrants to America, the Yemenis are middle peasants from marginal environments who were lured to America by the vision of wealth and prosperity. Seizing on America as the economic means for realizing the peasant dream of land and houses back home, they never intended to settle here permanently. With the passing of time and the evolution of Yemen's national and international economies, the economic advantages of maintaining their families in Yemen no longer outweighed the pain of long-term separation, and more and more men brought their families to America.

The arrival of women and children alleviated the migrants' loneliness but brought with it the responsibility of maintaining the religious and cultural integrity of these new dependents. To this end, many Yemeni immigrants have embraced fundamentalist Islam and its rejection of the Western tradition. While such a reaction is understandable, given the current socioeconomic circumstances it is also inevitably futile. Sadly, it will require several decades of struggle between the first and second generations before America's Yemenis accept and embrace their own unique synthetic version of American life.

NOTES

1. Most Yemenis would include Jizan, Asir, and Najran, which were seized by Saudi Arabia in 1934, as part of Greater Yemen.

2. Appalachia's crusty mountaineers are a more similar case in point. It is no accident that this part of America has been a bastion of individuality and regionalism since colonial times or that its people are famous for "feuding, fighting, and fussing."

3. Recently, archaeologists have concluded that the dam fell into disuse over an extended period of time due to a gradual buildup of silt.

4. In 1984, it was announced that Hunt Oil Company had discovered an oil field yielding as much as 300,000 barrels a day and that within a few years the Yemen Arab Republic would be a net exporter of petroleum (Burrowes 1985:313–14).

5. Estimates of the number of emigrants from Yemen range from the Swiss Airphoto Team's 1975 figure of 385,000 short-term and 250,000 long-term migrants (Central Planning Organization 1978:217) to the Cooperative Census of 1978, which claims a total of 1,394,778 emigrants.

6. The imams were religious secular leaders of Yemen for over a millennium. Overthrown in 1962, the last dynasty (Hamid ad-Din) struggled unsuccessfully to regain the throne until 1969.

7. For a more comprehensive discussion of the consequences of migration for Yemen, see Swanson (1979a, 1979b, 1982, and 1985).

8. Dweik (1980:3) has confirmed this on the basis of church records in the Buffalo area.

9. Very simply, Yemeni society is divided among warrior tribesmen (*qaba'il*), who are descendants of Qahtan, the legendary ancestor of all South Arabians, and two groups under their protection. One of these, the *sada*, is sacred and of higher status. It is made up of descendants of the Prophet Muhammad and is alleged to possess divine grace. The second group, which may be subdivided into a number of other endogamous categories, lacks a definable pedigree. Referred to by a number of names, including *khaddam* and *akhdam* from the verb *khadama* (to serve), it is associated with professions such as barbering, butchering, and sweeping, which are thought to be profane and of low status. All three of these groups are included among the immigrants to America, though tribesmen predominate.

10. The qat shrub is an important element in the economic and social life of Southwest Arabia. Its young leaves produce a pleasant sense of euphoria when chewed, and much of the nation's business is conducted during afternoon qat sessions. Since a day's supply can cost anywhere from three to thirty dollars, it is an important cash crop for many of Yemen's farmers. An exhaustive discussion of qat and its role in Yemeni society may be found in Weir (1985) and Kennedy (1987).

11. The evolution of the mosque as a social *and* religious center is also noted by Haddad (1983:22), who notes that although in the Old Country the mosque served primarily religious and political functions: "In the new country, it acquired a social and cultural meaning as the Arab Muslims struggled to maintain an Arab and Islamic identity in an alien culture. Not only are weddings and funerals conducted in the mosque, in keeping with American practices, but even fund-raising activities (primarily directed by women) such as mosque bazaars, bake sales, community dinners, and cultural events have been adopted as well. Occasionally, even folk dancing in the basement of a mosque has brought young people together in fellowship."

12. Haddad (1983) offers a general discussion of Islamic revival and reform in the United States.

13. During 1984, the Yemeni riyal declined from 4.5 to 7.3 to the U.S. dollar. In early 1987, the riyal stood at 12 to the dollar.

14. My comments on the Lebanese experience in America are based on my master's thesis (Swanson 1970) and knowledge gained from seven years' residence in the Arab Muslim community of Dearborn, Michigan. Studies of Lebanese Americans in addition to those cited in the paper include works by Aswad (1974) and Hagopian and Paden (1969).

15. Indeed, Elkholy (1966) in his comparison of the Lebanese Muslim communities in Toledo, Ohio, and Detroit, Michi-

gan, found that the more rigid and uncompromising the community, the greater the likelihood that its young people would assimilate.

SELECTED BIBLIOGRAPHY

Abraham, Nabeel Younis
    1978   "National and Local Politics: A Study of Political Conflict in the Yemeni Immigrant Community of Detroit, Michigan." Ph.D. dissertation. Ann Arbor: University of Michigan.
    1983   "The Yemeni Immigrant Community of Detroit: Background, Emigration, and Community Life." In *Arabs in the New World*. Detroit: Wayne State University Center for Urban Studies.

Aswad, Barbara C.
    1974   *Arabic Speaking Communities in American Cities*. New York: Center for Migration Studies and the Association of Arab American University Graduates.

Barth, Frederik
    1969   "Introduction." In *Ethnic Groups and Boundaries: The Social Organization of Cultural Differences*, ed. Frederik Barth. London: George Allen and Unwin.

Bisharat, Mary
    1975   "Yemeni Farmworkers in California." *MERIP Reports* (January): 22–26.

Burrowes, Robert D.
    1985   "The Yemen Arab Republic and the Ali Abdallah Salih Regime: 1978–1984." *Middle East Journal* 39(3):287–316.

Cohen, Abner
    1974   "Introduction." In *Urban Ethnicity*, ed. Abner Cohen. London: Tavistock.

Central Planning Organization, Yemen Arab Republic
    1978   *Final Report of the Airphoto Interpretation Project of the Swiss Technical Co-operation Service*. Berne: Swiss Technical Co-operation Service.
    1983   *Statistical Yearbook 1982*. Sanᶜa, Yemen Arab Republic: Central Planning Organization.

Dweik, Badr
    1980   *The Yemenites of Lackawanna, New York: A Community Profile*. Special Studies Series, 130. Buffalo: SUNY, Council on International Studies.

Elkholy, Abdo A.
    1966   *The Arab Moslems in the United States: Religion and Assimilation*. New Haven: College and University Press.

Haddad, Yvonne
    1983   "Arab Muslims and Islamic Institutions in America: Adaptation and Reform." In *Arabs in the New World*, ed. Samir Abraham and Nabeel Abraham. Detroit: Wayne State University Center for Urban Studies.

Hagopian, Elaine C., and Ann Paden
    1969   *The Arab Americans: Studies in Assimilation*. Wilmette, Ill.: Medina Press International.

Kennedy, John G.
    1987   *The Flower of Paradise: The Institutionalized Use of the Drug Qat in North Yemen*. Dordrecht: D. Reidel.

Kraut, Alan M.
    1982   *The Huddled Masses: the Immigrant in American Society, 1880–1921*. Arlington Hts., Ill.: Harlan Davidson.

Naff, Alixa
    1983   "Arabs in America: A Historical Overview." In *Arabs in the New World: Studies on Arab-American Communities*, ed. Samir Abraham and Nabeel Abraham. Detroit: Wayne State University Center for Urban Studies.
    1985   *Becoming American: The Early Arab Immigrant Experience*. Carbondale: Southern Illinois University Press.

Scott, Franklin D.
    1968   "Introduction: Migration in the Dynamics of History." In *World Migration in Modern Times*. Englewood Cliffs, N.J.: Prentice-Hall.

Swanson, Jon C.
    1970   "Mate Selection and Intermarriage in an American Muslim Community." Master's thesis in anthropology. Iowa City: University of Iowa.
    1979a   "Some Consequences of Emigration for Rural Economic Development in the Yemen Arab Republic." *Middle East Journal* 33(1):34–43.
    1979b   *Emigration and Economic Development: The Case of the Yemen Arab Republic*. Boulder: Westview Press.
    1982   "Histoire et conséquences de l'émigration hors la République Arabe du Yémen." In *La Péninsule arabique d'aujourd'hui*, ed. Paul Bonnenfant. Paris: Centre National de la Recherche Scientifique.
    1985   "Emigrant Remittances and Local Development: Cooperatives in the Y.A.R." In *Economy, Society and Culture in Contemporary Yemen*, ed. B. Pridham. London: Croom Helm.

Weir, Shelagh
    1985   *Qat in Yemen: Consumption and Social Change*. London: British Museum Publications.

Wolf, Eric
    1968   *Peasant Wars of the Twentieth Century*. New York: Harper Row.

Yemeni Farmworkers in California

RON KELLEY
Santa Monica, California

"What did the first American astronauts find when they first landed on the moon? Yemenis, looking for work." (Mohammed Saleh)[1]

"They caught a big fish in Japan. They cut it open and there was a Yemeni inside." (Ahmed Moharet)

Musaid (Moses) Saleh laughs now at his first work expectations as a new Yemeni immigrant to the United States.

> "We [new immigrants] were fooled," he says, reflecting on the morning of his first day of work as an apricot picker in California. "We didn't know what [kind of work] our Yemeni friends had been doing here. . . . I dressed up in a suit and necktie and a nice pair of shoes and walked in [amidst a group of Yemeni co-workers] and everyone started laughing. 'What the hell do you think you're going?' Well, I saw their clothes. I didn't have to see anything [else]. Regular clothes, apricot juice [all over them]. . . . They asked me if I was going to work in the White House." After redressing quickly in borrowed makeshift work clothes ["six pairs of socks to fit me in the shoes"], Moses spent his first work day in America, tired and humiliated, ready to return immediately to Yemen. Although he had quit the apricot job before the afternoon was over, Moses had no recourse but to stay and work in America. Having borrowed most of the money to get to this country, he had to remain at least until he could save up enough to pay off his debts and return home. For the next few years, he struggled in the fields, homesick and miserable, earning his way back

to Yemen. Twenty-two years later, Moses, unlike most of his countrymen, has yet to return home. Eventually, he landed a good-paying, full-time job in a cannery in Modesto, married an Anglo woman, who has since converted to Islam, took a few courses at a local junior college, and played an active role in the Teamsters Union. Recently, however, after seven years on the job, his work place shut down and he was laid off permanently, bringing his story of assimilation in America full circle.

Working in environments populated by competing ethnic minorities (predominately Hispanic), Yemeni farmworkers have labored quietly in rural America in recent years, invisible to the public eye. Given the lack of official records, it is difficult to assess the number of Arab farmworkers in California in 1984. Estimates run from 200 to 2,000, the higher number reflecting the constant flux of workers moving to and from Yemen. Specific to the Delano area, one useful index is the local ADC American-Arab Anti-Discrimination Committee) membership list, which claims about a thousand Yemenis. (Some of these members, of course, have escaped the fields.) In the early 1960s, a few Yemenis penetrated the Filipino control of the farmworker labor market in the Delano area to prove themselves to local companies as exceptionally hard-working and relatively trouble-free workers. Some Yemenis became established as fore-

69

men on a permanent or seasonal basis for corporate growers. Consequently, newly immigrating Yemenis routinely made their way to the same Delano and Stockton areas looking for job possibilities. The peak years for Yemeni farmworkers were in the late 1960s and early 1970s, when many took advantage of liberalized immigration laws to get a foothold in America. In recent years, the influx of migrants directly from their homeland to California has been reduced to a trickle. At the same time, many farmworkers have managed to escape the fields by getting better-paying or at least less physically taxing jobs as unskilled laborers in major urban areas. Many have pooled their savings and opened grocery stores; a few have started other small businesses. Some have changed their sojourn to a different—often Arab—country. Still others have returned to stay in Yemen. But even as many Yemenis are successfully finding alternatives to work in the fields, mass layoffs and deteriorating economic conditions in some urban areas, such as Detroit, are forcing some workers to return in desperation and for enormous cuts in pay to the same California farmlands where, years earlier, they began their sojourns.

Typically, the strategy of the Yemeni farmworkers is to immigrate to America for a three- to five-year sojourn, work hard, adopt a relatively spartan lifestyle, save money, and send a large portion of their earnings back home to Yemen. Once every few years, they grant themselves a return visit to their homeland, where they are accorded great attention and respect because of their improved economic status and are finally able to enjoy the fruits of their long labors. Usually, however, within a short time, their savings are exhausted on imported consumer goods, gifts for family and friends, new homes or renovations, and land expansions—and the pressures mount for them to leave Yemen again to maintain this standard of living. Sometimes this "vacation" at home lasts only a few months before the Yemenis are back in California following the harvests.

In the course of this long-term postponement of gratification in Yemen (and despite the omnipotence—even in the California labor camps—of television), some Yemenis have spent twenty to thirty years in the farmlands of California and still cannot speak a word of English. For many, the bleak, isolated labor camps located miles out of town in the middle of endless grape or asparagus fields are preferable to a typical American town's intensely bewildering socioeconomic pressures to acculturate and, hence, spend money. After all, to participate too much in the host society would be effectively to abandon the very rea-

son they immigrated to America in the first place—to provide for the family left behind in Yemen.

The Yemeni farmworkers tend to make their seasonal travels together in groups, car-pooling across the state, generally preferring, if possible, to work under the few Yemeni foremen employed by corporate growers. A typical routine is to pick grapes in the Delano/Porterville area from July to November; to prune grapevines in Delano, Shafter, or Arvin in January and February; to pick asparagus in Tracy (near Stockton) from February to May; and to pick cherries in downtown Sunnyvale in June. Alternatives include pruning and harvesting stone fruit in Shafter, early grape work in the Indio area, two or three months on the cannery lines in Modesto/Lodi, and spring carrot picking in Holtville. While the largest concentration of Yemenis can be found in the Delano/Porterville area during the grape harvesting season, smaller concentrations of Yemenis have also worked in Marysville, Woodland (Sacramento), and Salinas, pruning and picking various fruits and vegetables. One group seasonally leaves a Richgrove labor camp to travel to the employing company's Arizona grape operation located in desertlike conditions thirty miles from the closest town.

In 1983, the average field laborer was paid $4.70 an hour. At the peak of the grape season, the men work in the vineyard in teams of three or four, one man wrapping and packing the grapes as the others pick and haul them. Teams can augment their income by sharing a $0.28 per crate incentive bonus. Under optimal crop conditions, a good worker, laboring six days a week, can take home seasonally up to $350 per week after taxes. Some claimed that the hardiest farmworkers had earned $15,000 to $18,000 in a single good year; more typically, in helping a half-dozen men with IRS problems, I found yearly incomes ranging from $8,000 to $11,000.

Some companies, however, hire on a "contract" basis, where workers are not paid an hourly wage but by the quantity of crops they pick in a given day. Most Yemenis prefer this arrangement, because they can make more money per working day than they can at an hourly rate. Under "contract" work, breaks and sometimes lunches are ignored because workers are reluctant to waste time when they could be making money. Dawn to dusk working hours, sometimes seven days per week, are possible—and sometimes likely—under this system. If the weather is bad or the available harvest a poor one, however, contract work can backfire for the gambling farmworkers.

In the attempt to save the most money in the least amount of time, the worker is caught in the race to

47. Winter grapevine pruning, vineyards, Delano. *Ron Kelley*.

48. Yemeni work camp, Richgrove. *Ron Kelley*.

49. Vineyards, Delano. *Ron Kelley.*

50. Plowing the fields to improve irrigation, vineyards, Delano. *Ron Kelley.*

51. Vineyards, Delano. *Ron Kelley*.

52. Vineyards, Delano. *Ron Kelley*.

53. Early morning pruning, vineyards, Delano. *Ron Kelley*.

54. Grape harvest, vineyards, Delano. *Ron Kelley*.

55. Cherry picker, Sunnyvale. *Ron Kelley.*

56. Yemeni and Hispanic workers in plum orchard, Shafter. *Ron Kelley.*

accumulate as many pounds of grapes as possible (immature or otherwise) and secure the per-crate bonus. The employing company, however, insists that only the most optimally tasty and mature grapes be picked. Toward this end, Yemeni foremen spend most of the day inspecting the workers' gatherings and reprimanding those overly eager in picking slightly immature grapes or tasteless "water berries." For the first offense, a worker is officially warned with a pink slip and is suspended for the rest of the day without pay. Generally, the offender has car-pooled to work with co-workers and has no way to return the many miles to camp until his driver has finished the full work day. Thus, the suspended worker must idly wait out the rest of the afternoon in the shade of the grape leaves. The second such offense is penalized with another pink slip suspension; a third offense is grounds for being fired—a devastating blow to someone who has probably sunk deep in debt in order to come here from across the world expressly to work.

Harvesting grapes is a difficult, sometimes even hazardous, venture. All day long, clusters of grapes are meticulously inspected, picked, and laid in a large cardboard container. A full box weighs anywhere from thirty to fifty pounds depending upon a man's age and incentive. The box is then balanced on the head or slung to the shoulder and carried to the end of the vineyard row to the packer. This haul of anywhere from a few feet to fifty yards becomes increasingly precarious as the season wears on and discarded decaying grapes combine with damp grass, well-camouflaged holes, clods of dirt, and hidden irrigation canals to make the vineyard trails treacherous. It is easy to lose one's balance under these conditions, especially with up to fifty pounds balanced on one's head. Back injuries are common. After one such injury, an older man spent his long days in the barren camp, month after month, with no one to talk to and nothing to do, waiting for a resolution to his insurance claims.

Another major health problem is posed by the sulfur that is regularly sprayed throughout the vineyards to retard mildew and keep away insects. During the spraying season, as one drives up and down the rural highways through vineyards stretching from horizon to horizon, the pungent acrid smell of "silver" or "medicine," as the Yemenis call it, lingers everywhere. Even to the passing motorist, it smells as if it has been spilled in the back seat. Once sprayed, the liquid manifests itself as a ubiquitous white residue, conspicuous on the green leaves. As the grapes ripen, workers spend weeks slushing through the muddy vineyards, stripping leaves and grape buds off selected shoots, with a flurry of white "medicine" whirling in the air. Most workers respond to such close and regular contact with sneezing, watery eyes, and relentless itching, forced even on the hottest days to wear long sleeves to protect their arms from the dust.

It is no surprise, then, that many regular vineyard workers have asthma problems, brought on or aggravated by the ever-present white dust. One Yemeni foreman visited a number of doctors and scrupulously took every medicine prescribed for him. His symptoms became so severe, however, that he was advised that if he remained at his present job he risked death. He subsequently returned to Yemen, where, as he wrote friends, he was immediately cured of his misery. Another young farmworker, Ahmed Zamzami, was advised by a Bakersfield asthma specialist that he was allergic to everything from quackgrass to walnut trees. But, as Ahmed saw it, he had no choice but to continue to work in the fields, despite his tormented lungs, in order to provide for his family back home.

Work in the asparagus fields is no less demanding. The workers spend hours day after day, walking mile after mile in 110 degree heat, permanently hunched over, severing asparagus stalks. Chronic, sometimes permanent, back problems are a typical side effect of the asparagus harvest. One top foreman, still active in the fields, lives with the cumulative results of years spent picking the crop. He sleeps each night in a hospital bed adjusted for his back and visits spinal specialists regularly, seeking relief from the pain.

The Yemeni migration cycle includes five labor camps in the Delano/Porterville area (grapes), two in the Arvin area (grapes), four near Tracy and Stockton (asparagus), one in downtown Sunnyvale (cherries), and one in Arizona (grapes). For the most part, these company-owned camps are open for habitation only seasonally. In other areas of the state, the farmworkers usually live in groups in short-term, inexpensive rentals.

The Yemeni labor camps throughout California vary considerably. Few have pay telephones; only one has a washer and dryer; gang showers and nonprivate row toilets are universal, varying in upkeep and cleanliness. Most camps are located at least a few miles from the nearest town. In some such residences, two or three men share a small room. In others, a dozen or so men share a larger barracks. Usually, there is a dining area established somewhere in the camp with long wooden tables and benches, but in at least one camp, this dining area consists of a stove and card table at the end of two rows of beds.

57. Lunch break, vineyards, Delano. *Ron Kelley*.

58. Asparagus fields at sunrise, Richgrove. *Ron Kelley*.

One of the most rundown camps is the barracks in downtown Sunnyvale, a burgeoning suburb thirty miles south of San Francisco, serving the affluent employees of various high-tech industries. Here, across the street from a brand-new office building and next door to a camper shell dealer, are a small dilapidated shack and trailer where thirty Yemenis live for one month each year while they harvest cherries.

Generally, the employing company takes a deduction from the workers' paychecks to cover the cost of water, electricity, camp maintenance, and food. In some camps, one or two Yemenis are hired full-time as cooks. Breakfast typically consists of coffee and hard-boiled eggs. Lunch, which is carried to the fields in a large pot, is usually lamb, chicken, or beef and vegetable stew served over rice, with green onions and loaves of inexpensive white bread or tortillas. For dinner, this general format is repeated. Soda pop is by far the prevailing drink, always and everywhere. In most camps, food routines rarely vary.

At some of the more permanent camps, where farmworkers live year-round, small buildings have been built — or converted sleeping quarters have been officially designated — as mosques for prayer. This, I was told, was a fairly recent phenomenon of the past few years. Typically, the mosque is carpeted, but unfurnished; the Koran and a few Islamic books are stacked in a corner; a tattered, well-worn religious poster is taped on the wall; somewhere in the room is a small heater. The work regimen at the camps severely disrupts the day-long Islamic cycle of prayer, however. The tenets of Islam require a Muslim to pray at specific intervals five times a day, including noon, and to be clean while praying. While work habits in Yemen can be structured within Islamic law, workers cannot and do not pray in the California fields. Only a small minority of Yemenis actually fast for the holy month of Ramadan, during which Muslims are not supposed to eat or drink during sunlight hours. Few of even the most religious workers can endure the physical stress of such a fast while spending their daylight hours doing strenuous labor in over 100 degree heat.

Most Yemeni workers spend their nonworking hours in camp — playing cards, sleeping, or — for those who have it — watching television. Most smoke large quantities of cigarettes ("three packs a day since I was twelve years old," said Mohammed Saleh), and some chew tobacco. Most men go to bed at 9 or 10 o'clock and some wake at 4 A.M to pray in the mosque. In one camp, the inhabitants gathered regularly at a radio rigged to an Arabic news broadcast on a BBC channel, placing little trust in the American news media's interpretations of pan-Arab affairs. In another camp, a Yemeni foreman treats his crew periodically to the luxury of Egyptian movies with his video cassette recorder. On extended nonwork days, a few Yemenis take the Greyhound bus to visit friends and relatives in more hospitable living environments — usually the homes of grocery store owners.

Although most camps tend to be predominantly South or North Yemeni, northerners and southerners sometimes reside together in the exclusively Muslim camps, without letting the political differences of their respective countries interfere with their "same people" solidarity, expressing the hope that their countries will someday be reunited. For some, tensions do exist, however. One foreman from North Yemen, who had lost relatives in the recent border wars, was reluctant to hire those from the south. On occasion, non-Yemeni Arabs also reside in the camps. At one camp, over a two-year period, residents included a Moroccan, two Egyptians, two Jordanians, two Lebanese, and two Pakistanis. Three of the non-Yemenis were college students.

Most farm labor camps exclusively house one ethnic group or another, but there are exceptions. During the grape harvest, one camp I stayed in contained approximately eighty Yemenis and sixty Mexicans. The two groups, however, did not do a great deal of fraternizing, viewing each other with what one might kindly call a lack of appreciation for each other's habits. Since the man in charge of this particular camp was Yemeni, the camp life-style was structured to accommodate Arab needs, forcing the Mexican workers to make certain adjustments. On Yemeni holidays, for example, the Mexican workers were compelled to lose a day's pay or link up with Hispanic crews from other camps working for the same company. (Even a few Yemenis searched out work opportunities on Arab holidays.) Grumblings in Spanish could also be heard about the permanent camp injunction against going totally naked in the gang showers, in deference to Yemeni modesty. In terms of Western etiquette, it is a bit jarring to discover that there is no habit of knocking on doors among Yemenis; any door is routinely pushed open. Occasionally, tensions boiled over into violence. One night, a Yemeni shot a Mexican worker in the leg, claiming that he had pulled a knife during a dispute over the Mexican's allegedly reckless driving in camp. Another night found both Yemeni and Hispanic workers pinned in their sleeping quarters, unwilling to risk even going to the bathroom, as two Mexican workers drank and fired pistols into the late night air. The volatile racial possibilities in the

59. Delano work camp. *Ron Kelley*.

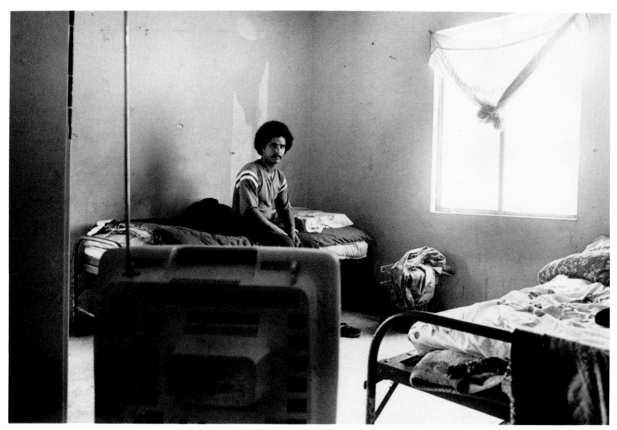

60. New arrival, Delano work camp. *Ron Kelley*.

61. Man reading Koran in workers' barracks, Tracy. *Ron Kelley*.

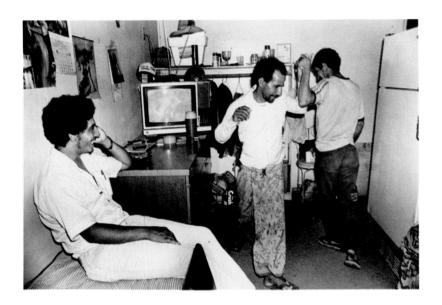

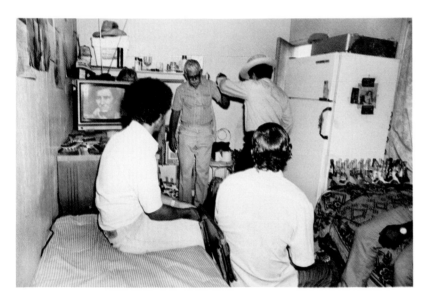

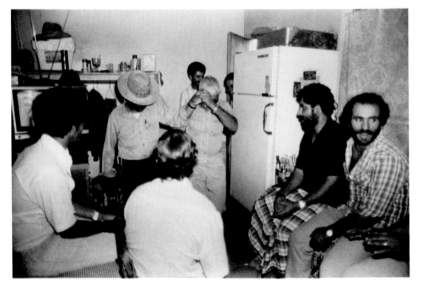

62, 63, 64. Delano work camp celebrating I^cd al-Fitr, the breaking of the Ramadan fast. *Ron Kelley*.

65. Yemeni foremen during work break, vineyards, Delano. *Ron Kelley.*

66. Interior hallway, Delano work camp. *Ron Kelley.*

67. Mosque, Yemeni work camp, Porterville. *Ron Kelley*.

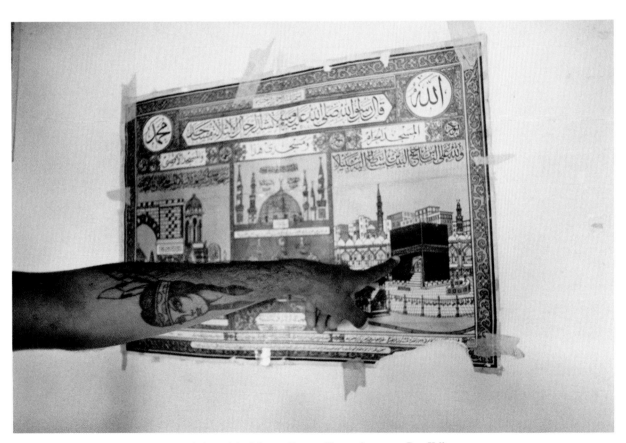

68. Poster of the sacred Kaᶜba (Black Stone) in Mecca. Porterville work camp. *Ron Kelley*.

69, 70, 71, 72. Sheep sacrifice, Iᶜd al-Fitr celebration, Delano work camp. *Ron Kelley*.

73. Carnival, Delano Harvest Festival. *Ron Kelley*.

74. Shriners from Anaheim, California, and Yemeni onlookers at National Date Festival Parade, Indio. *Ron Kelley*.

75, 76. Carnival workers, Delano Harvest Festival. *Ron Kelley*.

77. Delano, California. *Ron Kelley*.

78. Night class in English, Richmond high school. *Ron Kelley.*

79. Funeral, Delano. *Ron Kelley.*

80, 81. Yemeni work crew. *Ron Kelley*.

82. Yemeni farmworker, Delano work camp. *Ron Kelley.*

"internationalized" Delano area at-large—an area that seasonally includes substantial numbers of Arabs, Filipinos, Anglos, blacks, Mexicans, and Indians, among others—were angrily pointed out to me one night by the white owner of a local bar/dance hall who chastised me for taking photographs in his building "in such an explosive atmosphere," where, as he noted, representatives of every ethnic background gathered in groups, looking for women.

For the most part, however, the Yemenis and Mexicans get along well enough, if even only by necessity. Because their day-to-day contacts are more apt to be Hispanic than Anglo, some Yemenis speak better Spanish than English. When dressed up to go to town, many young Yemenis reflect the influence of fashion tastes of their Hispanic co-workers. In fact, Yemenis are often mistaken for Mexicans by rural residents. When correcting the mistake, knowing full well that few Americans have even heard of their homeland, most Yemenis refer to themselves as "Arabian."

In terms of stages of acculturation, the Yemeni farmworkers might be divided into three broad groups.

The first group consists primarily (but by no means entirely) of men between thirty-five and seventy years of age, who seclude themselves as much as possible from the taint of Western ways. (The oldest active Yemeni farmworker I met claimed to be seventy years old. The youngest person in the camps was a twelve-year-old boy who had just arrived from Yemen to live in the camp with his father and attend school.) The isolated camps, situated miles away from the nearest town, reinforce their resistance to assimilation. Here they can adhere with fair success to strict Muslim law, praying faithfully, avoiding alcohol and women, and often speaking little or no English. Wary and suspicious of outsiders, most have little conception of the workings of American society and little interest in investigating it. Their perceptions of America may be colored by extremely narrow and often bewildering experiences with some of the most nefarious elements of their host society—con artists, opportunists, drug dealers, and prostitutes—who aggressively solicit California's multiethnic farmworker communities. Indeed, for many Yemenis, their primary point of social interaction with rural America is the local bar subculture, where the only prerequisite for assimilation is a healthy wallet.

The second Yemeni group is more resigned to personal change while living in America. Many of these men, who commonly describe themselves as "lazy" in matters of the Koran, rarely pray in the camp mosque, actively court women, and frequent bars—while still paying at least lip service to Islamic teachings. Some wallow in American vices more discreetly, inhibited by the presence of conservative relatives in the camp ready to police and chastise them for sinful misbehavior. In America, they are inclined to partake in such commonly accepted activities as bar-hopping and women-chasing and to neglect Islamic ritual. One Yemeni foreman (who had recently lost $1,100 in Las Vegas) estimated that half of the Arab farmworkers in his camp drank alcohol (a practice forbidden in Yemen) at least occasionally. One enterprising Yemeni even sold soda pop and beer from his small room in the camp. Yet when they return to Yemen, they will—at least publicly—revert to forms of behavior appropriate to model Islamic citizens.

A small third group, consisting largely of young men, is the most notorious. These men neglect entirely the hallowed teachings of the Koran and publicly engage in a range of American vices. But most outrageously—as far as their fellow Yemenis are concerned—some of these men have abandoned the practice of sending remittances back home to their families in Yemen. Rather, they are more inclined to spend their hard-earned money on women, gambling, alcohol, fancy clothes, consumer goods, and the pursuit of an individualist identity in America. Within the camps, these men are referred to by the conservative Yemenis as "crazy." On one occasion, a group of Yemenis debated whether to help a countryman who was locked in jail for public drunkenness. Some argued that he deserved to be punished for such shameful behavior, and, abandoning the prevailing Yemeni ethic of mutual aid, refused to contribute to his bail.

One summer, a cross-cultural "new versus old" ideological confrontation took place, involving two Black Muslims from New York City who briefly worked in the fields with the Yemeni farmworkers. The Yemeni foreman had hired them—the first blacks who ever applied for fieldwork with the company—because he was intrigued with the New Yorkers' religious claims and wished to help out fellow Muslims. For two months, the newcomers roomed together and lived in the small Yemeni camp community. They were regarded with increasing fascination and fear by the Yemenis, especially after one of them—reputed to be a karate expert—was witnessed beating up a Mexican co-worker. Some Yemenis claimed that the blacks were false Muslims, pointing to their ignorance of Islamic ways and the way they shirked work, smoked marijuana, and behaved so aggressively. The blacks made counteraccusations, claiming that the Yemenis were themselves hypocrites. One Black Muslim reportedly took matters in his own hands and chased some soliciting prostitutes out of camp. By the summer's end, the two Black Muslims had been fired for missing work and being late too often.

> Ahmed Nagi shakes his head in disgusted disbelief. These Americans, he cannot understand them. Just last week he visited the nearby town of Delano, bringing an entire twenty-five-pound box of meticulously picked grapes as a gift to a woman he admired—a box that he had carefully scrutinized himself for quality ("Number 1 grapes!"), picked and carried beneath the merciless summer sun. In town, the woman, who owned a fast-food restaurant, was pleased with the gift, but wondered if Ahmed might procure yet another for her. The next day, he dutifully loaded another twenty-five pounds of grapes into his trunk and brought it to town. As the woman expressed her gratitude for the grapes, Ahmed, thirsty after ten hours in the fields, asked her if he might have a cup of Coca-Cola. The owner obliged, filled a cup with soda, and set it before him. "That'll be fifty cents," she said.

Coming from a culture that prides itself on generous hospitality, many Yemenis have difficulties adapting to the stringent, self-centered economic rigors of the American free marketplace. In Yemen, the immigrants attest, if a stranger—any stranger—comes to a foreign village, he will be offered food and lodgings gladly by any of the townsfolk. In a spirit of hospitable sacrifice, the townspeople may even compete for the honor of serving the needy stranger. For the new immigrant arriving at the labor camp, these expectations of interpersonal behavior quickly change when they are confronted with a $2 per ride transportation fee by the enterprising Yemeni car owners who pack their vehicles with as many riders as possible to and from work. Or the Filipino gentleman who will be happy to drive the five miles out to the labor camp and ferry him to Delano for $5 each way. Or the relentlessly entrepreneurial Yemeni who spends his work breaks selling bottles of soda out of an ice chest in the trunk of his car, for fifty cents per bottle. (He will spend the rest of his break retrieving the bottles to collect the ten cent deposit.)

The initial shocks that come from the Yemenis' first encounters with American society and their Americanized countrymen cause many to isolate themselves in the labor camps, content to be invisible to the public eye. Inevitably, however, the Yemenis are forced to deal with the host society in at least three areas: the United States Internal Revenue Service, the Immigration and Naturalization Service, and the local unemployment office.

Virtually no Yemeni farmworker can handle such a formidable task as a U.S. tax form; hence, they must go to, say, Delano, where many pay for their income taxes to be figured out by a favored Filipino accountant. Apparently, however, the IRS keeps fairly close tabs on the Yemenis as aliens and periodically harries them *en masse* over past tax returns, with dozens of Yemenis getting unpleasant surprises the same week in the mail. IRS demands for over $1,000 in back taxes are not uncommon, often revolving around complicated details surrounding the resident status of dependent family members in Yemen.

The majority of Yemenis also have to deal with the INS bureaucracy at some point. Fulfilling INS regulations to maintain their own legal status is complicated enough, but efforts to bring friends or relatives to the United States force the Yemenis to hire accountants, lawyers, and letter writers to meet immigration requirements.

Third, during slack working seasons, most Yemeni farmworkers end up standing in line to confront the befuddling bureaucratic demands of the local unemployment office. Of course, no one at any of these governmental offices—unemployment, IRS, or otherwise—speaks Arabic. The few Yemenis who do speak good English very rarely can even rudimentarily read or write it. Native-born Americans who struggle daily with the frustrating labyrinthian systems of bureaucratic entanglements, although knowing English may help a little, can only begin to imagine the anxiety and bewilderment that rural peasants must feel when confronted with such an overwhelming obstacle as a U.S. governmental bureaucracy.

In late 1982, the American-Arab Anti-Discrimination Committee (ADC) hired an educated South Yemeni, ex-farmworker, and former UFW organizer named Ahmed Shaibe to begin a tiny one-man operation in Delano. Between 1982 and 1985, he attempted to fill a void by helping the Yemeni farmworker community claim its rights in the surrounding non-Arab environment. In opening up the Delano branch, Shaibe felt that Yemeni needs had not been served well enough by the Hispanic-oriented UFW.[2] Although Yemeni farmworkers played a role in the United Farm Workers strikes of the 1960s and 1970s (one member, Nagi Daifullah, was killed by a county sheriff in Lamont), there were no Arab UFW organizers by 1982.

Given their experiences in an often hostile and insensitive American environment, Yemenis in the labor camps are wary of outsiders and suspicious of their intentions. Over the years of my visits to the camps, I was suspected by segments of the community at various times of being an agent for the INS seeking to ship some Yemenis home, a representative of Israel intent upon publicly portraying Arabs in a bad light, a spy for the vineyard company or the UFW, and an agent of North (or South) Yemen looking to make trouble. For most Yemeni farmworkers, my motives in living among them were incomprehensible. The rhetoric of secular humanism, anthropology, universities, and museums made no sense. Add to that the ultimately confounding fact that I was not being paid for the work I was doing, and my words seemed those of a fool or a lunatic. Or a liar.

Many Yemenis, of course, simply desire to be left alone to work toward returning to Yemen. Anyone coming to ask questions about their thoughts, history, or life-style is merely superfluous to the exhausting realities of day-to-day farm labor.

Of course, some do indeed have minor legal infractions to hide and are wary about the possibilities (real or imagined) of being sent home to Yemen. At least one man drove his car without a driver's license, for instance. And some Yemenis are from South Yemen — a country with a Marxist government, an extremely sensitive subject. Apparently, one needn't be in America too long to recognize what being stigmatized as "Communist" means.

Because I was an outsider — and wandering around with a camera too — I found the Yemenis very much on guard against bringing disgrace upon themselves as individuals, on their families, and, by extension, on the Yemenis as a people. In this regard, there are all kinds of taboos. Relatively few Yemenis, for instance, allowed themselves to be photographed at hard labor or even in the camps. No one wanted to be photographed, sweaty and dirty, hovering over the lunchtime bucket of stew brought to the fields. Many resisted attribution — on film or tape recorder — emphatically disliking any rendering of themselves in association with such a negative environment. One man even became extremely upset to find me walking around the camp taking pictures of dirty work boots. "Let me tell you," one Yemeni warned me out of earshot of the others, "never say the word 'dirty' around Yemenis." Indeed, many of the men have never explained to their dependent families in Yemen exactly what they do in America for money. One middle-aged man admitted that he never told his family what his life was really like in America. Only when his seventeen-year-old son arrived in America did the boy, totally shocked, finally find out.

One young Jordanian student in camp was quick to point out the differences between the Yemenis and other more Westernized Arabs. "One Yemeni's son is just sixteen years old, and he's going to let him marry in Yemen and then come over here. Imagine. He's going to get married over there. Just one month he will spend with his wife and he will spend four years here. What kind of life is that? Let him to come over here first. And then he will be twenty or twenty-five, let him to go back to marry and stay there. No way he has to be here. So what do you tell this people? You tell them this way and he says, 'No, no. I have a good idea.' When you argue with Yemenis about that, what do they say? 'I don't know. I don't know. Other people they did, I have to do.' "

Wary of being jeered at and sensitive to insinuations of being "backward," many Yemenis prefer most aspects of their distinctive private and cultural behavior to be hidden from public view in America. Most Yemenis, for example, wear traditional garments called *futas* when relaxing around the camps. These long skirts are inevitably mocked by Mexican co-workers as women's clothes. To Arabs, with their own high standards of machismo, this can be a source of extreme embarrassment. Similarly, Yemenis are reluctant to allow outsiders see them eating in their traditional manner — using rolled-up bread or tortillas to scoop food into their mouths. Fearful of seeming to "eat like an animal," some Yemenis make tortured efforts to use unaccustomed cutlery when eating in public. (I vividly recall one old man agonizing with a fork over a plate of Sambo's pancakes, unwilling to eat in the familiar Arab manner amid an American public.) Curiously, the Yemeni farmworkers as a group are much more reticent to reveal themselves to outside observers than even segments of the Mexican farmworker community that are obviously working in this country illegally.

Yet Yemenis are deeply proud of their homeland and quick to defend their ways. To listen to a group of Yemenis describe their country is to hear a virtual projection of paradise. They take great pride in the generous hospitality of their people, contrasting it with the mercenary business sense of the Americans they encounter. "In my village," one old man told me, a tableful of Yemenis nodding in agreement, "you leave some money in the street in the morning, at night it will be there waiting for you." Love of the homeland runs deep. One American-born twenty-year-old woman, working at her father's grocery store in Stockton, swore that before she died, she would not only visit her parents' Yemeni village, but live there.

When dealing with outsiders, Yemeni farmworkers are prone to act by consensus, with only the most radically Americanized deviating from group decision making and risking a blatantly individualist manner. Rather, they are apt to weigh the counsel of elders, family members, and friends before taking action. After all, the Yemeni community is a very tight network, where news travels fast to all quarters. No one risks being shamed. In the Yemeni villages, pressures to conform are ubiquitous—everyone knows everyone else's personal business. Public behavior is subject to constant control and censure. In America, enforced moral restrictions at the familial and community levels are much looser; within the ethic of individualist America, there is more toleration for eccentricities. Moral behavior is, hence, the responsibility of the decision-making individual and considerably less than an overseeing consensus group, as in Yemen. In the face of a Western "every man for himself" cultural edict, some Yemeni farmworkers retreat into the moral security of the world they grew up in. Others, however, flounder apart from their countrymen in confusion and crisis, lost in the tangle of both worlds.

> One top Yemeni foreman arrived in America in 1957 with $7 in his pocket, unable to read or write either Arabic or English. He has since fulfilled the American dream by working his way up to his current $60,000 + a year position. He married a Mexican American woman he met in the fields, and he is sending both of his children to college. Such success is not without its price, however. Twice during heightened labor disputes with farmworker unions he was shot at by disgruntled farmworkers, caught as the middleman between the company and workers. One night would-be assassins fired into his home not far from the camp, narrowly missing his daughter. Soon after he installed bullet-proof windows.

A milestone of success is to leave the labor camps and reside in town. While Yemeni foremen and workers who are involved with American women tend to live in towns near the fields, the largest group of Yemenis living out of the camps consists of small grocery store owners. In 1984, members of the Elsumeri clan alone owned thirteen grocery markets in Stanislaus County. There were estimates of dozens of Yemeni-owned food stores in Bakersfield, and several hundred scattered throughout the San Joaquin Valley, three as far south as Indio. Typically, two brothers or cousins work in the fields for a number of years, saving as much money as possible after sending remittances home. Borrowing whatever extra money they need—with no interest—from friends and relatives, they purchase a small grocery store, usually in the poorer part of town. Friends or relatives may be hired at $900–$1,000 a month to help run the store, joining the owners in working twelve to fourteen hours a day, seven days a week. ("We get a vacation when we go home to Yemen.") Because of the total dedication and long hours invested in the businesses, these stores usually become profitable and in some cases extremely successful.

Running these grocery stores has, for many, a particular moral cost. While it is expressly forbidden by Islam (and outlawed in Yemen), economic survival in America requires the Yemenis to sell liquor—the marketing lifeblood of the small grocery store. A few Yemenis even own liquor stores. This compromising of Islamic values within the "whatever it takes to succeed" American moral matrix certainly must produce a Pandora's box of psychological dilemmas. Few, if any, of the families left behind in Yemen know to what extent their men have sacrificed (morally and spiritually, let alone physically in the fields) to provide for their material well-being.

Because of the locations of their stores, Yemenis quickly become familiar with crime and racial tensions. Most Yemenis have stories to recount about friends and family members who were robbed or murdered in America. Many others tell of occasions when they were the victims of racial prejudice or violence. Large cities like Oakland and Bakersfield have dangerous reputations, but even a small Yemeni store in Earlimart, for example, was robbed three times in a year. Consequently, an armed Yemeni guard was hired to survey the store from a hole in the rear wall. One man related the story of being expelled from school in Lodi for chasing two boys with a knife, though they had beaten him up the previous day for daring to speak to an American girl. He also told of scaring off a mob of looters with a warning shot when they attempted to break into the grocery store he once co-owned in Brooklyn during the famous New York blackout. Over the short period he ran the store, he says he was robbed at gunpoint three times, the last time "with a .357 to my neck, my .38 five feet away." The police caught the robber, who threatened vengeance upon the Yemeni. A few weeks later, the store owner saw the robber back on the street. ("There's no law in this country," he complained, contrasting the American legal system with Islam's swift and severe justice.) He quickly decided not to press his luck in the grocery business too much longer. Yet another Yemeni in Modesto is still bitter over the night during the 1979 Iranian hostage crisis when a gang of Anglo thugs mistook him for an Iranian and beat him up. While these may not necessarily represent the typical Yemeni immigrant's experiences in America, such incidents are far from uncommon.

Some of those who establish themselves successfully in grocery stores feel economically and socially secure enough to bring their wives and children to America and share in the material, health, and educational benefits afforded here. For all of these Yemeni women, the transition from Yemen to America will mean abrupt changes. Some will remain cloistered in their husbands' homes, never leaving except for doctor's visits, seeing only family members and close friends. Their communication with the few other Yemeni women in neighboring towns will be largely by phone. Others, in order to save money on salaries, will share the work at the cash register with their husbands, engaging in a kind of public interaction that is unheard of in their native villages.

In November 1982, fifty-year-old Ahmed Mohammed and another Yemeni were drinking alcohol in a car that failed to yield for a stop sign, causing an accident in which Ahmed was killed. Ahmed had recently migrated to the California fields after being laid off from a job in Detroit. In Detroit, he had married an American woman to expedite acquiring U.S. citizenship. Like most men from Yemen, he believed that someday he would return to his beloved homeland to reap the benefits of his many hard years in America. In a chilly fall drizzle, Ahmed's brother from New York City and 200 Yemeni farmworkers gathered in a bleak Delano cemetery to pay their last respects to him and reflect upon the harsh will of Allah in bountiful, albeit crazy, America. For a people whose universe is defined by their family circle, Ahmed's burial in foreign soil with only a brother present magnified the excruciating loneliness, isolation, and fragmentation of immigrant experience in the farmlands of California. A pink coffin and commemorative card inscribed with Shakespearean verse epitomized the cultural alienation of Ahmed and his mourners in this foreign land. "It's a sad thing—a very sad thing—to die out of your village," lamented Gamil Shohati, visibly shaken, as he watched the coffin sink into its American grave.

Removed from the family unit and familiar surroundings, the Yemeni farmworker experience in America is largely one of stress and, for some, cultural disintegration. One nineteen-year-old farmworker, raised and educated for the past seven years in America, was uncertain whether he was American or Yemeni, confiding that he was always "nervous."

Although he wished to get married soon to a Yemeni woman, the high cost of dowry these days was prohibitive.

In an area completely devoid of Arab cultural activity, one summer, a group of North Yemeni entertainers rented the Delano High School auditorium to present an evening of Yemeni music and song in celebration of the 1962 North Yemen revolution. Of the hundreds of Yemenis in the area for the grape harvest, less than twenty showed up for the performance. As one man said, "I'd rather watch the boxing match that night on TV."[3]

When asked where they plan to be in the next few months, most Yemenis shrug their shoulders, uncertain, some alluding to a faith in Allah to guide them. After all, a wide range of variables beyond their control is involved in their decisions—the weather, harvest projections for a given area, rumors of trouble of one kind or another, the potential foreman's reputation, the consensus of others, the expected wages, transportation, and the work options available at any given time. In essence, the farmworker must evaluate how he can best string together a series of wage-earning situations that may well overlap without ruining possibilities for each successive season. Most Yemenis migrate when and where the strongest (albeit uncertain) economic winds take them, wavering between the lures of Yemen and America, uncertain when they will ever return home.

NOTES

1. In deference to the fact that many Yemenis dislike direct attribution, most of their names have been changed in this essay.

2. As of this writing, the ADC office in Delano is already defunct.

3. With the persistent economic and organizational efforts of one of the local foremen and the rare appearance by the Yemeni ambassador from Washington, D.C., a much larger crowd turned out for the recent twenty-fifth anniversary celebration of the establishment of the Yemen Arab Republic.

The Workers Speak

"If God helps you no one can overcome you."
(Koran III:160)

Ali, in his mid-forties, spent his first years in the United States in the fields but, in more recent history, has worked a steady job in a cannery in a major San Joaquin Valley city, gone to night school, married an Anglo woman, and, atypically for the Yemeni migrant, has not returned to Yemen since 1962.

Q: When did you first come to this country?

A: I come in 1962.

Q: What did you think America was going to be like?

A: I was in Bahrain then, the Arabian Gulf. America, it's not what I heard. America is great country. But the things are for certain people, the things are not for everybody. You got to understand the beautiful things in any country are not meant for everybody—they're meant for certain people. There's a lot of Americans, it doesn't do them much good being here, you know.

Q: Rich and poor?

A: Yeah, there's rich and poor. Levels between people. There is selfishness and satisfaction also. Where I came from, people don't have too much. We didn't have much to eat there, you know, in Yemen. Just little things. But we were happy, really happy. If you understand your life or what life is all about . . .

it's good for your life. You work for your life like you're never going to die. And you work for your afterdeath like you going to die tomorrow.

Q: Do the families of the workers know how hard it is here for them?

A: When I came to America from Yemen, within those people, there is pride. If one of them is working as a janitor here, or pruning the trees—real hard labor—when they come back to Yemen, they will not say what they was doing. This is pride. They think if you doing those things, it's something you should be ashamed of. It's something for uncivilized people, or you way behind, and they don't like to admit that to themselves. We be—I don't know how to put it—"fooled" of what's going on. We were fooled. When people came back to Yemen after three to five years doing hard labor, they come back and they don't like to say what they were doing. The rest of us saw they come back—at that time—with $4,000-$5,000, at that time a lot of money. They come from America. America is the heaven, really. It's like they making the money just like that! We becoming fooled. We don't know how they making the money. When I was in Bahrain and Qatar, the Arab Gulf, I was making ten rupees a day at the most and that was about $3 in 1960, '61.

Q: You immigrated from Yemen to Bahrain?

A: Qatar, then Bahrain. When I went away, I went away from Yemen. It was something you wanted to do as a young kid. Just like young people here, they run away from one state to another. When I got to Qatar, that was the beginning of the immigration. I go to school in the morning and work in the afternoon as a janitor and post boy, deliver the mail. After that, I went to Bahrain. In Bahrain, I also went to school and what you call special class. Not daily school, special class to learn a little bit English and Arabic also. I was working for a company that digging in the ocean. I was making good money on that. But actually, when I see the boxes of apricots, apples, oranges, peaches, grapes . . . you see "California, U.S.A."

Q: When you say Yemenis were "fooling" other Yemenis, this is because they were so proud?

A: They were so proud of themself, they don't like to admit what they were doing.

Q: Why is that?

A: I don't know. Myself, I think it's stupid. It's not shame, any way you make a living—as long as you make it other than robbery, prostitution, you know, if it's a decent thing to do—do it. No matter how hard the job is.

Q: Did you feel the same way when you first came here?

A: It's hard to adjust from one country to another. When I came here, I know there's peach trees. I know there's apricot trees, things like that. . . . I come to California, I'm not prepared for what they are doing. . . . My cousin was the foreman. He showed me how to get on the ladder, how to pick and which to pick. I could never make it. As soon as you get on top of the ladder, you fall! I fell back three or four times. I was very stubborn. I said, "I'm not going to do it. I quit!" First day I told them, "If I come from there to do this, I think I want to go back." I have $600 that I brought in with me. But some of it was sent to me, was a loan. And I was thinking at that time, if I can not to pay them back, just go back! I wanted to go back home for almost a year and a half. I wanted to go back! But . . . I didn't have any money to pay for the airplane ticket. That was $700, I think, at the time. It was pretty expensive. So, they said, why don't you go to Delano? That's where it's easy job—grape harvest. They working grapes and stuff like that. I said alright. I went in there and everyplace you go there's Yemeni people that you know, you get to know. I was there working grapes. At least you didn't have to climb ladders. I stayed there for a season time of picking grapes. And you get used to it. I wouldn't say you like it, but you get used to it. After you get used to

what you're doing, then you get to know things you don't have back home. Going to the shows, real nice-looking girls . . . things like that. . . .

Q: In Yemen, a lot of women still can't go out in public without a veil. What were your thoughts when you first came here and saw women in bikinis and everything?

A: Between now and the sixties, when I came, it's different. You don't direct your eyes on those things when you coming because you still hanging on to the habits you got [from Yemen]. I came here just like blind. I wasn't even thinking about those things. I come from an airplane, to Greyhound, from Greyhound to camp. And you don't get to see what's going on. But after a while when you get used to, you go from the camp. You go to the show. You start drinking and we're not even supposed to drink, you know. And we start to see those things and life here that we can't get in there. And then we find your self-satisfaction. You want to be happy, you want to do this, that. And lot of us just slip and stayed for so many years because of the freedom, I think, or looseness or whatever it is.

Q: Yemenis change a lot, drinking beer and all that?

A: Some of them do. A lot of them do. Yeah. They substitute their happiness back there. Substitution. When you get to miss your family. Some of them stay here two, three, four years or more. They get depressed and somebody come with the wrong advice: "Why don't you have a couple of beers? Maybe that'll make you feel better." And when you try it, it's just like that potato chips commercial. You know, "you can't just eat one." You have to try it and then you get used to it and there you go, you slide from the top of the mountain all the way down.

Q: When the men come to this country and do these things that are bad according to the Koran, when they go back to Yemen, do they have troubles? Don't they change a lot in this country?

A: They have a stuff in there they chew—qat, we call it. That's the worst thing really disturbing the country. It prevents men from working. Some of the government workers, they go to work at nine o'clock, they work for one hour, start getting lunch. And then after lunch they look for qat to chew. And start chewing it from one o'clock or two o'clock to maybe three o'clock in the morning! If the World War III started in Yemen in the afternoon, they never realize it. I don't think so. It's bad thing, really. And when they come here, they forget about that. And then some of them start drinking—it's stuff that's been forbid. In our religion it's forbid. We're not supposed to drink, we're not

83. Yemeni pruning crew, vineyards, Delano. *Ron Kelley.*

supposed to gamble, steal. It's just like the ten commandments. But like I say, most of us, they read the Koran. But it's interpretation, oceans of interpretation. You have to understand what the verse is about in Koran. The Koran is a school that you can never finish. It's one verse, you can interpret it to mean many different things. And when we read it in there [Yemen], we're taught by somebody who doesn't even know the meaning. They know how to read it and write it, but, actually, the meaning of that, they don't know. And then we come here, we don't know what's sin and what's right. We don't know which is which. For example, some people start selling liquor and beer and stuff like that in here. Lots of them. They don't even know it's a sin to sell it. Now I'm sure they do because we got a lot of group that come to teach what's right and wrong. But when somebody buy grocery store with alcohol in it, then your business goes in alcohol. If you discontinue selling alcohol, you're out of business. If you give it up, you're giving $200,000–$300,000 for nothing. You're lost.

Q: Do most families back home know that in order to get all the money, the stores have to sell beer and stuff?

A: I don't think so. See, what happens, you judge people by the way you feel. There's business people there [in Yemen], they have business, and when you

say I have a business in America, they think it's the same things as they got in there. To give alcohol or liquor is unacceptable to God. It's forbid, even Christians aren't supposed to drink it. Well, what's happening when people start substituting their loneliness for alcohol. There is no advice. There is no advice from friends, relatives, or somebody that knows about Islam or religion.

Q: Doesn't each camp elect an imam [religious leader]?

A: Even prayers. There never used to be prayers until recent years, about two to three years ago when people started praying in here. . . . I never used to pray myself. Not after I came here. You came first to fall and you start worrying about how you're going to settle. And then there's no mosque here, nobody to call for prayers. And then you see one person praying and you start getting lazy. The devil gets on top of you. Well, maybe tomorrow, maybe the day after. Until you slip. You start doing the wrong things. You get to think, "I wonder if that prayers are so or just some tradition?" Like I said, we weren't really taught the meaning of the Koran. We read it, but we didn't know the meaning.

Q: A lot of Yemenis have told me that when they come over here, they feel that they get stuck here. Do you know what they mean by that?

A: . . . I wouldn't say anybody gets stuck here unless they follow to have good times, to forget about your culture or whatever. I don't know. I feel that wherever you go, it's not "I stuck." I think while you becoming family man or you get married, a man supposed to change the world, OK? For example, a lot of them think they get stuck because they started working in here and they don't make enough money to pay what they owe when they come to America. They borrow a lot of money. They have to go through so many difficult things that cost you. Very costly. . . .

Q: Now it's not costly?

A: Well, now not too many new people coming here. A lot of them learn the truth of what it is you have to do in America to make a living. And people don't like it. And then, also, Yemen now start opening up. There's construction in there that a lot of people can live, make their own living in there. You can work now for electric company, oil company. Yemen is on the beginning of the "life"; people start make living there and realize that what you can do in different country, you can do in Yemen and make living. But most of it is selfishness. And the cost of when they came, they owe a lot of money. A person coming here, he has to work three to four years to pay what he owe. Well, you work three months out of a year, so it's no regular job. Two months in Delano, another month in asparagus. Something like that. Travel just like gypsies. Couple of months in different area. Most of the time, what you earn in grape season or otherwise you end up wasting or spending it.

Q: People in Yemen think the Yemenis here make easy money?

A: Used to. Like I said, when I came, we were fooled. I was thinking you come here to just make money. . . . People don't like to mention what they were doing. My uncle used to be in America. I never bothered to ask him what he was doing and he never told me. He didn't know I was coming to America. I ran away from North Yemen to Arabian Gulf. I was thinking of two years to come to America and make a lot of money and go. . . . The first two years in America, I was sad. I wanted to go back but I didn't have the money. If you don't have the money, you stuck. But, also, if you go back, where you going to pay back what you owe to coming here? For example, if I sponsor somebody to bring him in, it would cost me gas money, this money, that money to go to the immigration and get his papers, for notary public, attorney. . . . I have to charge that person to bring him here. And then he has to keep going from the village to the capital to pay 600 or 700 riyals for the jeep to take him back and forth, to go to the Embassy, the

84, 85. Snapshot of emigrant standing on the roof of his house in the Yemeni highlands. Image on facing page depicts him seated in his room at the Delano work camp. *Ron Kelley*.

U.S. consul in San°a, or other part. You go to the consul and nothing comes real quick. The U.S. consul—and the people that work there, Arab or otherwise—don't have the feelings for those people. They keep coming from the village every day or so to let them go so quick. "You come back next week" or "You come back next month." "You need visa" or "whatever's not ready yet." Why? Because in Yemen they learn . . . what you call it? Bribe. Bribe the secretary or something. And if you don't have that kind of money to give to the interpreter of the U.S. consul, then "Come back within two months" or something. I don't know if the U.S. consul take part in it, but I don't think so. The people that interpret for the U.S. consul—for any part, not just Yemen—the people have learned. The salary in there is very poor. Well, if I can come and give him $500 to put me first, he will take that $500 because it's going to take two months to earn it. They got that; they expect it from a lot of people. There's nothing you can do about it. . . .

Koranic verse taped to the wall reads: "If God helps you no one can overcome you" (Sura 3:160).

Q: Is there a lot of pressure on the men in the fields to send money home?

A: It's not really pressure. It's "comparison." It's comparison among the people themselves. Like, for example, I have grocery store and I'm selling liquor and beer — something I'm not supposed to be doing. I make maybe $500 a day. I send $10,000 a month to Yemen and you work in the field and you're making $10–$20 a day. You want to compare with me. If I build mansion, you want to do the same. This is comparison between the people.

Q: Is this about pride? About shame?

A: This is something between the group themselves in here. You go to San Francisco, there's a lot of the boys work as a janitor. They don't like to tell they're janitors. They think it's a shame to do that. That's pride. OK. But as far as money to go back with — not much money or something like that, it's not pride, it's too much selfishness. People take things different. I take it as selfishness. I want to compare with you because you have so much money and I try to kill

myself to compare with you. That's not right; that's selfishness. I'll give you an example for this. There's maybe two families with two men coming here and they have two fathers in Yemen. That two fathers maybe don't have much money to buy qat or something, but one of the boys come here, start earning money and sends it to his father. The other kid start earning money and has good time with it. Now when that kid sends money to his father, his father starts chewing qat, buying nice turban, one of those knives . . . he starts wearing fancy clothes. The other man will get jealous: he have good son, he send him all kinds of money, and he have none! "You stupid! You a total loss! It's no use to ever have you for a son!" Those are the things that are happening. We were both the same before, but now he's a couple steps ahead of me. How come my son is not as good as his? It's comparison. I don't think that has anything to do with pride. It's selfishness. It's jealousy. Just like here.

Q: You came here in 1962 and you planned on being here for two years. Tell me what happened since then. How old are you?

A: I think I was twenty, twenty-one years old when I come. The first step was in New York airport. I went to a barbershop. Real handsome guys in there, a barber man and stuff. I was looking at myself in the mirror. I said, "Gee, what an ugly face there! Look at those nice people." They were talking to me a little bit. I understand some. And he said, "You come from Saudi Arabia or something?" I said, "No. Bahrain." He said, "Do you like it here?" I don't know. I said, "Yes," but in myself I was thinking "How in hell the guy ask me?" He know I just come in here in the airport. How do I like it? I just got here! I don't know if I like it yet. I haven't seen nothing. I see good-looking people in here, but that's not what I come here for. And this question, I never heard it before: "How do you like this country?" That's the only thing they ask you here. Wherever you go, this is the first thing an American asks you. . . . I'm not saying I don't like it. I like it here and I like it there [Yemen], but there is satisfaction. . . . You have to be satisfied. I'm putting myself on the spot right now. I have families in there [Yemen], brothers, sisters. . . . They would love for me to be there, more than anything. I would say that. I like to be there too. I wanted to go. But I'm not going to say, "Hey. I'm going to get my family in America and go because they want to see me." It's up to God. If it meant for me to be go, I would go. If I can afford to go visit, I'll take my family if they like to go. If not, I have option to go. Last year, my oldest daughter wants to go. I let her go because

I have seen of Yemen, what it's like in the Arab world. And I thought for her it's important to go see how people live on the other side of the world.

Q: What did she find? What did she tell you?

A: She find things different than what people talk in the school about Arabia in Yemen. She likes things and she don't like things, just like any other country. She wants to stay in there. As a matter of fact, now she's saying that when she finished high school, she'll go there.

Q: To live?

A: I think so. I hope. Myself, I said I hope, not I want to get rid of her. When she learn something in here, she could be helpful in there. School person goes from here and can be helpful in there because they need doctors, nurses. . . . Attorney is not necessary because the law in here does not exist in there. The law does not exist. Western style law. It's court of law. . . . Some of them still ruled by the way of the Koran. Some of the law. And when you becoming an attorney to defend criminal that you already know, or there's a witness that he had committed crime, killing, stealing, adultery, anything (adultery is crime in there, not like here), and you defend the criminal person, then you be a criminal yourself. You try to prosecute someone that is innocent, that's a crime also.

Q: When did you start thinking that you might want to stay here? You originally wanted to be here for two years. When did you change?

A: It's not change. It's satisfaction. Let's put it this way. Not even an hour I'm not there with my mind in Yemen. Mostly about the prayers, the religious, the call for prayers five times a day. I think about that. I think about the closeness of friendships. There, how your friend would sacrifice for you! . . . The friendship is closer than the family. The prayers, it's a life in there. I like it here. I love my family in here. And I also wanted to stay but I wanted to go also. But it doesn't bother me to the point that I wanted to go anyway. I like to go and I like to stay. Either one, it's fine with me.

Q: For the first two years you said you didn't like it here. But then you started getting used to it?

A: Well, you start getting used to it and then you like it. They got to like it. Anybody say they don't like it, that's a lie. OK. If I don't like it here, I wouldn't stay, even if I owed a lot of money. I'd go back. I would sacrifice my time working day and night until I make that airplane ticket and go. But some of them, they do have to stay to pay what they owe. But it's future, after they pay and go back, they stay for a while, and they come back again. It's like an alco-

holic. The immigration among Yemen people is like an alcohol. When you're an alcoholic, you're very difficult to quitting. The immigration with Yemeni people is very difficult to quit.

Q: Why?

A: I really don't know if I have answer to this or not. I think it used to [be], before the revolution, people were just like in the cage. No schools, no hospitals, no medical. And barely you make a living. You were happy with what you got because you didn't know anything else. And they start the immigration and they go to "free world," you call it. There's too many things in here that there isn't there, that you never seen. OK. Now people still sleep in bed that's made from rope? Real hard bed sleeping, and people have water beds here. (But the water bed is already in Yemen too, this time. They got Sheraton Hotel in there, most perfect place in the world to live, you know?) At that time when people leave Yemen for the immigration, they see world that has schools, hospitals. . . . Mainly it was medical treatment that they don't have in Yemen. And they got that in their minds that this is never going to happen in Yemen. They used to immigrate to Saigon, Vietnam. It used to be under French rule before it was destruct. A lot of Yemeni people used to immigrate there and join the French force. Police, guards, things like that. Lot of Yemeni people still in Vietnam.

Q: I was told that a lot Yemenis got Vietnamese wives and brought them back to Yemen.

A: Yeah. Lots of them.

Q: How are those Vietnamese women treated in Yemen?

A: I've been away for so many years — over twenty-two years — but at the time, you know, with certain nationalities like that, all you know is the human. You don't go by color, by shirts, by . . . people have discrimination on "class."

Q: I understand there's a caste system in Yemen. The butchers and barbers are the lower class.

A: Well, the gypsies are low class. The butcher, barber . . . a few things. It's not low class. I think it's the ignorance. Used to be in the low class. For example, you would not marry your daughter to a barber or butcher but that's already been erased. That was in the time of the kingdom.

Q: Why do so many Yemenis come to this country when some of them tell me they could go to Saudi Arabia and make much more money?

A: There is over a million of us in Saudi Arabia that working and a lot of them used to be here and went back to Saudi Arabia. Yes, you can make a lot of money in there. It's true. But the life is miserable in there in Saudi Arabia. I think, first of all, there is disrespect for the Yemeni people. There is something between the two parties—Saudis and Yemenis—which is politics. There is some of the Yemeni land being taken by Saudi and used as oil well right now. Now the government of Saudi paying the government of North Yemen to keep it quiet, let it go as it is. And the people of Yemen don't like that. The people of Yemen very revolutionary. They would go to Saudi but they also like to live free. They don't like to be insult. Now the Saudi people have no respect for nobody other than Saudi. They call you "outsider." They call you "infidel" because you not that area, that part of the world. There will never be friendship as long as what's going on stay as it is. And to go to Saudi Arabia and work and make a lot of money, some of the people don't feel comfortable to stay. Some don't have the opportunity to go because there's restrictions on the country, how many goes to Saudi Arabia, sometimes from the government of North Yemen to how many can go. People can do things here they can't do in Saudi Arabia. Free to do what they want to do. They go out, have fun, those are the things that a lot of them like. Nobody can tell me they're forced to stay here. They must like it here.

Q: You've married an American woman and she's converted to Islam. Can you tell me how you met?

A: Well, when we met, I wasn't doing too good myself on Islam. I was just like her, I wasn't praying. I wasn't reading the Koran. I wasn't bothering with Islam. But it's something in your life. . . .

Q: You told me a friend of yours was mistaken one night by some punks for an Iranian and they beat him up.

A: Well, they said, "Are you Iranian?" and he said, "What do you care who I am?" For something like that. . . . Young kids, about fifteen were drinking. Actually, they're lost. It's the way they were taught, to discriminate. But to come to me and say, "Are you Iranian?"—no, I'm not Iranian. I'm Arab. "Well, we don't like you neither." "Well, it's not much I can do about it. I'm not so crazy about you neither, but there's nothing you can do about it if we're both here." "You want to fight?" "No, thank you." If I can run, I run. But you have to have a positive attitude about things. "Are you Iranian?" "No, what do you care what I am?"—that gives the other side more determination to get to you and they know it's not one to one. It's maybe twelve to one, fifteen to one. They got you beat. They got him; they beat him pretty good.

It happened to me one time. We have some problems with people that don't like Arab people. We used to live by the airport. They used to come and throw rocks at us, and spoons and forks, at our house. We called the police. I even went to the City Hall and the county supervisor and there isn't much they can do about it. They said, "If we can't catch somebody, we can't do nothing about it." I figure if we [Yemenis] come to a group and we can take care of ourselves, maybe we do something. So we get together and we wait in a dark area by the house and when they come, we face them and what they're doing to us. But after that, the problem becomes worse. They went and brought a bus full—maybe forty people came. They came and threatened they going to shoot us and this and that. In 1970, I lived with some Yemeni friends in a house in Modesto. And then those people that attack us were a bunch of ignorants, uncivilized. They don't like Arabs, they say. The police and sheriff said there wasn't much they could do about it. I said, "Well, you come with your uniform. You can catch them." I went and bought a gun and I told them I will take care of it myself and they follow me, you know. I said, "You welcome to use my car and use regular clothes and you find out what happened." Two sheriffs come and they stay in my car, and there was eleven of them in one night. Twenty-three years old, grown men, not young kids, you know.

Well, when they were arrested, they remember the car. It was my car that the sheriff came from. They followed me two months later to a drive-in. I went to get a hamburger. It was 10 o'clock in the evening. I have pistol—it was in the car. And there were six of them, four in the car and two right by me and he said, "Hey. We going to beat the hell out of you." I think he was six feet high, another big guy on the other side. I said, "Why? What did I do now?" He said, "We just don't like you." I said, "You can't beat someone because you don't like him. There's a lot of people in this world I don't like." He said, "The sheriff used your car." Well, I thank God, I have instant reaction. I knew I was beaten if I. . . . I said, "Hey, could you be a witness? I'm suing the sheriff for that." He said, "You're lying." I said, "No. I have papers to show you." Actually, I don't have papers. He said, "Where are they?" I said, "They're on the sun visor on the car. Go get them." He said, "You go get them." I said, "Why should I? You go get them." You see, if I make him believe I want him to go, he might give me a chance to go so I can get my gun. The gun was on the seat. He said, "No, you go get them." I said "OK." The other guy said, "Don't let him go. He's going to run away." I said, "No. Here's the car keys." I give him the car keys. I said, "You go get them if you don't believe me." He said, "Go get them." He fol-

86. *Ron Kelley.*

lowed me and I grabbed the gun. He said, "Son of a bitch!" I said, "No way. Now, who is son of a bitch? You sit your ass in there."

And then I have all six sitting there; I run the customers out. That was one bad thing, the customers started moving from the place. It was a hamburger drive-in. I got all six on a bench and we have nice talk. And I said, you know, as far as I'm concerned I can get all six of you right now. And all I can pay is for one crime—I go to jail. It's worth it if I want to be as stupid as you are. But why don't you just leave me alone and go? I still have the papers from what happened. "Oh, we just wanted to talk to you." "You fool. Bullshit." I said, "You want to talk to me? You attempt to beat me up. But now, your life is in my hands, right here. I beat you. You not about to say what you said a while ago." "Oh, we were just talking." "I know you were just talking. So am I." We have a nice little talk and I got my hamburger and my change from the lady at the place and I went home. I said, "Don't ever follow me again because next time it's not going to be talk."

I left and fifteen minutes later four or five policemen came with big flashlights looking for me. Those people already knew me, they took the car number and they call them. When I got home I call the sheriff and I told them what happened and they said it's up to the police. They said, "They looking for you already. Somebody call and accuse you of robbery or something." I took them my address, then came police officer, he's on the prejudicial side, he said, "Where is your gun?" I said, "What gun?" He said, "You had gun. You rob people." I said, "Rob people? Where?" He said, "By the drive-in." "Who were they?" He give me the names. I said, "It's stupid to believe these people have any money. They look forward to go to jail to have dinner." He said, "We not going to take that into consideration, but we like to see the pistol." I said, "It's a water gun." He said, "Where is it?" I said, "It's right on the table." I did have it on the table because I already know they're going to come to look for it. But I took the clip out. He said, "Oh, that's a nice water gun." .380. New, I just bought it. The case was dismissed, you know. He said, "We have to take your gun." I said, "No, you're not. You take my gun, you take me." He said, "That's the law." I said, "I will not let go of the gun unless you take me with you." A police officer said, "We'll take it for the night until the morning—8 o'clock, you can pick it up." I said, "Good. You leave an officer outside my house till 8 o'clock in the morning." I mean it too. I know the rest of the people are out of their mind. Those people don't have food. They not accepted on welfare because they're single people. They like to cause trouble so they can go to jail and it's a fact, to eat. That's the main reason for them to bother people. Three meals, color TV, bed . . . which they don't have.

Q: Most Yemenis who come to this country plan on going back to stay, right?

A: I think, Yemenis people, especially, their connection to their country is the most strong connection of any other human.

Q: Why is that?

A: That's something within the people. They could be having problems between themselves but when it's something about Yemen, they would be together. Connection with the families is very close. They'll do anything for the families.

Q: What's it like in the fields?

A: . . . it's not easy to work in the field. We argue. Sometimes we argue like we get in fight. It's not that we hate each other. Did you ever see how they work in asparagus? That's the worse job that could ever be done by a human. When you go to work, for example, in 100 degrees or 95 degrees and in that land is real dusty and it's about a mile to go to keep cutting. You always bending from end to another. There's no water for a while, you can't drink water till you get to the other end. When you finish that row you're cutting, you really don't even like to live. . . .

Mohammed, a foreman in his late forties, lives in town with his Mexican American wife. Since this interview he suffered a serious heart attack and spent considerable time in the hospital.

Q: When did you come here?

A: Oh, I come here in 1963. Long time ago and I'm an American citizen. I married over here and I got family. I am happy.

Q: What was it like when you first came here? Do you remember? Did you speak English?

A: No. No. No. I take one year to go to the restaurants to eat and the waitress comes to me and told me, "May I help you?" I told her yes. "What do you want?" I told her "fried chicken" for dinner. In the morning, I ask for two eggs. That's all. For one year I ate only fried chicken and eggs because I don't know how to order anything else. . . .

Q: So how did you get over here? Did you have relatives here?

A: Yes, before, twenty years ago, if you have uncles or friends, they fix papers for you and get you over to the United States but I think around fifteen years ago they change the law—nobody can get friends or anybody else, can get nobody—only the fathers and brothers.

Q: It's difficult to practice Islam here, isn't it?

A: Well, the Muslims—every one of the boys—they know about the religious because over there back home, first thing we do in school is to learn about the religious. And even like my baby, she's four years old, and she now pray at home, you know? When they are four years old up they was going with them parents to the church—we call it *masjid.* And they learn how to pray and just something beautiful! Everyone knows about them religious, is not hard for the religious over here. The hard is the language.

Q: You married an American or Mexican woman?

A: She's American and Mexican.

Q: And you have a daughter. . . .

A: I have a daughter. Four years old.

Q: Are you interested in raising her Muslim?

A: Well, I hope for that, but it's very difficult for me, really, because she watching TV and even the Arabic language is very hard for her. I talk with her mother in English and I can't teach her to speak Arabic. It's very difficult for me because I'm the only one.

If I talk to her once, she forget what I tell her. She watching TV and play with kids like her, talking with her mother and grandparents in English. She don't know anything else, only English. And I wish for her, maybe in the future, if God bless me, I make some money and can send her to Arabia to one of the colleges over there like my friend. He send his daughter to Cairo and she stayed over there for a while and she knows some Arabic now and she praying in Muslim's religious.

Q: Do most Yemenis here want to stay here, or do they want to go back to Yemen?

A: Well, they go back and forth. Some of them stay two years and they going back, some of them three years, four years, five years. It depends. I'm the only one stuck. Some of them stuck—the ones that come in the beginning, long time ago. The wages was only $1.10 an hour. You know what I mean? And we was working for $10 a day and ten hours. Now, you have to pay for the groceries. You have to go to the show, to town, to the restaurant. . . . You spend it all. Nothing, you know? And after what I take—ten years—I decide to get married because it was long time for me to go back and I can't go back. I stuck! And I don't have no choice.

Q: Why were you stuck?

A: Because I didn't have no money to go back! That's why! That's why I stay here. Our country—if you know the truth—is rich country. Even I don't have to come to the United States if I looking for the money only because Saudi Arabia is close to us, is our neighbor. And we going without visa or anything. It's same country—we go back and forth, no problem. And they got paid in Saudi Arabia more than what they get paid in the United States. In Arabian Gulf also, like Qatar, Bahrain, Kuwait. . . . They're rich places also.

Q: Why do Yemenis come here then?

A: That's what I tell you! The name of the United States is big over there. You know what I mean? And everyone to wish to come to the United States. And when they coming over here, the people that was here and going back to Arabia they explain how the United States is a free country and got beautiful girls like those that comes here, you know? You know what I mean? If you look like that to the window [at a woman in Yemen] and somebody else see you, they might shot you! And, besides, most of the womans they stay inside. Just only the young generation, now, they beginning to working with the people, going outside without cover on themselves. You know what I mean? That is the religious. The woman—that in our Bible, the Koran—have to cover up herself, not to show her beauty to anybody else. Only to her husband. That is in our religious. Over there in back home, if anybody else going with a woman and somebody else see them, then they hit him 100 times with green stick, you know, till when they take the skin out. Then they take him to the hospital and the next week, [he does] something. That twice. Then, if he did one more time, they bring four big trucks of rocks and then they hit him with the rocks until when they bury him in that place. That's it. If anybody else steals one box of matches, they cut his hand off! It doesn't matter if you drop your money over there—somebody else pass by and go the other way till when the police pass by and they pick up that things. Anybody come to the police station and pick up what he lost. The United States is a beautiful country *but* one condition: they don't protect the people. They have to make some protection. They got lot of Mafia over here. You go anyplace, you can't trust yourself to be alive if you have a good ring on your finger! Somebody will see that ring on your finger and shot you and take it from your hand! Or he can kill you even for $10! If he take what you got without hurting you, it don't make no difference. Over there in my country, we believe in our religious and the Koran. If you kill anybody else, you going to the hell. That what the Koran says.

Q: Do the families of all the Yemenis here understand how hard the men have to work here in this country?

A: I don't think so. The one that over there—they didn't come over here yet—they don't know how hard the job over here. Even the boys over here, they don't tell them exactly how hard it is. Anybody else is stuck here and go back home tell him different kind of story! They want him to be the same man what he be. You know what I mean? They talk about the United States perfect. That's why most of them come over here.

Q: Do you remember coming over here in 1963? Do you remember seeing cars and jets and TVs . . . ?

A: Of course! We have those things in Yemen, all over in Arabia. Just only some villages in Yemen, they don't have no car because they don't fix trails for the cars to go to the village's hard places, high mountains. You know, the mountains over there in my country very, very high. Something like 20,000 feet high. It very difficult to go over top of mountains to villages.

Q: When you first came here, what did you think this country was going to be like?

A: Well, it just exactly like I would expect because there was too many people that tell us how and we watch sometimes on the TV. I know New York, how New York was, how buildings is, the towers over there, the Empire States. . . . I see it over there back home before I come. At that time, even people of the United States very good people, but now they change. They have [had] soft hearts. I remember I come in the beginning to the New York airport and just come out from the airplane and one girl hold my hand and take me to the Immigration and Naturalization Service. The immigration leave one girl with me, be afraid for me to get lost. Then they ask me about address, what kind of relatives I got over here, what place I can go; they just took look to my pockets. They find the address of my uncle. Then they call the taxi and that girl didn't leave till she put me inside the taxi. She told the driver, "You are responsible for this boy to take him to this address. Anything bad happen to him, you are the responsibility." And then he takes me to my uncle's house exactly. And she told me, "You have the money for taxi?" I told her I have around $500 in my pocket and I take all the money in my hand and she told me, "No, don't take the money outside all like that! I'm going to take the money and I give it to him." She give him $7 and she put the rest of the money in my pocket. I was didn't know nothing. I take all the money in my hand! I was thinking like it was Arabia—it doesn't matter what you got in your hand, what you carry, nobody can attack you or rob you or do anything. I stay in New York twenty-five days with my uncles and friends. They took me to the Empire States, to all the places over there beautiful to show me and then I fly from New York to San Francisco. I stay in San Francisco thirty days with friends over there. Then I come to Stockton.

Q: Why Stockton?

A: To looking for a job on farm because I didn't know nothing how to speak. I got too many friends in New York who want me to help him in the stores, but I don't even know how to talk to the customer. I don't know nothing about it! Then I said, well, I'm going to work in the farm. Better for me. There's no problem; they got Arabians working over there. I come to Stockton, they were working on asparagus and I try two hours. I can't do nothing! I wasn't working as hard a job in my life! Never! Then I leave Stockton and come with other friends over here to Delano. We was working in the grapes. I working sometimes and sometimes I didn't work, I think, like that for about two years. Then I push myself. I don't have no ways. It don't matter how hard the job. I have to work. I have to make money to live, you know? That's it. Well, I was working—like what I told you—ten years. I didn't make nothing, just only to even. And I decided to get married over here. Whatever I make, I

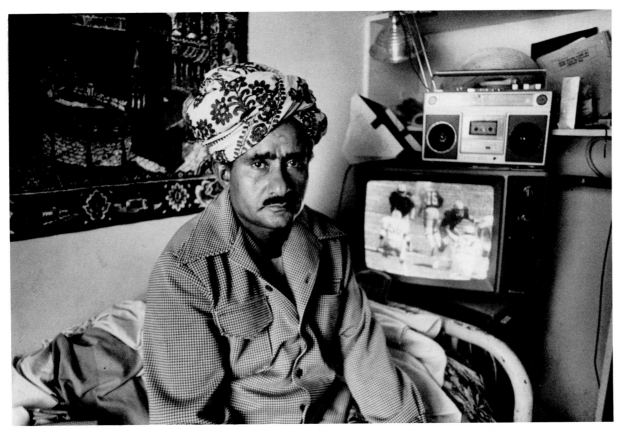

87. *Ron Kelley.*

just spend it! I spend it to go around town, to eat in the restaurant, to go to the show. . . .

Q: You send money back to Yemen?

A: I didn't have no money to send back! Like what I told you, the wages was $1.10 an hour.

Q: You have a bad back, right?

A: Oh, yeah!

Q: Tell me what happened.

A: Well, still I'm now training with the doctors and use beds for pains and I don't know what to do. I have appointment to see the doctor next week in Bakersfield, special.

Q: How did it happen?

A: In the job. I'm foreman to cross the row, check on the job. And I have too many new boys and I'm afraid they going make mistake on the job and I cross the row very fast and hit my head on the arm of the vine and go to the back. And I hurt my back. It's very badly now. This is [was] 1981, almost three years. Three years pass since I hurt my back and have this problem. All this problem is killing me! I can't sit down one hour I don't have pain! Is very hard. The doctor told me don't carry over twenty pounds. The pain is killing me.

Q: There are some men in the camp who don't speak English.

A: Some of them. Some of them know just a little bit.

Q: And those men who want to learn English, they want to go back to Yemen. . . .

A: Some of them even if they know how to speak English perfect, they going back to Arabia back and forth. Because them family back home. They going back home to stay one year, some of them two years. The ones they are American citizens, some of them stay ten years. . . .

Q: Why does anyone want to become American citizens then?

A: Some of them . . . I think each one wants to become American citizen but some of them is very hard for them to answer the questions. They don't know how to speak English and answer the questions. American history, who discovered the United States? You can answer, "Mr. Christopher Columbus." And when did he come to this country? You tell them "19 . . . 1492." What he come to looking for? "He comes looking for the gold." Who make the flag of the United States? Who was the chief of the United States? Who's our chief over here in California? How many senators? You know, lots of questions, some of them don't know how to answer this kind of questions.

Q: When did you become a citizen?

A: Oh, 1969. Fifteen years.

Q: Were there a lot more Yemenis here in 1969, in the camps, in the fields?

A: Yeah, but the camp here, I don't think so. The rest are in different area like in Merced, Stockton, Oakland, San Francisco, Detroit, Michigan, and most of them in New York City. They got business over there. Too many stores over there. Arabian. They leave farmwork and they buy stores because. . . . I like the way we are. We stick together. We help together. Not like over here. When you are not Yemeni and you have something important to you and you need some money, you go to the finance company or you go to the bank and you want to draw $2,000 or $3,000 or $5,000, I don't know how much interest they make off you. But we help together. If I have money and my friends come and asks me for $10,000 or $20,000, I give him without interest and anytime he have the money, he give me back the money.

Q: Even a friend? It doesn't have to be a relative?

A: Just friends! Yemenis, that's all! That's our way. That way, most of the Yemenis, they make stores. . . . And most of them, now they have store. Every town in this area. I tell you an example: in Richgrove, they got two Arabian stores there. Three! Porterville, Poplar, Woodville, Pixley, Delano, Fresno, Bakersfield, everywhere and every town, they got Arabian stores. They happy and they make money.

Q: Do many think about bringing their families from Yemen over to here?

A: Some of them do. The ones that get a stores. But the ones that working on the farm, no. It's very difficult for them. They can't make enough money. Gas, telephone, here and there, car and insurance for the family—he can't do all this responsibility from the farm. But the ones in the stores, yeah. All of them, they get their family over here.

Q: What can you tell me about the imam [Yemen's former ruler, deposed in 1962]?

A: Oh, he's the one left the country behind! The United States going to the moon and we didn't know anything over there in Arabia. That was what he was doing, keep the people like animal. Don't know anything. Most of the people in my home in Yemen, they didn't know nothing. He didn't make no schools, no streets, no hospitals. Nothing! . . . But, now, the boys, they talk. [The ones that] come from Arabia in Yemen. I can't even believe it. Is very beautiful, more over there than the United States!

Q: What do they say?

A: They fix the streets, they make the trees on the streets, lights. . . . Only the heaven, you know? And they build towards business. Everything is perfect.

Q: What was it like when you were there?

A: Well, little schools to learn about the religious only.

Q: You told me you saw the imam's palace and you weren't supposed to look. Do you remember that story?

A: Of course. . . . When we were going to Aden, south of Yemen, to fix our paper with America ambassador in Aden and we was pass by close his castle in Taʿizz. He has castle over there everywhere in Yemen. They told us before we reach to the castle not look to the imam castle. I told him, "Why?" They said they come and catch you and put you in jail. I said, "Even if I am a kid?" He told me it doesn't matter, kid or big or old man or whatever. He [the imam] was have two lions. Over there in the castle and he leave one guy to take care of the lions and to clean them places and he was feed him himself in the nighttime. . . . He come in the nighttime to feed the lions and he train them only like the circus over here. Then they listen to him. Whatever he said, they do to what he train them. One time he told the guy take care of them, leave the door open for the lions to go out into the street to prove it to the population that means he's just like a god. The lions come outside, every one of them bigger than a cow because they feed them lambs. And the population be scared. Children, womans, man, they run. Everyone run away. Every one of us have to carry weapons, guns, rifles, machine guns, it doesn't matter. That custom. But we can't shoot because it's the king's lions. And [the king] come outside and he say, "Put them back!" and they know his voice and get back in his place. Golly, even the king of the animals listen to our lord!

Q: The imam.

A: Yeah. And sometimes he brings the buses of people over there. They have big families in Arabia, especially like in Yemen. Like four or five towns, they got 5,000–10,000 people and one guy is the leader for them. And [the imam] gets all the leaders of this families and invites them for dinner at his house. When they are eating the dinner he has toy guns just like they make in Hollywood. They shoot without bullets. And he says, "Oh, I have heart problem! Open the fire to my chest!" And ten guys they just come up and shoot. The families' leaders, they hear the noise from their rifles and they don't know they got no bullets. They think they shoot real. "Thanks be to God, I'm alright now!" [The people] said, "Jesus Christ! Wouldn't you pray to God to send us to heaven, our lord imam?" That was what he was doing! They make that revolution against him. This guys they get guys from Iraq, Cairo, Egypt. . . . And they know how the rest of the countries they do, how they make parliaments like a congress, and there and there. Not only one guy to control all the country himself. And they come back to Yemen and they make the revolution secret. They talk to the leaders of the police and control everything and then they make the revolution and they kicked him out. Make the Yemen Arab Republic.

Ahmed, in his late thirties or early forties, lost two fingers in a Detroit factory accident. At the time of this interview, he worked as a cook in one of the camps.

Q: How long have you been in this country?

A: I come over this country in 1972 and I live in Detroit, Michigan. I'm working from 1972 to 1975 in factory—Ford Motor Company, and after about one year I go home my country. I stay there maybe one year and I come back to Detroit. I can't find job. I come to California. I'm working from 1980 in California. I'm working packing and asparagus. It's a hard job but what you going to do?

Q: When you were in Yemen, what did you hear about America?

A: . . . everybody working over there told me America is good, is lot of fun, a lot of money, free country, something like this, you know?

Q: Did you speak English when you came here?

A: No. I go sometime to school two hours a day, two days, three days a week and from the work I got a lot of friends, American people. You talk a little bit. I don't speak English very good, you know, just a little bit.

Q: What are some of the differences between Yemen and America? What's important to you?

A: Well, the difference is America is free country and is lot a job over there but in Yemen is good but if you work too much you make a lot of money like here. Same thing, no difference.

Q: How is there more freedom in this country?

A: Here is a lot of fun over here.

Q: No fun in Yemen?

A: Yeah, is fun in Yemen but lot of trouble sometimes with people, family. That's why.

Q: Do you have a wife and children in Yemen?

A: Yes.

Q: When was the last time you saw them?

A: 1982.

Q: When will you see them again?

A: Maybe this year. Maybe four or five years more I go to my country.

Q: Are you happy here in America?

A: No. I don't happy here. I like to go back my country. My family, I don't see him. My wife, my mother, my father. . . . I miss everybody. America is nice, I'm alright here. I got a lot of friends here, but I miss my family.

Q: Did you know when you came over here to America that it was going to be such hard work?

A: No. If I know is hard work over here, I not come here. Everybody tell me easy job, take money easy. If somebody come here from my country, in America before, and he come back to my country, he make maybe $10,000, $11,000. He say, "Easy money. I'm working job easy." That's why. If somebody told me truth, is America hard job like this, I not come here. No. No way.

Q: When you go back, do you tell them that you work hard or it's easy . . . ?

A: No. Myself, I told them, "Hard job." My brother, he wants to come here. I say, "No." He say, "Why? You not like me?" I say, "Yeah, I like you but I don't want to give you hard job like me." He drives car, he makes 7,000 riyals in my country. Easy job. Just drive a truck, that's it. What do you think, for the pruning? I can't work for the pruning. Make $100 a day. I can't. I don't like it. Too hard. My arms, everything. . . .

Q: What was it like in the factories in Detroit? Easier?

A: Not easy, but better than here. Work hard little bit eight hours and go home. Make a lot of money too. If I make $4.50 an hours here, I make in Detroit $11 an hour.

Q: They'll call you back?

A: I don't think so. I don't have seniority too much. Just three years. Some people working seven years not come back. People working ten, eleven, twelve years, maybe call him back.

Q: Tell me the story about your seventy-five-year-old cousin.

A: This guy named Ahmed. He one time *salat* [praying] home, you know, in California. I don't know what city. One American guy he opens the door and comes with big knife in his hand. He hold my cousin, wants the money. He say "Al right. After I finish my *salat*, I give you money." And he stand up, he break his [the robber's] hand. He call the police. The police come, they say, "Why, you crazy! You kill yourself!

88. *Ron Kelley.*

Give him the money." He say, "I don't want to give him. I'm working hard job. Why I give him my money? If I give him my money like this, is no good. I have to kill him or kill me. I don't want to give him the money. I working hard job on the ranch, all the week, seven days a week. I make $75 this week. I have to kill him or kill me, I don't care." He broke the robber's arm. And he took him the knife. My country is not like this. If somebody wants some money, he told you, "Give me 100 riyals and I give you back." My friend for New York City, he got a store, small store, grocery store. He buy it. He sold beer and wine, cigarettes, newspapers. Some people come takes some cigarettes and some wine and he got a short maybe $1.50. My friend he told him, "I don't know you. I don't give you credit because I don't know you. You have to pay me." He says, "No, I don't have no money." "Well, if you don't have no money, next time. Come back. Don't take my beer like this." He say, "Alright. I'll see you later." And another day he come back, he hold him, he got a gun. He say, "Let's go. Give me the money." My friend, he got a gun too. My friend he take a gun and the people shoot him — this American, black one. He shoot him two shots. He's die. Flatbush Street. Four years ago. And right here in California too, maybe three months ago in

Oakland. Some people, he go to Yemeni store. Not Arabian guy, he working with Arabians in store and sombody — black one, two — he come and he shoots him. He kill him.

Ahmed Shaibe of South Yemen, ex-farmworker and UFW organizer, is currently working as the American-Arab Anti-Discrimination Committee (ADC) representative in Delano, California.

Q: Could you tell me something about yourself, when you came here, why you came here, and so forth?

A: Well, I came here in 1972. I come here to go to school and work in the same times. And when I arrive here I worked as a farmworker in the beginning for a couple of years. I worked as a farmworker in the daytime, at nighttime I went to night school. At that time, the UFW and farmworkers was very strong and they didn't have an Arabic organizer to organize Yemeni farmworkers and I work with them as a part-time organizer. I did it off and on from 1973 to 1981.

Q: You're an educated man.

A: Yes, in Yemen I graduated from there. But it's difficult for me to do the same job I was doing in Yemen because of the language. It's college there, but more like junior college here.

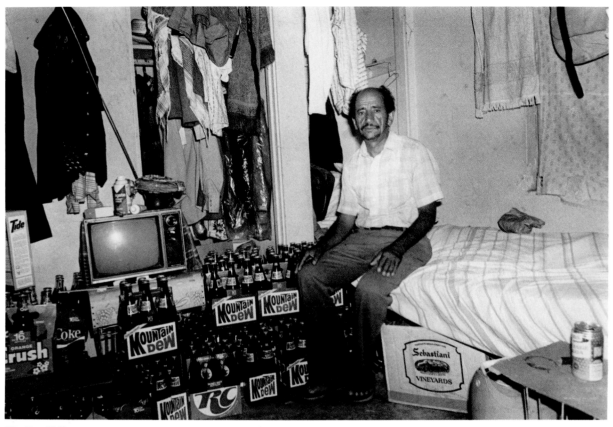

89. *Ron Kelley.*

Q: Have Yemenis always been supportive of the UFW?

A: It's a long history. In the seventies, the Yemenis farmworkers, they back up the UFW very, very strong. And the UFW, they used to be very strong for the Yemenis at the same times. But when the Teamsters came, that's when the UFW start to be weak and the Yemenis workers continue to support the UFW. But we lost in a lot of places and lot of Yemenis get fired from their jobs. And that is all. They dismiss their cases and, after that, they didn't do too much for the UFW.

Q: How many Yemeni organizers were there?

A: There were two before me and the same times when I join working for the UFW, they have two organizers come from Detroit for the season. Then they went back.

Q: Are there any Yemeni UFW organizers now?

A: No. There is none. They used to have a lot of contracts under where the Yemenis farmworker used to work. Now, we have one contract. There are a few Arabs working on it.

Q: Why did you come to this country?

A: To see America first! To work and I was thinking to finish college here. It was a lot of problems. I have my family back home and I have to support

them and didn't get a chance to go to college. I might go and finish in the future.

Q: When you gave up the UFW job, what did you start doing?

A: I didn't give it up. I had to resign. I was asked by the ADC [American-Arab Anti-Discrimination Committee] to come and open up an office in this Delano area.

Q: As the local ADC representative, do you see a lot of problems?

A: Oh, yeah! A lot!

Q: Could you give me some examples of problems that Yemenis face?

A: Well, the first problem they're having is the language. They're having too many problems with the Internal Revenue, income taxes. . . . They have problems with the Motor Vehicles and Unemployment Department. And the doctor's offices. They need translations, all those things. I'm doing my best to help, but I'm not doing 100 percent. I'm not an attorney, like when they have cases with the court or Internal Revenue. They need to have an attorney who speak Arabic language. We're working on it to provide them an attorney and doctor. We have a few Arabic doctors that came from Los Angeles to this area to see if there's enough people to open offices and

clinics here in Delano. They're thinking about opening offices in Bakersfield or Porterville. That's the last
decision we heard. Anyway, I'm doing my best to help
them in some issues like translations. Some of them
have accidents, injuries at work, and we settle cases—
some of them—with the insurance. Some of them get
a lot of money. Another way which our organization is
willing to do for them is underwriting life/accident
insurance and cheap ticket fares to Yemen.

Q: What did the Yemenis do before you were here
to help?

A: A lot of them were stuck. A lot of them were
injured on the job. A lot of them have a lot of problems and go back to work and not bother anything—
the insurance or anybody else—because they don't
know language and nobody could help them. Some of
them get help from other friends who speak some
English. And some of them go to attorneys before
once they know how to speak some English.

Q: How many Yemeni farmworkers do you think
speak English well enough to do these sort of things—
10 percent?

A: No, no, no. I couldn't tell you exactly but we
have a few who speak some, like two or three in each
camp, but if you want them to translate for you, these
things, you have to pay them for the work they miss
plus gas and food and things. But it's different if they
come to us. It doesn't cost anything—just $15 a year.

Q: How many Yemenis do you have on the ADC
list around here?

A: We have a lot, enough. We're working to sign a
lot more.

Q: What did you expect when you first came to
America?

A: I was thinking it was going to be a lot better
than I was expecting. I was thinking when I go to
work in the field, I have to wear a tie. Honestly. I was
not thinking about the language. America is nice but
you need to know your rights.

Q: When Yemenis go home, do they tell their families how hard it is here?

A: Oh, yes. People told us before. My brother, he
told me. He came here twenty-one years ago. When
he came back in 1970 he told me it was very hard and
I said, "I don't believe him." I thought I want to come
to the United States—even if it's hard. And then till
when I came here and found it's very hard and very
difficult, I went back, same thing, and told the other
ones and they didn't pay any attention to that.

Q: A lot of guys have told me they've gotten stuck
here.

A: We have people stuck and not able to go back.

Q: Why?

A: Well, first, they are not saving money. They
spend it and send some back home. You need a lot of
money to go back home. It costs you now $2,500 just
for the plane.

Q: What changes do Yemenis go through when
they come from Muslim Yemen to here? Were you
shocked when you first came here?

A: I was shocked because they take me to the
fields and at that time it was the season for the grapes
and I have to go inside the vines and cut two full
boxes of grapes. My arms! When I get outside to the
packer to pack the grapes, I was very tired. I worked
all day. I was tired. This is not America. I thought it
was not like that.

Q: Did you think about going home? Were you
upset?

A: I was very upset! I don't want to go home right
away; I was telling myself I wish I study more English
there, a lot more, so I come here and do another kind
of job. Because this is very difficult working on the
farm.

Q: Most Yemenis here in the fields don't have
much education.

A: No, the oldest ones don't go to school at all.
They only read the Koran.

Q: Is it true most Yemenis can't read or write in
English or Arabic?

A: Some of them can't read or write Arabic. The
oldest ones. But the younger ones, they know.

Q: You recently brought your family here. Does
that mean you're going to stay here? What sort of
things are on your mind?

A: Well, I was thinking about this for a long, long
time. And I decide is very hard for me and my family
that I am here and they are in Yemen and is very
difficult if I go there every three years and I stay there
for six months. I decide that's not enough. Since I find
this job and I'm satisfied with it, I'm making some
money and I save some, I decide to go home and
bring my family with me. I did that and that helps me
a lot.

Q: Do Yemenis change a lot in the camps? In
terms of being Muslims, you're not supposed to drink,
you're supposed to pray five times a day . . . those
things seem to change in the camps.

A: OK. In Yemen, in your villages, you heard the
mosque's prayer five times a day. You're not doing
heavy job. You're speaking your language. There is
no beer. There is no dance. There is no things to do
like here. And you see a lot of people praying every
day in their culture. When the Yemenis come here,
some of them—very few—they used to pray, they
used to be religious, not go to bars and all those

90, 91. Youngster in Sanᶜa, Yemen (studio photograph), and at work in the vineyards, Delano, California. *Ron Kelley*.

things. But when they come here, they begin to see things here and start to forget about praying and like Americans have drinking beer and dancing and those things.

Q: Why do Yemenis come to America when they can make more money in Saudi Arabia?

A: This question has a lot of answers. First, I think you heard in the 1970s in Saudi Arabia there is a lot of jobs and they're making more money than whatever is here. And lots of people go there. Not only to America. More than a million Yemenis go to Saudi Arabia and even there are some who quit working in Saudi Arabia and come here. I think—I'm not sure—they heard that America is beautiful and nicer than Saudi Arabia and is more freedom and more money too. But this was wrong. When they came here they found out it's better in Saudi Arabia. Some of them they did go back and some of them they didn't because, right now, I heard it's very difficult to get work in Saudi Arabia.

Q: Is there a lot of pressure to send money home?

A: Oh, yeah! . . . If you are a good man, you have to send to your poor family there. They're not very poor—they're not dying, starving, but they need the money. And about 90 percent of the Yemenis—not only the farmworkers, but who work in the factories in the U.S.—they have to send at least half of their income a year to their family.

Q: What would happen to the Yemeni guy who went back home with no money? Would he be shamed?

A: Well, they make fun of him. Over there not like here. If something happened like this, all the people in the village know. That guy is not good to his family. When he goes back there, sure, they'll make fun of him and have no respect for him.

Q: In this project, I've found it's very difficult to be allowed to take pictures of Yemenis, say, working in the field. They don't want to be photographed being "dirty" and all that. Could you talk about what's going on here?

A: OK. I think it's simple. We have people who came, like you, working for magazines, organizations, and they take pictures and they did stories on the Yemeni farmworker and they put them in the ugly spot.

Q: What do you mean?

A: There's magazines and they put the bad pictures in their books and bad stories and when the Yemenis heard about that, they don't like it. From I see about you, you've been here a long time, they be friendly with you. They take a lot of pictures

because they trust you because they know you're not going to do something like that. You will tell the truth.

Q: What can you tell me about this picture on the wall [a local newspaper photograph of a Yemeni]? Someone told me the people were upset about him being photographed in a *futa* [Yemeni skirt].

A: I am very upset. Those clothes the guy is wearing . . . we believe it's not nice to take a picture without tell us he's going to take this picture and put it in a newspaper because this is for inside. He wear it in the camp around Yemeni farmworkers. But he cannot wear that in town or in village.

Q: I also heard there was another problem with a picture of men playing cards because of gambling or something like that.

A: That's kind of silly. I don't know there is a problem on that. I don't think so. . . .

Q: In Yemen, what do people there think is the proper way to have a photograph taken? You don't take candid pictures, you ask permission, right?

A: Well, nobody give you permission in Yemen. Nobody allowed you to do that, especially with the family there. . . . If you are in Yemen, it doesn't matter what pictures you took because you are there. But here they think if you take a picture like this, it looks funny to the other people. That's what they think, which I don't agree with.

Q: A lot of Yemenis are afraid of embarrassment?

A: Right. The other thing is, like, people come and take pictures of them in the fields and they think, "Why didn't they go to town and take somebody who is nice-looking and have a tie and suit and take my picture in town? I could do that. How come I have to be the ugly one in the field?" They don't know.

Q: Are there any tensions between North and South Yemenis here?

A: Our experience to our knowledge here is we are from Yemen. We are from Yemen; there is only one. The British and the imam divided the Yemen but we believe there is one Yemen and we are here. Like me. They call me from the south. I serve the north more than the people from the south. And we don't believe there is south. We come here to work.

Q: A lot of Yemenis live in the camps. Do they prefer it there?

A: No! They don't want to, but they have to. They don't like it even one hour! If they have a chance to, if they speak the language and they have transportation and all those things, they don't want to stay in the camps. You see who speak the language and have cars. They don't live in the camps.

Q: Did you ever hear of any Yemenis who came here and it was so hard and different than they thought that they left right away?

A: Oh, yeah. Not too many, but I've heard about a few.

Q: What are the most common injury problems in the fields?

A: Backs, broken arms, accidents falling from trees. . . . We have the problem with a lot of people with the spray. Chemicals in the field. A lot of people sneezing, tears from their eyes, a lot of allergies. I have that too from the fields. Now if I go to see any workers in the field, I can't breathe very good. I never had the problem before. My eyes and my nose and my chest. I think it's when I pulled leaves. When they spray the chemicals to the trees, that's when I have that. I've been sick and too many doctors not helping me any good. We have one old man, he have to leave the country because of that. We fight his case for four months. We lost. He applied for social security benefits.

Q: Tell me what's involved in Yemeni society with taking a picture of a man's wife.

A: In two seconds she be divorced.

Q: Why is that?

A: In Yemen, they follow the Koran. They're very religious. I don't know if it's the Koran or they make it up. I'm not sure. She supposed to wear clothes so nobody could see her. She's supposed to be a house-wife and nobody allowed to come and take a picture of any wife of somebody just like that. It's very diffi-cult. I think it was the same thing in America for first woman who take a picture—she have same feeling we do. Because we don't have any magazines with pic-tures of women there. Maybe in the future it's going to be natural. But right now it's still difficult to take a picture without her husband. She won't let you take her picture.

Musaid, in his late thirties, one of the best English speakers in the camp.

Q: When did you come to this country?

A: I come to this country in 1974.

Q: To where?

A: To New York.

Q: Did you speak English?

A: No. I didn't know how to ask for water.

Q: How did you ask for help or directions?

A: I live with American friends. I get around with Americans, with Mexicans.

Q: How come you came to this country?

A: I like this country.

Q: Why? Why did you want to come here?

A: Because I'm freedom here. In my country, you're not free. You don't have freedom there.

Q: Why?

A: You can't do nothing there! They cut your head there. This is truth, honest. You can't do nothing there.

Q: Like what?

A: You know like what. You can't hang around with womans. . . .

Q: In Yemen you can't see women?

A: You can see women but you can't do nothing. If you need a woman you have to have a lot of money. You have to have over 80,000. No money, no honey! You can't have no honey if you don't have no money. Believe me.

Q: How did you come here? How did you end up in the fields?

A: To the U.S.? My father brought me.

Q: Your father doesn't speak English.

A: No.

Q: How long has he been here?

A: About sixteen years. He live in the labor camp only with Yemenis.

Q: Why?

A: Well, he doesn't like it. He's old. Arabian Yemenis, they different when they over thirty years, didn't go to school. If I tell him, "Go to school," he say, "I'm too old to go to school."

Q: He doesn't know English at all?

A: Maybe he knows "Cómo estás" in Spanish. I know Spanish.

Q: How long have you been in California? Do you like working in the fields?

A: Yeah, I like it. I like to work in the fields.

Q: Why?

A: That way you save your money. You don't have to pay for rent. You don't have to pay for food. When you work, they cut from your check for the food over here. Then you save money and then you free. In case if you get sick or you want to take rest the next day, you don't have to go to work. Exam-ple, if I work in the city, if I want to take one day off, I have to have a reason. Because if I take a day off and next day go to work in the city, you need doctor's excuse. But over here, we don't need no doctor's excuse.

Q: You have a wife in Yemen?

A: Right. And three kids.

Q: When was the last time you saw them?

A: 1981.

Q: You send money home?

A: Sure, all my money. I save money in case we have problem between Yemen and the United States. Yeah, if they throw me out of the country, I have money.

Q: What do you think of Saudi Arabia?

A: Saudi Arabia, good and bad. The bad because the Saudi make a fight between Yemeni country. Between South Yemen and North Yemen. Lot of people get killed in North Yemen, between North and South Yemen. Why? Because of Saudi. The Saudi support the shaikh. You know shaikh? And then they fight with the poor people in South Yemen. The poor people receive weapons from the Russians and North Yemen from the U.S. All the civilians in North Yemen, they have weapons, Russian weapons. AK-47. Why? I don't know. Why they have the Russian weapon?

Q: Do you have one?

A: Yeah, I have one. I have one at home. And we have one from this country. This country support North Yemen with weapons. But all the civilians have Russian weapons.

Q: Why did you come to this country exactly? Why didn't you go to Saudi Arabia?

A: I like the U.S.

Q: You want to bring your wife here?

A: No. I'm going to have a wife over here. . . .

Q: So you might divorce your Yemeni wife and stay here?

A: No, just leave her there. Yeah, she'll wait for me. Ten, fifteen years. She can't go anywhere because I pay money for her. I buy her from her father.

Q: But you might have a wife here too?

A: Sure. But I don't have to let her know I have another wife in the Middle East.

Q: Don't you have to be a rich man to have two wives?

A: Everybody has money there. Everybody. These people, they have money. They have property, they have fields, they have animals. They have everything. All Yemenis.

Q: Is your father going to stay here for many more years?

A: No. Maybe next year we're going back home.

Q: For good? Or you'll be back?

A: Maybe I be back.

Q: How often do you see your wife in Yemen?

A: Every four or five years. The first time I came over here in 1974. '75, '76 . . . to 1981. I went home in 1981.

Q: What do you tell them when you go back to Yemen? Do they think you've got an easy job?

A: She knows I've got another woman over here.

Q: Your wife? How does she know?

A: Because I take the baby away from the lady over here. The baby's back home in Yemen.

Q: Your baby from America?

A: In Yemen.

Q: Was she half Yemeni and half . . .

A: White.

Q: Your Yemeni wife doesn't care?

A: She loves him. He's six. He's in school already.

Q: The mother here didn't care?

A: I don't know. I take him from her because I need him and she didn't need him. She's going to find another baby in the street or somewhere. . . . Yeah, I need it.

Q: What do your wife and family think you do here?

A: They know's hard job over here. We told them everything, how we're doing over here. But we like it. We like to work over here. If we work in Saudi Arabia we make more money than over here.

Q: Every now and then you just leave this place, you go to Denver. . . . You told me that every now and then you get bored or tired. . . .

A: I get nervous over here because I get bored in the camp. I can't do nothing over here. My dad is here. He's a Muslim man. He believes in God, Allah. I believe in God but I have to have fun. I like to enjoy myself. . . .

Q: What do people in Yemen think America is like?

A: They see American television over there. They know lot of bums over here.

Q: When you first came here, were you scared or nervous?

A: Happy.

Q: Why?

A: Because I like to be over here. Because the Number One country, believe me. Two countries control the world, the U.S. and Russia, but the U.S. Number One. Because they care. They care about you, about me, about civilians. . . . The Russians, they don't care.

Q: Do they care in Yemen?

A: Sure, we care. If we rich, we help people. But we didn't have enough money. Small country, Yemen. I like the U.S.

Q: Do most Yemenis pray and do all the Muslim things in this camp?

A: Everybody over here. Me? No.

Q: Everybody?

A: Yeah.

92. *Ron Kelley.*

Q: Who did you go with?

A: Anyplace by myself. Walking the street, get in and listen.

Q: What did they say?

A: No difference between a Muslim and Christianity. Only difference, the Muslim has to pray five times a day, Christianity only Sunday, sometime. And Christianity, they drink—alcoholic, heroin, drugs, marijuana, everything. This is against the law. Because it says in the Bible if you want to be in heaven you have to believe Jesus is the son of God. I said, "No." I don't believe he son. I believe in God, and Jesus a prophet of God.

Q: Are you a Muslim?

A: Yeah. I'm a Muslim. I don't believe the son of God.

Q: But you don't pray very much. . . .

A: Too much. God, he knows I pray, but nobody see me. God, he know. Nobody see me, but God see me. I pray. I don't know which to believe, Christianity or Muslim or Buddha. I don't know. Because nobody prove it. Nobody went to heaven and come back. You see, how do you know we have heaven? Nobody knows. Can you prove it?

Q: Who taught you all this? This isn't what they say in the Koran.

A: This what they say in Delano.

Q: You don't go to prayer?

A: Nah, I get lazy. When I'm in the city I went to the church of Jesus Christ. Go have fun and listen the Bible and learn about God.

Editor's note: These accounts were excerpted from interviews conducted by Ron Kelley in the San Joaquin Valley, 1983–84. The accompanying photographs do not literally represent the workers interviewed.

Portfolio
Michigan, 1982–83

TONY MAINE

93. Autoworkers' residence, Coldwater, Michigan.

94. Yemeni industrial workers on lunch break, assembly feeder satellite, Dearborn.

95. Cutting steel, South Dearborn.

96, 97. Zinc smelting plant, Detroit.

98, 99. Frame assembly line, Ford River Rouge complex, Dearborn.

100, 101, 102. Stamping plant, Ford River Rouge complex, Dearborn.

103. Chrysler engine line, Detroit.

104. Spot welder, Chrysler truck plant, Detroit.

105, 106. Industrial spray painter, Dearborn.

107. Yemeni grocery, Joseph Campeau Boulevard, Hamtramck.

108. Yemeni soccer team at halftime, Dearborn.

109. Arabic instruction, Yemeni school, Hamtramck.

Portfolio
Yemini Steelworkers' Community
Lackawanna, New York, 1977

MILTON ROGOVIN

110.

111.

112. Family dressed for Ramadan.

113. Women dressed for Ramadan.

114. Woman made-up for her daughter's wedding.

115. Woman with prayer shawl.

116. Grocery store owners.

117. Koranic school.

118. Ramadan sermon in a Yemeni mosque, formerly a Greek Orthodox church.

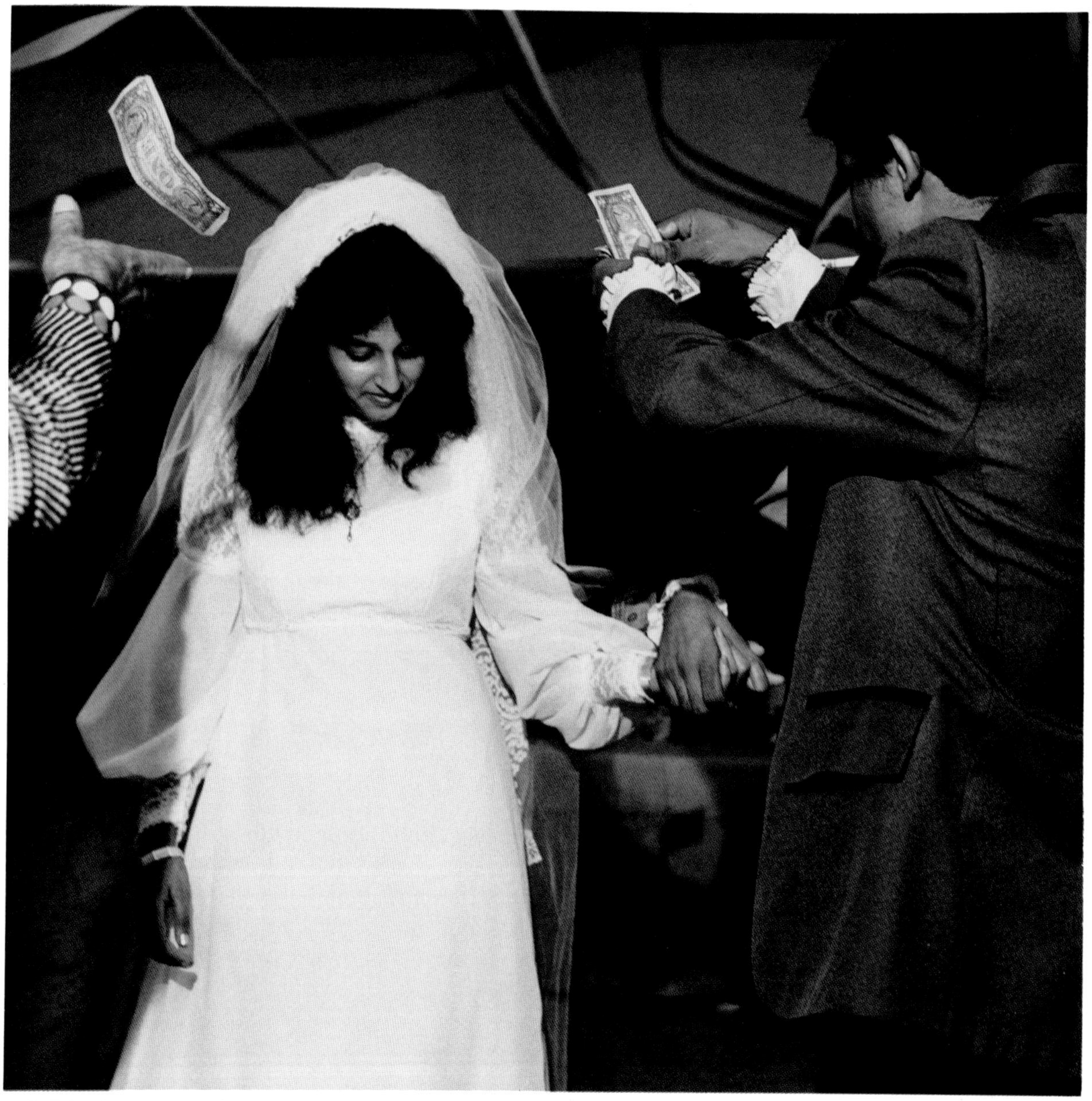

119. Wedding dance.

The Settlement of Yemeni Immigrants in the United States

GEORGES SABAGH AND MEHDI BOZORGMEHR
Department of Sociology
University of California, Los Angeles

INTRODUCTION

The prevailing wisdom about Yemenis in the United States is that they have been a predominantly sojourning, "recurrent" or "circular" immigrant group consisting mainly of young men (Aswad 1974). This view is supported by existing studies of Yemenis in Detroit, Buffalo, and the San Joaquin Valley, where the Yemenis are most visible. Aswad (1974:62) partially attributes the preponderance of Yemeni men in Detroit to restrictive laws in Yemen on the emigration of women, although she adds that "these laws are currently being modified." Abraham (1983) infers that since the majority of the Yemenis in the Detroit area had become separated from their families, while retaining their farmland in Yemen, their case is a typical "recurrent migration." Similarly, Dweik (1980) suggests that most of the Yemenis in a small ward of Buffalo were originally sojourners, although his portrait of the community comes closer to a settled population (see also the photographs by Milton Rogovin in this volume). According to a small survey conducted in the Central Valley in California, three-fourths of the fifty Yemeni farmworkers who were interviewed intended to return home, but were unable to visit Yemen frequently because of the high cost of travel (Sanchez and Solache 1980; see also

Bisharat 1975). It should be noted that the three states of Michigan, New York, and California account for 82.8 percent of the 2,491 North Yemenis and a somewhat smaller 63.6 percent of the 602 South Yemenis enumerated in 1980 in the U.S. Census (table 1).

While it might appear that these studies reflect the Yemeni, particularly North Yemeni, experience in the United States, they have focused on workers on the farm and in the automobile and steel industries, who may constitute the bulk of sojourners. In addition, the sojourning thesis either is inferred from the indicators mentioned above or is based on the opinion of a nonrandom sample of Yemenis. A knowledgeable Yemeni candidly told the junior author that Yemenis are very proud of their heritage; when asked by strangers about their intentions to return to Yemen, most of them will answer in the affirmative. Thus, sojourning intentions may not be the definitive indicators of return to the country of origin. These should be checked against objective measures of settlement in the country of immigration. Furthermore, the validity of the findings of these earlier studies needs to be tested with data for Yemenis from all classes and locations in the United States. At present, the only sources of these data are the 1980 U.S. Census and the Immigration and Naturalization Service (INS).

Table 1. Distribution of Persons Born in North and South Yemen by State of Residence in 1980 and Year of Immigration, United States, 1980

State	Percent Distribution North Yemen (San^ca) Year of Immigration					Percent Distribution South Yemen (PDRY — Aden) Year of Immigration				
	1975–80	1970–74	1965–69	Pre-1965	Total	1975–80	1970–74	1965–69	Pre-1965	Total
Michigan	39.9	51.6	31.9	9.3	39.7	19.4	56.0	22.3	16.7	32.1
New York	21.2	13.9	42.0	58.0	25.6	48.8	14.5	6.4	11.9	25.2
California	11.3	25.5	14.6	14.3	17.5	12.4	2.4	0	7.1	6.3
New Jersey	3.3	1.4	1.5	1.7	2.1	0	4.8	6.4	7.1	3.7
Ohio	.5	1.5	0	14.0	2.4	0	0	0	20.2	2.8
Illinois	.4	0	1.2	1.3	.5	2.8	6.3	28.7	0	7.6
Other states	23.4	6.1	8.8	1.4	12.2	16.6	16.0	36.2	37.0	22.3
N	905	957	329	300	2,491	217	207	94	84	602

Source: U.S. Census of Population, 1980 (1985).

The primary aim of this chapter is to use census and INS data to test the hypothesis that Yemenis, unlike many other immigrant groups in the United States, have experienced little or no settlement. A secondary objective is to describe, for the first time, immigration trends from Yemen to the United States and to present the salient demographic and socioeconomic characteristics of this immigrant group.

The most serious problem with the census is undercount, especially of farmworkers and transient workers employed in the auto and steel industries. The farm laborers live in group quarters and are counted separately by the Census Bureau. Unfortunately, data on ethnicity of the population living in group quarters are only available for major groups such as Hispanics. Yet, despite its shortcomings, the census is the most comprehensive nationwide and systematic source of information on the demographic and socioeconomic characteristics of Yemenis. Census and immigration data used in this analysis are for persons born in both North Yemen (Yemen Arab Republic) and South Yemen (People's Democratic Republic of Yemen). The comparison between the two Yemens provides a further measure of control because it has been claimed that, unlike persons from North Yemen, South Yemenis come to the United States to settle permanently (Abraham 1983).

Before presenting the results of our analysis of immigration and census data, we give a brief discussion of the process of immigrant settlement and its measurement as discussed by a number of social scientists.

THE PROCESS OF IMMIGRANT SETTLEMENT AND ITS MEASUREMENT

Bohning (1972) and Piore (1979) have formulated, but not tested, the hypothesis that labor migration matures over time as immigrants gain more experience in the host society, and eventually results in their settlement. According to Piore (1979:59–60), the settlement process involves the transition of temporary migrants into permanent residents, including their native-born children. Similarly, Birks and Sinclair (1981:449) have asserted that "while migration for employment is always seen as a temporary phenomenon by both the receiving country and by the individual migrant, a metamorphosis into permanence generally occurs sooner or later."

The maturation of temporary migrants into a settled population involves demographic, economic, and social transformation of the immigrant streams. Bohning — as well as Birks and Sinclair — argues that demographic changes pertain to the age, sex, and marital structure of the immigrant population. In the early stages of labor migration, the young and single males predominate. Later, married men join the migration stream. Feeling torn from immediate family members, these men bring over their wives and children, followed by brothers and sisters. Since married people in general are older, this partially accounts for the aging of the migrant stream. The original sex imbalance is somewhat corrected with the occurrence of family reunification. In the long run, the unit of migration changes from single individuals to families involving chain migration and a self-feeding process, independent of the demand for labor. Demographic settlement and maturation are accompanied by the development of immigrant institutions to satisfy special demands of the members of the ethnic group. At this stage, there is also a movement of immigrant workers from specific occupations to many sectors of the economy.

Bohning's and Piore's hypothesis was confirmed by Massey (1985, 1986) on the basis of data collected in a survey of Mexican migrants to the United States: the best predictor of settlement seems to be the "cumulative amount of U.S. migrant experience." Other important variables are sex ratio, family and friendship ties, friendship ties with members of the host society, shift from agriculture to industrial and service jobs, permanent resident status, English language ability, use of U.S. social services (e.g., unemployment compensation and medical facilities), and payment of taxes. All of these factors point to increasing social and economic integration of immigrants in American society. Massey's definition of a settler is "a migrant who has lived for three *continuous* years in the United States"; a sojourner is one who has not (1986:681, emphasis in original). According to a classic sociological definition, a sojourner is "one who clings to the cultural heritage of his own ethnic group and tends to live in isolation, hindering his assimilation to the society in which he resides, often for many years. The sojourn is conceived by the sojourner as a 'job' which is to be finished in the shortest possible time. As an alternative to that end he travels back to his homeland every few years" (Siu 1952:34). While such a definition is subjective and very difficult to operationalize, it suggests the need to go beyond length of residence. Jasso and Rosenzweig (forthcoming) have proposed that "of all an immigrant's behaviors worthy of examination, two are of special importance. These two—naturalization and emigration— are conceptually polar opposites, signifying, for the one, the end of alienage and entrance into the fullest participation in American life possible to a foreign-born person and, for the other, abandonment of residence in the United States." The sojourner is, of course, much more likely to return to his or her country of origin than the naturalized immigrant. Consequently, in the present analysis, we define a settler as a foreign-born person who has been naturalized and a sojourner as one who has not. It has been argued that some immigrants become naturalized in order to have the rights of U.S. citizenship rather than to settle in the United States. On the other hand, with a few exceptions (e.g., holding a U.S. passport), the desire to acquire these rights implies an inclination to settle. This applies particularly to the Yemenis who became citizens in order to bring their families over.

Because of prevailing views that they are sojourners, Yemenis offer a theoretically interesting case to test the hypothesis advanced by Bohning, Piore, and Massey. Unlike the Mexicans studied by Massey, many Yemenis enter the United States as legal immigrants. Therefore, the contention that Yemenis are sojourners becomes even more tenuous, given the fact that many Yemenis have the legal option to settle here. Another distinction between the Yemenis and Mexicans is the long distance and high cost of travel between the United States and Yemen, reducing the frequency of back and forth trips. In this sense, for the Yemenis length of residence in the United States is a better indicator of settlement than number of trips to the United States.

The analysis of INS and census data is divided into two sections, reflecting the nature of these data. First, we consider general trends in the number of Yemenis admitted as immigrants and naturalized for the period 1971–84, the only years for which INS data on Yemeni immigrants admitted and naturalized have been published. Second, we test the hypothesis of settlement by utilizing demographic and socioeconomic data on Yemenis from the 1980 U.S. Census. Data on the characteristics of Yemenis at the time of immigration are available from INS, but they have been published only since 1978. This information is used to supplement the analysis of census data.

YEMENI IMMIGRATION TO THE UNITED STATES, 1971–84

Immigration from Yemen to the United States is a trickle compared to the flood of emigration from that country.[1] According to Steffen and Blanc (1982:98–99), there were an estimated 250,000 "long-term emigrants" from North Yemen in 1975, of whom 20,000 were presumed to be in the United States, and 385,000 "short-term emigrants." During 1971–84, a total of 6,297 and 1,922 Yemeni immigrants were admitted to the United States from North and South Yemen, respectively (table 2).

More North Yemenis than South Yemenis came to the United States in every year during this period except 1980 and 1981. Although INS published data on Yemenis are only available for 1971–84, they appear to cover a large segment of the Yemeni immigration to the United States. According to the 1980 census, over 70 percent of the Yemenis from both North and South Yemen immigrated between 1970 and 1980.

The most drastic change in immigration from North Yemen occurred in 1974. From 1971 to 1973, the number of immigrants more than doubled; but this number was halved in 1974 to almost its original 1971 level. The number of immigrants further declined by more than 50 percent in 1975 (table 2). Since 1974 was the year when the price of oil rose fourfold in the world market, the oil-rich Gulf states

Table 2. Yemeni (Aden and San^{c}a) Immigrants Admitted and Persons Naturalized, United States, 1971–84

Year[a]	Immigrants Admitted		Persons Naturalized	
	North Yemen (San^{c}a)	South Yemen (Aden)	North Yemen (San^{c}a)	South Yemen (Aden)
1971	564	38	NA[b]	NA
1972	920	94	NA	NA
1973	1,219	139	157	2
1974	561	113	140	29
1975	227	97	197	83
1976	549	48	89	150
TQ1976[c]	133	12	52	49
1977	376	48	195	130
1978	258	126	308	115
1979	203	174	453	197
1980	160	261	358	128
1981	230	347	286	207
1982	305	179	181	230
1983	268	239	221	145
1984	324	7	79	156
Total	6,297	1,922	2,716	1,621

Source: Immigration and Naturalization Service (1980, 1982, 1984).
[a] The definition of fiscal year changed after 1977 from year ended June 30 to year ended September 30.
[b] Not available.
[c] Transition quarter July–September.

became a more attractive destination for Yemenis than the United States. Furthermore, in late 1975, the government of the Yemen Arab Republic instituted strict controls on labor emigration and issued passports only to students, businessmen, and pilgrims in order to stem the tide of migration to Saudi Arabia (Steffen 1979). Although immigration from North Yemen to the United States rose once again in 1976 to about 550, it seems to have stabilized around 300 in more recent years. A knowledgeable Yemeni interviewed by the junior author in the Central Valley of California attributed the recent decline in Yemeni immigration to the United States to the difficulty of obtaining an American visa.

While immigration from North Yemen declined after 1973, one of the earliest Yemeni immigrants told the junior author that most of the Yemenis came to the San Joaquin Valley after 1973. This is not incompatible with immigration trends from North Yemen, because many of these Yemenis could have come to California's agricultural valley via Detroit and not directly from Yemen. Detroit's auto industry experienced a major recession in the aftermath of the oil price hikes, thus reducing the availability of jobs in this industry. It is an irony of the world economy that the oil embargo should create more opportunities for Yemenis in the oil-exporting countries of the Arabian

Peninsula while costing other Yemenis their jobs in Detroit.

Immigration from South Yemen almost follows North Yemen's pattern, but the shift in trend is less marked due to its small numbers. In contrast to reports of the early studies that Yemenis from the south immigrated earlier than Yemenis from the north, table 2 shows that nearly 70 percent of the former immigrated in 1978 and after, whereas only 28 percent of the latter arrived in the same period. Therefore, immigration levels are reversed for these two immigrant groups in the two periods 1971–78 and 1978–84. Inexplicably, only seven immigrants were admitted from South Yemen in 1984.

Table 2 also presents data on the Yemenis who became naturalized American citizens during 1973–84. The totals of 2,716 naturalizations for North Yemenis and 1,621 for South Yemenis are substantial compared to the total numbers of Yemeni immigrants admitted. Since immigrants are generally eligible for American citizenship after five years (or three years if they are married to a U.S. citizen), and since many immigrants may wait longer to be naturalized, only approximate rates of naturalization can be calculated from the data given in table 2. Data on rate of naturalizations from the 1980 census are more reliable and easier to derive.

CHARACTERISTICS OF YEMENI IMMIGRANT COHORTS IN 1980

While immigration data present a picture for all Yemenis who were admitted legally to the United States during 1971–84, the 1980 census pertains only to a residual group of Yemenis who stayed in the United States until 1980. Thus, sojourners who went back home could not be included in the census. Also, as was suggested earlier, a number of Yemenis were either living in group quarters at the time of the census or were not enumerated. The 1970–80 immigration cohort of 2,286 Yemenis enumerated in 1980 is much smaller than the INS count of 6,320 Yemeni immigrants for the period July 1, 1970–September 30, 1980. The difference between the two numbers reflects not only the return of many immigrants to Yemen, or the deaths of Yemenis by 1980, but also the undercount of Yemenis in the 1980 census. Unfortunately, it is impossible to disaggregate these two effects. Even the INS alien registration figure of 1,135 for 1980 cannot help to resolve this matter, because it is also subject to severe underregistration. Nevertheless, the main advantage of the census is that it provides information on the pre-1980 period. By analyzing the changes in demographic and socioeconomic structure for the five immigration cohorts of 1975–80, 1970–74, 1965–69, 1960–64, and pre-1960, we may be able to establish the timing and extent of the settlement of Yemenis. As suggested by Massey,[2] assuming that the 1980 census question on year of immigration was answered in terms of year of last rather than first entry, and that Yemeni migration to the United States is circular, then recent immigration cohorts would include more sojourners than the earlier ones. In other words, settlers would report an earlier year of entry and sojourners a later year. But, in view of the cost of travel between Yemen and the United States, it is not likely that many Yemenis engaged in extensive circular mobility. Consequently, any increase in the proportion of sojourners between the earlier and the later Yemeni immigration cohorts could not be attributed to a response effect.

Massey's work provides a basis for selecting indicators of settlement. Among the variables that he uses in his research (Massey 1985, 1986), the following are available from INS data and the 1980 U.S. Census and are applicable to the Yemeni experience: immigration trends (especially number of immigrants admitted), immigration of immediate relatives of U.S. citizens and permanent residents, rates of naturalization, age and sex distributions, English language pro-

ficiency, occupational shift from seasonal work such as agriculture to more stable jobs, hours worked per week, and income. One variable that Massey does not include in his analysis is student status. Among Yemenis and other Middle Easterners who come to the United States for higher education, college students constitute a special group of "sojourners" (Sabagh and Bozorgmehr 1987). In Massey's analysis, the indicators of settlement show a steady progression with increasing years of experience in the United States. We expect a similar trend between the 1980 census measures of settlement and length of residence of Yemenis in the United States.

Published INS data on the characteristics of Yemeni immigrants are only available since 1978 for some variables and since 1980 for others. Nevertheless, they provide information not available in the 1980 census, particularly trends in family reunification. Consequently, they are used to derive additional indicators of settlement.

Rates of Naturalization of Immigration Cohorts

As mentioned earlier, Jasso and Rosenzweig (forthcoming) assert that the acquisition of U.S. citizenship by immigrants is one of the best indicators of settlement and integration in the receiving society. In his descriptions of the settled Mexican workers in the United States, Massey (1986:671) indicates that "most of them have obtained legal residence documents." Naturalization is a step beyond legalization of residence and applies only to those persons who have been admitted to the United States or reclassified as immigrants for three or five years or more.

It is very clear from the data in table 3 that Yemenis who were in the United States prior to 1970 availed themselves of their rights to acquire U.S. citizenship. With the exception of North Yemeni women who arrived before 1965, the rates of naturalization are all in excess of 80 percent and sometimes reach the 100 percent mark for those who came before 1970. But, even for North Yemeni women who immigrated before 1965, the rate of naturalization is 78 percent. The rates are somewhat higher for North than South Yemenis. If similar data were available for all Yemenis in 1970, it is likely that they would have had a much lower level of naturalization at the time. This is suggested by the fact that, for all Yemenis, about 41 percent of the 1970–74 cohort and only 8 percent of the 1975–80 cohort had been naturalized by 1980. Consequently, the 1980 census data do not contradict the findings of Aswad, Abraham, and Dweik about

Table 3. Percent Naturalized, Persons Born in North and South Yemen, by Sex and Year of Immigration, United States, 1980

Country of Birth	Percent Males Naturalized Year of Immigration					Percent Females Naturalized Year of Immigration				
	1975–80	1970–74	1965–69	Pre-1965	Total	1975–80	1970–74	1965–69	Pre-1965	Total
North Yemen (San^{c}a)										
All ages	9.3	45.1	95.9	91.0	45.9	7.4	30.3	84.1	77.9	31.3
N	622	782	266	223	1,893	283	175	63	77	598
South Yemen (PDRY – Aden)										
All ages	0	45.2	84.0	100.0	37.2	10.0	9.4	100.0	91.2	43.9
N	137	135	50	27	349	80	72	44	57	253

Source: U.S. Census of Population, 1980 (1985).

the predominance of sojourners among Yemenis in the early 1970s. It may be noted, however, that in 1972–74, the earliest years for which INS data are available for our population, there were already 608 naturalized Yemenis. Census data also imply that, with the passage of time, Yemeni sojourners who remained in this country became settlers. In this sense, Yemenis behave very much like other sojourners. Thus, the rate of naturalization of 45.9 percent for North Yemeni males is close to the comparable rate of 52.2 percent for all foreign-born males in 1980 (Jasso and Rosenzweig forthcoming).

INS data for 1978–84 suggest that recently admitted Yemeni immigrants are very likely to settle in the United States. A total of 1,748 North Yemenis were admitted in 1978–84, most of whom were new arrivals and 51.9 percent of whom were exempt from numerical limitation. Almost all of those exempted from these limitations were spouses and children of U.S. citizens (table 4). If we include both exempt and nonexempt categories, a total of 97.7 percent of North Yemenis immigrated as relatives of U.S. citizens (71.5 percent) or relatives of permanent residents of the U.S. (26.2 percent). A similar pattern occurs for South Yemenis. Of the total of 1,333 South Yemeni immigrants admitted in 1978–84, 51.7 percent were numerically exempt and a total of 95.9 percent were either relatives of U.S. citizens (69.7 percent) or relatives of permanent residents (26.2 percent). Thus, based on these data, it is very clear that Yemeni immigration is almost exclusively based on family reunification. The immigration of immediate family members is a major step toward permanent settlement in the United States.

Data on Yemeni nonimmigrants are available only since 1980. There were almost three times as many nonimmigrant Yemenis admitted in 1980–84 as immigrants (6,303 compared to 2,320). Among these, over half were temporary visitors for pleasure, about 10 percent were temporary visitors for business, and roughly the same percentage were students. Given the high cost of travel between Yemen and the United States, it is unlikely that Yemenis are only vacationing; rather, they are visiting relatives and/or close friends. These data suggest that the pattern of travel is not unidirectional from the United States to Yemen, but works in both directions. In other words, not only are Yemenis in the United States making trips back and forth to Yemen, but their friends and relatives are also visiting them in the United States.

In the latest period, 1975–80, however, a new type of Yemeni "sojourner" was coming to the United States. College students constituted 27 percent of the North Yemeni males and 31 percent of South Yemeni males aged twenty and over who arrived in 1975–80. This is a trend that appears to be continuing, since students accounted for about 10 percent of Yemeni nonimmigrants admitted in 1982–84. It is possible, of course, that students who remain for a long time may ultimately settle in this country.

It may be recalled that, for the years 1971–80, the number of Yemenis reported by the U.S. Census was smaller than the number of persons recorded as Yemeni by the INS. Thus, it is likely that many Yemenis who were sojourners returned to Yemen or were not enumerated in the 1980 census. But the data on naturalizations indicate that those who stayed were in process of becoming settled. In one sense, the seemingly contradictory statements that "Yemenis are sojourners" and "Yemenis are settlers" may both be correct but might refer to different phases of the settlement process. According to Massey (1986), the

Table 4. Percent New Arrivals, Percent Relatives of U.S. Citizens, and Percent Relatives of Permanent Residents, Immigrants from North and South Yemen, United States, 1978–84

| Year and Country | Immigrants Admitted[a] | Percent New Arrivals[b] | Percent of Immigrants | | | All Relatives |
			Immediate Relatives of U.S. Citizens[c]	Other Relatives of U.S. Citizens[d]	Relatives of Resident Aliens[e]	
North Yemen (San^c a)						
1978	258	NA[f]	25.2	25.2	48.4	98.8
1979	203	NA	39.4	42.4	18.2	100.0
1980	160	89.4	41.3	25.0	25.6	91.9
1981	230	89.6	47.8	21.3	28.7	97.8
1982	305	86.2	67.5	12.5	17.4	97.4
1983	268	92.9	60.4	10.8	26.9	98.1
1984	324	88.9	67.3	11.1	19.7	98.1
1978–84	1,748	—	51.9	19.6	26.2	97.7
South Yemen (PDRY — Aden)						
1978	126	NA	NA	NA	NA	NA
1979	174	NA	NA	NA	NA	NA
1980	261	85.4	47.9	20.7	25.3	93.9
1981	347	89.9	44.4	20.2	33.7	98.3
1982	179	79.9	61.4	12.3	22.3	96.0
1983	239	82.4	61.1	16.7	20.1	97.9
1984	7	g	g	g	g	g
1980–84	1,333[h]	—	51.7	18.0	26.2	95.9

Source: Immigration and Naturalization Service (1980, 1982, 1984).

[a] All immigrants, including adjustments of status.

[b] Percent of all immigrants who were new arrivals.

[c] Percent of all immigrants not subject to numerical limitations, includes mainly spouses and children of U.S. citizens.

[d] Percent of all immigrants subject to numerical limitations, other relatives of U.S. citizens.

[e] Percent of all immigrants subject to numerical limitations, relatives of permanent residents (spouses, unmarried children of resident aliens, and their children).

[f] Not available.

[g] Base too small for calculation of percentages.

[h] For 1978–84.

three phases of integration process are sojourner, transition, and settlement. Conducted earlier, the studies on Yemenis may have captured the Yemeni experience in its inception, the sojourner or transition phase, whereas the more recent census and INS data reflect the settlement phase. But these data also reflect the presence of the college student as a new type of "sojourner" among the Yemenis. However, before we reach any definitive conclusion about the hypothesis of settlement, we should consider the trends in sex ratios, age distribution, English speaking ability, education, labor force status, occupation, and earnings.

Sex Ratios and Age Structure of Immigration Cohorts

As a migration stream matures and labor migrants become settled, they tend to bring over their wives, children, and older relatives (Bohning 1972;

Birks and Sinclair 1981; Massey 1986). Consequently, we would expect, over time, the ratio of males to females (sex ratio) to decrease and the age distribution to become more balanced by including more children and older persons.

Using age in 1980 as a starting point, age at migration was derived for the 1975–80, 1970–74, and 1960–69 periods. The distribution of age at migration and the corresponding sex ratios by age groups are given in table 5. The sex ratio of 220 for the most recent cohort (1975–80) from North Yemen is substantially lower than the sex ratios of 447 and 336 for the previous cohorts. This trend is even more marked for the most migratory ages, fifteen to twenty-nine. As indicated above, the cohort of 1975–80 includes a high percent of students (mostly college) among South Yemenis. If we exclude students, the sex ratio of Yemenis aged sixteen and over in 1980 decreases noticeably from 480 in 1970–74 to 165 in 1975–80.

Table 5. Persons Born in North and South Yemen by Sex, Age at Migration, and Year of Immigration, United States, 1980

Age at Migration	Percent Distribution Year of Immigration				Males per 100 Females Year of Immigration			
	1975–80	1970–74	1960–69	Pre-1960	1975–80	1970–74	1960–69	Pre-1960
North Yemen (San^c a)								
0–14	18.9	4.5	9.2	a	205	139	660	a
15–29	53.2	53.7	58.6	a	241	534	386	a
30–44	23.1	34.0	30.6	a	254	564	218	a
45 +	4.9	7.8	1.7	a	63	178	b	a
Total	100.1	100.0	100.1	-	220	447	336	376
N	905	957	415	214	283^c	175^c	95^c	45^c
South Yemen (PDRY — Aden)								
0–14	13.4	28.5	18.6	a	0	59	243	a
15–29	55.8	49.3	56.6	a	290	437	38	a
30–44	18.9	19.8	20.2	a	105	273	333	a
45 +	12.0	2.4	4.6	a	b	0	b	a
Total	100.1	100.0	100.0	-	171	188	95	40
N	217	207	129	49	80^c	72^c	66^c	35^c

Source: U.S. Census of Population, 1980 (1985).

[a] In view of the wide time interval, age at migration could not be calculated.

[b] Rate is infinite; there are no women in age group.

[c] Number of females.

The latter figure is close to the sex ratio of 177 for North Yemenis who immigrated in 1980–84. Unfortunately, the distribution of North or South Yemeni immigrants by males and females was not published prior to 1982. For the much smaller South Yemeni stream, the sex ratio increased from 95 to 188 and then decreased to 171 for the three cohorts of 1960–69, 1970–74, and 1975–80, respectively. This figure is also close to the sex ratio of 181 for South Yemenis who immigrated in 1982–84. The pattern is accentuated in the age group fifteen to twenty-nine, and a very low sex ratio of 38 is observed for the 1960–69 cohort. Since the sex ratios for South Yemenis are based on small numbers, it would be hazardous to develop any elaborate interpretation of the differences in the trends in sex ratios between the two Yemens. The very low sex ratio for 1960–69 could reflect the greater return migration of males and lower census coverage of South Yemeni males who arrived in this period.

For North Yemenis, recent immigration cohorts have a more balanced age distribution than earlier ones. Thus, children under fifteen years of age constituted 18.9 percent of the 1975–80 cohort as compared to 4.5 and 9.2 percent for the 1970–74 and 1960–69 cohorts. The percentage aged forty-five and over increased from 1.7 in 1960–69 to around 6–7 in the 1970s. For the most migratory age cohort of fifteen to twenty-nine years, there is only a slight decrease from 58.6 percent from the earliest cohort to 53.2 percent for the latest one. But 1975–80 immigrants in this age group have the highest percentage of Yemeni students of all other comparable cohorts (table 8). If we had data on the age distribution of nonstudents,[3] it is likely that the 1975–80 cohort would have a lesser proportion in ages fifteen to twenty-nine than shown in table 5. The age distribution patterns for South Yemenis are much more irregular, partly because the percent of students in the 1975–80 cohort is much higher than for North Yemenis (the percentages of males and females aged sixteen and over who are students are, respectively, 49.3 and 46.2 for South Yemen and 32.9 and 10.3 for North Yemen). If this factor could be taken into account, there is no doubt that the 1975–80 cohort of immigrants from South Yemen would have had a more balanced age distribution.

INS data on the age distribution of North and South Yemenis who immigrated in 1980–84 indicate an even greater importance of children in the recent Yemeni migration stream (data not given in a table). For 1981, 23 percent of North Yemeni and 26 percent

Table 6. Percent of Persons Age 5 + Knowing English Well or Very Well, Born in North and South Yemen, by Sex and Year of Immigration, United States, 1980

Country of Birth	Percent Males Speaking English Well or Very Well Year of Immigration					Percent Females Speaking English Well or Very Well Year of Immigration				
	1975–80	1970–74	1965–69	Pre-1965	Total	1975–80	1970–74	1965–69	Pre-1965	Total
North Yemen (San^{c}a)										
Age 5 +	56.0	70.7	86.8	86.6	70.2	38.5	52.6	60.3	55.4	47.2
N	555	732	251	202	1,740	265	175	63	65	568
South Yemen (PDRY — Aden)										
Age 5 +	78.2	80.0	81.8	100.0	81.0	66.2	83.1	100.0	100.0	83.0
N	101	130	44	20	295	80	65	44	35	224

Source: U.S. Census of Population, 1980 (1985).

of South Yemeni immigrants were children under fifteen years of age, figures that are somewhat higher than those derived from census data for the 1975–80 cohort. For the whole 1980–82 period, comparable data are only available for the age group under twenty. This population constituted 47.7 percent of North Yemeni and 45.8 percent of South Yemeni immigrants in this period. The same data show that the largest proportions of males are in the age groups under twenty and twenty to twenty-nine years, respectively. Thus, the bulk of male immigrants are under twenty-nine years. However, for women the proportions are evenly distributed among the above two age groups and thirty to thirty-nine years. Therefore, more older women than men are immigrating. Combining this information with the knowledge that relatives are immigrating, it becomes clear that many of these are wives of Yemenis already in the United States. At the same time, more younger men than women and male children than female children are coming to the United States.

In general, the data given in table 5, as well as INS published data not given in a table, support the conclusion that, with the passage of time, Yemenis have brought their wives and children over or gotten married and raised a family in the United States.

It should be noted that age, as derived in table 5, and sex are the only 1980 census characteristics that can be determined at the time of immigration. All other variables, including ability to speak English, education, labor force status, occupation, and income, are measured in 1980. They reflect the cumulated experience of the immigration cohorts.

Ability to Speak English and Educational Achievement of Immigration Cohorts

Good knowledge of English and higher education should increase the human capital of immigrants and facilitate the process of moving from being sojourners to being settlers. If we rely solely on the studies of Yemenis in Buffalo, Detroit, and the San Joaquin Valley of California, we would have to be doubtful about Yemenis' prospects for settlement. These studies claim that first-generation Yemenis in these three areas have little or no education and no knowledge of the English language. The 1980 census, however, gives us, on the whole, quite a different picture of the Yemenis' knowledge of English and education.

In view of the fact that South Yemen was occupied by the British from 1839 until 1968, it is not surprising that 81.0 percent of South Yemeni males as compared to 70.2 of North Yemeni men and 83.0 percent of South Yemeni women as compared to 47.2 percent of North Yemeni women stated that they know English well or very well (table 6). There is a definite increasing trend in the knowledge of English with time spent in this country, so that at least 80 percent of North and South Yemeni men and South Yemeni women who came before 1970 stated that they know English well or very well. This pattern undoubtedly facilitated their acquisition of U.S. citizenship and adaptation to American society.

It is clear from table 7 that Yemenis have much higher educational achievement than reported in the early studies of farm and industrial workers. About 78 percent of South Yemeni and 66 percent of North

Table 7. Percent of Persons Age 20 + by Years of School Completed, Born in North and South Yemen, by Sex and Year of Immigration, United States, 1980

Country of Birth	Percent Males by Years of School Completed Year of Immigration					Percent Females by Years of School Completed Year of Immigration				
	1975–80	1970–74	1965–69	Pre-1965	Total	1975–80	1970–74	1965–69	Pre-1965	Total
North Yemen (San°a)										
Years of School Completed										
Under 9	21.5	41.5	40.6	24.7	33.8	61.2	53.5	65.5	50.6	57.7
9–12	48.5	40.8	48.8	58.7	46.4	21.0	35.0	22.4	42.9	28.9
13 +	30.0	17.7	10.6	16.6	19.8	17.8	11.5	12.1	6.5	13.4
N	447	757	254	223	1,681	214	157	58	77	506
South Yemen (PDRY—Aden)										
Years of School Completed										
Under 9	18.5	17.7	24.2	51.9	21.9	27.4	45.7	35.1	40.4	36.7
9–12	31.9	55.8	18.2	25.9	39.0	37.3	14.3	0	38.6	25.5
13 +	49.6	26.5	57.6	22.2	39.0	35.3	40.0	64.9	21.0	37.8
N	119	113	33	27	292	51	35	37	57	180

Source: U.S. Census of Population, 1980 (1985).

Yemeni males have at least an elementary school education. In fact, while these percentages are lower for women (63 and 42 percent for South and North Yemen, respectively) they are still higher than expected. The trends in educational achievement are generally opposite to what would be predicted by the settlement hypothesis. On the whole, educational levels are higher for the later than the earlier cohorts. Thus, for North Yemeni males, the percentage with at least one year of college increased from 16.6 in the earliest cohort to 30.0 in 1975–80. But as indicated above, the fairly large percentage of students in this latest group, who were mostly in college, would tend to inflate the educational achievement of this cohort. If we had data for nonstudents, they might well show an increase in educational achievement with increasing length of stay in the United States. However, in view of the rapid development of educational facilities in both North and South Yemen, one would expect a higher level of education for the later than the earlier cohorts. The total number of students enrolled in all schools and universities in North Yemen increased from 194,412 in 1973–74 to 454,474 in 1980–81 at an annual rate far exceeding that of population growth (United Nations 1985). Indeed, what the data in table 7 may show is the combined effects of two opposite trends.

Both naturalization and knowledge of English data suggest a marked increase in the Yemenis' propensity to settle with increasing length of stay in this country. The findings on educational achievement are somewhat less clear, but they do not contradict this conclusion.

Labor Force Status, Occupations, and Earnings of Immigration Cohorts

Increased participation in the labor force, more stable and higher-level occupations, and higher earnings are all factors that would increase the propensity for settlement (Massey 1986). Since Yemeni women have a much lower rate of labor force participation than men (table 8), this argument is more applicable to male migrants. Consequently, the economic data given in table 9 are for men only. It should be noted that trends in labor force participation are confounded by the larger proportion of students in the later cohorts and the higher percent of retired persons in the earliest cohorts. Also, the categories of "labor force" and "school" in table 8 are not mutually exclusive. Nevertheless, there appears to be some increase in labor force participation with increasing length of residence (table 8). There is also an increase in the steadiness of work for North Yemeni men over time.

Table 8. Percent of Persons Age 16 + in School or in the Labor Force, Born in North and South Yemen, by Year of Immigration, United States, 1980

Country of Birth	Percent Males Age 16 + in School or Labor Force[a] Year of Immigration					Percent Females Age 16 + in School or Labor Force[a] Year of Immigration				
	1975–80	1970–74	1965–69	Pre–1965	Total	1975–80	1970–74	1965–69	Pre–1965	Total
North Yemen (San^c a)										
Persons Age 16 + in School	32.9	10.4	9.4	2.2	15.6	10.3	10.6	7.9	0	8.4
Labor Force	62.2	87.9	86.5	94.6	81.2	25.1	11.2	11.1	26.7	19.5
N	516	781	297	223	1,817	223	161	63	90	537
South Yemen (PDRY — Aden)										
Persons Age 16 + in School	49.3	10.3	8.2[b]	—	25.8	46.2	31.6	12.9[b]		27.1
Labor Force	61.6	97.6	64.4[b]	—	75.7	36.5	31.6	49.5[b]		41.4
N	138	126	73	—	337	52	57	101	—	210

Source: U.S. Census of Population, 1980 (1985).

[a] The percentages may add up to more than 100 since some students are also in the labor force.

[b] Before 1970.

The percent of men who worked full-time all year round increased from 40.5 in 1975–80 to 65.3 in the pre-1965 years (table 9). Surprisingly, throughout this period, South Yemenis had a much lower level of steady work (in the 21.7 to 28.2 percent range) than North Yemeni men.

As might be expected, the 1980 census data on the occupational distribution of Yemenis contradict the earlier studies of farm and industrial workers. As many as 21.6 percent of North Yemeni men and 51.7 percent of South Yemeni men reported white-collar occupations in 1980 (table 9). But, even if we consider the data for Yemenis who arrived before 1970 (i.e., the groups included in the existing studies), a very similar pattern is observed. Indeed, 27.3 percent of North Yemenis and 57.6 percent of South Yemenis who arrived before 1970 had white-collar occupations in 1980 (table 9). It might be argued that this trend reflects both selective return migration to Yemen and upward occupational mobility of Yemenis who remained in the United States. But, contrary to expectations, the longer the Yemenis have been in the United States, the lower their occupational achievement. The percentage in occupational category IV (operators, fabricators, and laborers) increased steadily from 32.2 for the 1975–80 cohort to 50.9 for

North Yemeni men who came before 1970. For South Yemeni men, the trend is even more accentuated from 15.2 to 42.4 percent between the two cohorts.

At the same time, and paradoxically, there is some increase in the percentage of Yemeni men in the top white-collar occupational level I (executives, administrators, managers, and professionals) with increasing residence in the United States, though this trend is not consistent. These trends are, of course, consistent with the data on education given in table 7. Since naturalization rates are higher for the earlier immigration cohorts, these findings suggest that an increasing propensity for settlement does not necessarily imply higher educational or occupational achievement. It may also be noted that the self-employment rate among North Yemenis was highest for men who arrived before 1965 (16.7 percent). It declined to 2.6 for the 1970–74 cohort but increased again to 9.3 percent for the 1975–80 cohort. No self-employment was reported by the South Yemenis. It may well be that for Yemenis the extent of self-employment is a better indicator of settlement than either educational or occupational levels.

In contrast to occupational achievement, income as reported for 1979 increased with length of residence, particularly for men who worked full-time all

Table 9. Percent of Males Age 16 + by Occupational Levels, Self-Employment, and Median Income, Born in North and South Yemen, by Year of Immigration, United States, 1980

Country of Birth	Year of Immigration				
	1975–80	1970–74	1965–69	Pre–1965	Total
North Yemen (San[c]a)					
Percent of Men Age 16 + in Occupational Levels					
I	7.2	4.2	16.3	9.9	7.9
II	20.3	9.7	15.7	13.1	13.7
III	33.9	35.5	20.8	22.5	30.3
IV	32.2	41.8	47.1	54.5	42.8
Farming	6.4	8.8	0	0	5.3
Percent of Men Age 16 + Self-employed	9.3	2.6	8.4	16.7	7.6
N	236	454	178	191	1,059
Median Income of Men Age 15 +					
All	$ 8,535	$10,450	$11,473	$17,961	$10,734
Year-round full-time workers	$11,775	$12,199	$15,625[a]	—	$13,025
Percent working year-round full-time	40.5	34.2	47.9	65.3	42.1
N	363	755	257	219	1,594
South Yemen (PDRY — Aden)					
Percent of Men Age 16 + in Occupational Levels					
I	25.8	50.7	39.4[a]	—	38.8
II	12.1	11.3	18.2[a]	—	12.9
III	47.0	19.7	0[a]	—	26.5
IV	15.2	18.3	42.4[a]	—	21.8
Farming	0	0	0[a]	—	—
Percent of Men Age 16 + Self-employed	0	0	0	—	0
N	66	71	33[a]	—	170
Median Income of Men ages 15 +					
All	$ 8,698	$10,069	$11,072[a]	—	$ 9,500
Year-round full-time workers	$17,500	$12,143	$25,715	—	$14,911
Percent working year-round full-time	28.2	26.0	21.7[a]	—	25.7
N	85	123	60	—	268

Source: U.S. Census of Population, 1980 (1985).
Occupational Levels
  I: Executive, Administrative, and Managerial; Professional Specialty
 II: Technical, Sales, Administrative Support (including Clerical)
III: Total Service; Precision, Production, Craft, and Repair
IV: Total Operators, Fabricators, and Laborers
[a] Pre-1970.

year round. However, occupational achievement is for all males in the labor force, including the unemployed and those working part-time. For North Yemeni full-time working men, the median income rose from $11,775 for the most recent cohort to $15,625 for the pre-1970 cohort (table 9). The comparable figures for South Yemenis are $17,500 and $25,715. The latter figure, however, is based on a small number of cases.

CONCLUSION

This chapter has presented data on the demographic, social, and economic characteristics of

Yemeni immigrant cohorts in the United States. This quantitative profile of all Yemenis in the United States is a supplement to the few existing studies of Yemenis in Detroit, Buffalo, and the San Joaquin Valley in California. But the major objective of this chapter is to use these data to test the hypotheses or propositions advanced by some social scientists about the transition process from temporary migrants or sojourners to permanent migrants or settlers. The Yemenis are an interesting case for such a test because of the prevailing view that they are sojourners. They are consistently reported as sojourners and "circular" or "recurrent" migrants in the literature on the basis of such evidence as intentions to repatriate, retention of family land in Yemen, and trips back and forth. But as suggested by Piore (1979) and Massey (1985, 1986), the process of settlement involves an accumulation over time of economic, social, and other experiences in the receiving country by migrants who originally came as sojourners. Only a study in Buffalo describes what appears to be a settled Yemeni community (Dweik 1980). Abraham (1983), however, partially acknowledges that some Yemenis have settled in Detroit and states that they tend to be urban-based Adenis, men married to American women, and successful merchants. The last category implies that only the successful migrants tend to settle, a conclusion questioned by Piore (1979). In a recent study of Yemeni women in Dearborn, Michigan, Aswad (n.d.) documents the settlement of Yemenis.

Earlier studies have been limited in that they have focused on workers on farms and in the automobile and steel industries, who may constitute the bulk of sojourners. An adequate test of the hypothesis about the process and determinants of settlement has to be based on data for all Yemenis from all social classes in all regions of the United States. The 1980 U.S. Census is, at present, the best source of such data, but it is not without its limitations. First, evidence presented in this chapter suggests an appreciable undercount of Yemenis by this census. Second, selective return migration of Yemenis in the 1960s and the early 1970s means that pre-1975 immigration cohorts in the 1980 census included many more settlers than sojourners. Finally, the information provided by the census is limited and does not encompass all the indicators needed for an adequate test of the settlement hypothesis. Thus, the analysis of census data had to be supplemented by available INS data on Yemeni immigrants.

A brief description of the trends in Yemeni immigration to the United States based on Immigration and Naturalization Service data preceded the analysis of census data. During 1971–84, a total of 6,297 and 1,922 persons from North and South Yemen, respectively, were admitted as immigrants to the United States, or reclassified their legal status to immigrants in this country. In the earlier years, more North Yemenis than South Yemenis immigrated. There was a rapid increase in immigration of North Yemenis until 1974, when their numbers started to decrease, partly due to the alternative opportunities created in the oil-exporting Gulf states as a result of the oil crisis.

The census provides a social and economic profile of the Yemenis that is at odds with those delineated by existing ethnographies. This was expected, since those studies mainly focused on blue-collar workers or farmworkers. Yemenis, on the whole, are far from an immigrant group with little or no education and knowledge of English, predominantly occupying unskilled manual jobs. About 67 percent of North Yemeni and 78 percent of South Yemeni males have at least an elementary school education. Almost all the South Yemenis and about two-thirds of the North Yemenis speak English well or very well. Finally, only 18 percent of the South Yemenis and 42 percent of the North Yemenis hold unskilled manual jobs.

While census and INS data do not contradict the findings of the existing studies, they clearly imply that we should reject the hypothesis that Yemenis have experienced little or no settlement in the United States. The rate of naturalization was used as the main indicator of settlement. It was shown that almost all the Yemenis who arrived before 1970 were naturalized by 1980 and, hence, settled. There is no doubt, however, that early Yemeni immigrant cohorts were initially temporary migrants. Their experience has formed the basis of conclusions about Yemenis as sojourners. But, with the passage of time, some sojourners probably returned home, and the Yemenis who remained in the United States became settlers. The census and INS data also document the emergence of college students as a new type of Yemeni sojourner.

An analysis of the demographic and socioeconomic data for the successive Yemeni immigrant cohorts provides additional, though not always unambiguous, evidence in support of the settlement hypothesis. These data reflect, in part, the cumulated migration experience of the Yemenis in the United States. The demographic data indicate that, with the passage of time, both the sex ratios and the age distributions became more balanced, suggesting an increase in the number of wives and children and family formation in the United States. Also, over time, Yemenis tended to acquire a better knowledge of

English, thus facilitating naturalization and settlement.

As Massey (1986) has argued, higher-status and better-paying occupations constitute a strong incentive for settlement. The findings for Yemenis are somewhat contradictory. The earliest cohorts have both higher rates of naturalization and lower educational and occupational status than the later ones. But they also have a higher level of self-employment (for North Yemenis) and a higher income. Unfortunately, it was not possible to control for the confounding effect of the large number of college students in the most recent cohort. Nevertheless, it is possible that for Yemenis, and other comparable immigrant groups, self-employment and income are more predictive of settlement than education and occupation.

NOTES

We are indebted to Barbara Aswad, Nancy Jabbra, Dixie King, Carolyn Rosenstein, Jon Swanson, and particularly Douglas Massey for their many comments and helpful suggestions.

1. Swanson's chapter in this volume places the Yemeni immigration to the United States in its historical and global perspective.

2. We are grateful to Massey for this argument.

3. Student and nonstudent categories cannot be disentangled from the 1980 census published material and can only be determined from census tapes. But because these tapes are based on a sample of 5 percent of the total population (i.e., 155 cases for all Yemenis in the United States), the sample was too small for analysis.

BIBLIOGRAPHY

Abraham, Nabeel
    1983   "The Yemeni Immigrant Community of Detroit: Background, Emigration, and Community Life." In *Arabs in the New World*, ed. S. and N. Abraham, 110–34. Detroit: Wayne State University Press.

Aswad, Barbara
    1974   "The Southeast Dearborn Arab Community Struggles for Survival against Urban 'Renewal.' " In *Arabic Speaking Communities in American Cities*, ed. B. Aswad, 53–83. Staten Island, N.Y.: Center for Migration Studies.
    n.d.   "Yemeni and Lebanese Muslim Immigrant Women in Dearborn, Michigan." In *Muslim Families in America*, ed. Earle Waugh and Karen Abu-Laban. Beverly Hills: Sage. In press.

Birks, J., and C. A. Sinclair
    1981   "Demographic Settling amongst Migrant Workers." In *International Population Conference*, 733–52. Liège, Belgium: International Union for the Scientific Study of Population.

Bisharat, Mary
    1975   "Yemeni Migrant Workers in California." In *Arabs in America: Myths and Realities*, ed. B. Abu-Laban and F. Zeady, 202–9. Wilmette, Ill.: Medina University Press International.

Bohning, Wolf R.
    1972   *The Migration of Workers in the United Kingdom and the European Community*. London: Oxford University Press.

Dweik, Badr
    1980   "The Yemenis of Lackawanna, New York: A Community Profile." Special Studies Series, 130. Buffalo: SUNY, Council on International Studies.

Immigration and Naturalization Service
    1978–84 *Statistical Yearbooks*. Washington, D.C.: U.S. Government Printing Office

Jasso, Guillermina, and Mark R. Rosenzweig
    n.d.   "Taking Root: Naturalization." Chapter 2 in *Immigrants in the United States*. New York: Social Science Research Council, 1980 Census Monograph Series. In press.

Massey, Douglas S.
    1985   "The Settlement Process among Mexican Migrants to the United States: New Methods and Findings." In *Immigration Statistics: A Story of Neglect*, ed. D. B. Levine, K. Hill, and R. Warren, 255–92. Washington, D.C.: National Academy Press.
    1986   "The Settlement Process among Mexican Migrants to the United States." *American Sociological Review* 51:670–84.

Piore, Michael J.
    1979   *Birds of Passage: Migrant Labor and Industrial Societies*. New York: Cambridge University Press.

Sabagh, Georges, and Mehdi Bozorgmehr
    1987   "Are the Characteristics of Exiles Different from Immigrants? The Case of Iranians in Los Angeles." *Sociology and Social Research* 71:77–84.

Sanchez, Juan, and Saul Solache
    1980   "Yemeni Agricultural Workers in California: Migration Impact." *Journal of Ethnic Studies* 8:85–94.

Siu, Paul
    1952   "The Sojourner." *American Journal of Sociology* 58:34–44.

Steffen, Hans
    1979   *Population Geography of the Yemen Arab Republic*. Wiesbaden: Reichart.

Steffen, Hans, and Olivier Blanc
    1982   "La démographie de la République Arabe du Yémen." In *La Péninsule arabique d'aujourdhui*, ed. P. Bonnenfant, 73–106. Paris: Centre National de la Recherche Scientifique.

United Nations
    1985   *Statistical Abstract of the Region of the Economic and Social Commission for Western Asia 1974–1983*. Baghdad: Economic and Social Commission for Western Asia.

United States, U.S. Census of Population, 1980
    1985   *Foreign-Born Population in the United States*. Microfiche. Washington, D.C.: U.S. Bureau of the Census.

Yemenis in New York City: Emigrant Folklore and Social Identity

SHALOM STAUB
Pennsylvania Heritage Affairs Commission

Faced with minimal opportunities for economic development at home, villagers from the southern highlands of the Yemen Arab Republic have turned to emigration and remittance as a strategy for survival and advancement.[1] Men, generally traveling without their families, seek employment and send the bulk of their wages to support their wives and children left behind. An ideology of return offers the Yemeni villager a way to structure his foreign labor experience. By primarily associating with other Yemenis and showing reluctance to participate extensively in foreign social and cultural activities and institutions, the Yemeni emigrant creates his social identity from a repertoire of Old World social categories and boundaries. Family, village, tribe, region, sect, and religion — all salient social identities in Yemen — can continue to form the basis for interaction among emigrants, together with other, broader social categories — as Yemenis, Arabs, or Muslims. This essay explores the ways Yemeni workers in New York City express a range of social identities and views of their sojourn through traditional genres of their folkloric repertoire.

I focus on these Yemeni social identities as they are enacted in the emigrant community. The Yemenis' patterns of interaction and their shared folklore repertoire reveal how these workers confront and manage the social and cultural disruption imposed by their emigration. Yemeni workers arrive in the United States with little physical evidence of their accustomed village ways other than photographs of their family and home. Yet, despite the lack of the traditional public markers of social identity, Yemeni emigrants draw upon a repertoire of stories, jokes, songs, poetry, foodways, and other folkloric forms to recreate their traditional village identities in the radically different American urban environment.

The vast majority of Yemenis in New York today have arrived since the late 1960s. Their region of origin is generally the Yemeni southern highlands, specifically the districts Ba'adan and Riyashiyah. Most of the men among whom I worked were from Riyashiyah, a district subdivided into six units: Wadi ar-Riyashiyah, al-Jabal, ath-Thuman, Harif, al-Kharba, and Lahab.

It is impossible to judge exactly how many Yemenis live in New York City, since no accurate census figures are available. Estimates by Yemenis varied widely. Some modestly identified the size of the New York Yemeni population at 1,500, some suggested 5,000–6,000, and one man offered the unlikely figure of 13,000. Unlike other Yemeni communities in the United States where many Yemenis are employed in a single industry and consequently live in relative prox-

120. Yemenis and other Arab-Muslim residents of the Atlantic Avenue district of Brooklyn return from Friday prayer at the local mosque. *Ron Kelley.*

imity, the New York Yemeni community is character-ized by a pattern of dispersed employment and resi-dence throughout the greater metropolitan area. Yemeni workers in New York are employed in posi-tions that require little job training or language skill: as guards, elevator operators, busboys, dishwashers, janitors, and office cleaning crew. Some run small grocery stores in Brooklyn, Queens, Manhattan, and the Bronx, or 24-hour candy and news shops in Man-hattan. These grocery stores and candy shops are more lucrative than the jobs mentioned above, but are also considered undesirable by many Yemenis since urban crime and violence have taken their toll on Yemeni store owners. Some Yemenis own or work in Middle Eastern restaurants. During the period of my field research, there were eight Yemeni-owned and -operated restaurants, primarily in the Atlantic Ave-nue section of Brooklyn. Over the years, Yemeni-owned restaurants have opened in Brooklyn, Manhat-tan, and New Jersey.[2]

THE EMIGRANT IDENTITY

Emigration and its associated experiences of social dislocation are common themes in Yemeni

interaction. Workers are constantly seeking news about their families from those emigrants who have just arrived; these newcomers, in turn, look to the veterans for information and advice about jobs and lodging. In addition to this exchange of instrumental information, emigration also figures prominently as an expressive folkloric motif. This "folklore of emigration" takes many forms, including personal narratives that offer reasons why an individual emi-grates and how that foreign sojourn is viewed, stories about the historical role Yemenis played in the early Islamic expansion, bitter anecdotes about how Yemenis feel they are treated by other Arabs in oil-rich states, and jokes that play on the Yemeni's status as an international migrant worker.

There is a long historical precedent for Yemeni emigration. One Yemeni storyteller in the New York area placed the current generation in relation to a tradition of fourteen centuries of emigration by citing the legend about the bursting of the dam at Marib in the latter part of the sixth century as causing the beginning of Yemeni emigration. Scholars have ques-tioned this folk etiology, only to suggest that prior emigration from that region preceded and contributed to the neglect and later destruction of the Marib dam.

121. Yemeni women and children, Atlantic Avenue bus stop, Brooklyn. Arabs settled in the New York metropolitan area at the turn of the twentieth century beginning with the migration of Syrian and Lebanese Christians to the Wall Street district. A secondary community was established with its core on Atlantic Avenue. The Yemenis are the latest in the wave of Middle Easterners who inhabit this Brooklyn neighborhood. *Ron Kelley.*

Researchers have documented migration from the southwestern corner of the Arabian Peninsula to even earlier times, tracing the destinations to Ethiopia, Sudan, Nubia, Egypt, Oman, and East Africa.[3]

Similarly, this storyteller and others recounted the role of his fellow countrymen in conquering and populating the Middle East and North Africa during the Islamic expansion in the seventh century. Yemenis were among the first to accept the Prophet Muhammad's call, and later joined the armies of Islam.[4] Telling the story of the Yemeni's role in the Islamic expansion recalls an earlier, more glorious time of Yemen's place in world affairs. When these events are recounted by an emigrant narrator, it is clear that "emigration" is a salient category of Yemeni historical consciousness.

REFLECTIONS ON THE YEMENI EMIGRANT EXPERIENCE IN THE UNITED STATES

Before they arrive in the United States, Yemenis tend to have an unrealistic view of what their life will be like. Idyllic images of easy money in the United States are frequent, fueled by the seeming affluence of returning workers bearing suitcases of gifts for family members and money in their pockets to begin building a house. The emigrants themselves are not likely to reveal too many details about their occupational life, since their often menial jobs would be considered low in status and possibly shameful for a proud Yemeni tribesman. Once in the United States, the idyllic images are transformed to bitter reflection, as revealed here in a discussion with two Yemeni workers:

M. H.: Listen, United States, especially New York, Big Apples, yeah, the Big Apples, when you're out of the United States, what do you think about here? You think it's easy to just come here, get job.

S. S.: What kind of stories do the people tell in Yemen about what it's going to be like in America?

M. H.: It's too much different. . . . I mean, it's not only in Yemen, it's everywhere, the way the United States [looks]. It's big you know, they make the great country. . . . But I mean it's different, it's different anyway. When you're there, . . . you think when you come from there, you're going to come to the heaven. And not to here. To the heaven. We come here, and look for job. I look for job six months.

122. Yemeni and other Arab restaurants often serve as a place of business for American patrons, as a meeting place for fellow villagers, and as a source of employment for the newly arrived immigrants. *Ron Kelley.*

No really, six months. Six months, and this, you know, "come back tomorrow." I went two day work, dishwasher, in the restaurant. What is this? Dishwasher? My hands, the skin . . .

S. S.: falling off . . .

M. H.: . . . fell off from my hand. From the dish-washer. Two days! What is this?

M. U.: Believe me, last week, I been looking for a job. I was, I was. And I have no money in my pocket. You know, I was walking, looking for a job. And I stop, and finally I hate life. I swear it. I hated life, I swear it. I would go to hell rather than to look for job . . .

M. H.: You're in the hell, don't worry about it.

Confronting the gap between the image and the reality, Yemeni workers face the harshness of their situation. Their attitude toward a "bleak future" is expressed later in the discussion:

M. U.: Believe me, specifically the Yemenis, we are victims.

S. S.: Victims of what?

M. U.: Victims, we make no progress.

S. S.: Victims in Yemen, or . . .

M. U. and M. H.: Everywhere.

M. U.: Everywhere, we are victims of God. I came here eight years ago. My uncle was there, in Michigan. So when I came here, everyone told me to go, and I was thinking I should go to school. And he support me, and

he said, "Keep going to school." But the gang, the com-rades that I came with, I saw them work and make money at Chrysler. They speak to me, "Yeah, we make a lot of money, $150 a week." That's great! So, I went there and ask for a job. And I was looking young at the time, I was like sixteen years. And he looked at me, and he accepted me. Then, get in the assembly line with the most, you know, worst people, the most bad people work the assembly line. They just work and drink and smoke. So, additional to that, hard job, hard job, you know, assembly line. So, I worked there and make some money, and go to school, and go back [to Yemen] and come here and go back. And now, they kick us out. Now there is no experience, nothing, no future, no future, bleak, here in America or there. To me, it's a bleak future. You know, I am young, I can do anything, but I feel that [it is] the end, it's all over. Here or there. We are victims of that guy upstairs. . . . I know thousands like I, who feel the same way.

Such a fatalistic prognosis is not completely a product of their emigrant experience; nevertheless, their foreign work experiences confirm an attitude that is shared by many Yemenis. For instance, there is a general resentment against the Saudis related to a perception that Saudi Arabia is somehow profiting from oil reserves that are actually beneath Yemeni territory. Yemen's proximity to some of the world's richest oil fields juxtaposed with its own lack of resources certainly has contributed to a feeling of being cheated by God. Many Yemenis are convinced that rich oil and mineral deposits lie beneath their soil, but they believe there is an international conspiracy to prevent them from discovering and mining their resources. From their distant vantage point, Yemeni emigrants paint an idyllic image of their homeland, complete with references to buried treasures, precious mineral deposits exposed on mountainsides, and places where black crude oil oozes from the ground.

The glory of past history and the untapped richness of the land stand in contrast to a tone of despair and helplessness that is evident in the folkloric repertoire referring to Yemen and to its future development. The following recorded narrative evokes the bitter humor shared by Yemeni workers.

> Okay, one time, all the presidents held a meeting that they're going to see God, and you know, climb up the ladder and ask him a few questions. So, President Charles DeGaulle got up the ladder and he went to see God. And he was asking God, "When will my country be like the U.S., so advanced?" God said, "Not during your reign, Mr. DeGaulle." So DeGaulle came down crying. Then President Nasser came up, and he was saying, "God, when will my country be in the stage of flying a rocket to the moon?" God said, "Not during your reign, Nasser." So Nasser came down the ladder crying. Then, at that time the president of Yemen was al-Iryani, so he got up the ladder, and he was asking God, "When will my country be advanced?" So God himself started crying, and he said, "Not during my reign."[5]

The emigrants' bitter reflections are tempered by a self-awareness that allows them to distance themselves from their difficult situation. Yemeni workers tell jokes, for example, that through absurd exaggeration offer a way to laugh at their circumstances. The worker who remarked bitterly about his situation told the following joke on another occasion: "The Americans and Russians have both landed on the moon to do exploration. A Yemeni arrives, and he asks, 'Do you have any jobs up here for me?' "[6]

The emigrants draw strength from their ideology of return and the maintenance of contact with their families and villages. This commitment to return offers a structure and means of coping with their long periods of separation. As these emigrant narratives have revealed, Yemenis in the United States are driven by their commitments to support their families while struggling with the difficult working conditions and sacrificing personal fulfillment.

SYMBOLIC EXPRESSION OF THE ESOTERIC "EMIGRANT" IDENTITY

In addition to the personal narratives, stories, and jokes already mentioned, Yemeni emigrants make use of their folk poetic tradition to express both their frustrations and aspirations. Through composition and performance, Yemeni poets, singers, and audiences create and achieve this shared social identity. The sacrifices and hardships of this life, with its prolonged separation from family, find expression in a folk poetry of emigration. There are a number of emigrant folk poets, such as al-Mansub and Muhammad ʿAbdallah ʿUmaysan in Detroit and Musa ar-Ruhani and ʿAbdallah Nasr in New York. Muhammad Ha'il, a singer and oud player popular among Yemenis in the United States, sings the compositions of several of these poets when he plays for parties in New York, Detroit, and Buffalo. His song book contains handcopied versions of such songs as *Yaum al-Widaʿ* (The Day of Farewell) and *Khayal Mugtarib* (The Emigrant's Imagination) by Musa ar-Ruhani and *Ah ya Amrikan Kaffa* (Oh You American, Enough) by ʿUmaysan. The songs address the emigrant's problems, his longing for return, and his frustration upon separation from family.

Aya Allah Qum ya Tayyar (By God, Get Up, O Pilot) is one of the songs ʿAbdallah Nasr wrote to express the emigrant's situation. Its composition was prompted by a personal experience, as ʿAbdallah Nasr relates:

> [This one] is based upon someone who I accompanied to Kennedy airport and was ready to take off for Yemen. He was ready to go back. At that time, he was with me, his body was with us, but he was already back home. So the way I analyzed the situation he was in, he could not wait even the next ten minutes until the plane take off. So I started talking to him, and he was telling me that he could not wait and all that. I asked him several questions about how he feels and all that. He responded that he would miss his friends, but at that time he could not control himself, because he was already gone. . . .
>
> So what happened, I wrote it afterwards, and composed it. I got a lot of reaction from the public, and I would say that was the best song I had that year [1975]. And up to today every time I sing, most people ask me to sing that song.

With ʿAbdallah Nasr's assistance, the following text is a translation of the song. Note that ʿAbdallah Nasr utilizes Yemeni place names and images of its physical environment to create the sense of longing felt by the emigrant.

By God, get up, O pilot, why are you delaying me?
Separation from the family is like a fire [burning within me]; the longing overcomes me.
O pilot, my heart is flying, take me directly to San͑a.
First to San͑a, and whatever happens will happen; its atmosphere surpasses me.
Its climate overcomes me like a wizard, if you come with me you will see.
You'll see Haddah with its trees, you'll feel what is within me.
O God, begin the trip, tell the plane, "start up."
Yearning, longing for news from his Yemeni lover.
I am patient, there is none more patient to endure what is within me.
In New York, my burden is heavy; a tear falls from my eye.
My heart always confused, it keeps me awake all night.
My longing makes the oud strings play, and the strings will make you cry.

The emigrant maintains a primary orientation to the homeland, so it is not surprising that the folk poets choose to elaborate on two key experiences: the day of departure and the day of return. The emigrant's longing and desire for return finds expression in this carefully composed and stylized folk poetry. Although this orientation to the homeland dominates Yemeni social identity and interaction, as an emigrant the Yemeni worker inevitably confronts the confusing foreign culture of the United States.

FOLK HUMOR OF THE EMIGRANT EXPERIENCE

The encounter with American ways is expressed among workers in humorous, and sometimes scatological, stories about an emigrant's lack of familiarity with American language and social custom. For instance, one worker who always kept an Arabic-English dictionary beside him so he could look up new words became the butt of the other workers' humorous attention. The workers were starting their afternoon meal, but the one worker was still looking up a word. The workers kidded him that he wouldn't eat his food until he could find the word. This same worker started telling the others about something he had seen, but instead of saying he saw it in the *New York Post* he mistakenly said the "post office." The kidding started again. One of the veteran workers present told a joke about an Italian immigrant who is taking a citizenship test and is asked, "Who is the first president of the United States?" The Italian answers, "George Washington Bridge."

Yemeni workers enjoy other narratives recounting the emigrant's blunders in the United States. On a

separate occasion, the same storyteller told of another Italian immigrant's experience:

An Italian came to the United States and set up a fruit stand. His cousin taught him how to say the name of the fruit, how much it costs, and to tell the customer that if he doesn't like the price he can go elsewhere. Someone comes up to this new fruitman, and asks him, "What time is it?" The immigrant tells him he has apples and pears, how much they cost, and "If you don't like it, go somewhere else."

While the storyteller focused his jokes on another immigrant community, the tales ring true for many Yemeni workers, who may master only the most rudimentary English language communication even after years of residence in the United States.

Sitting among a group of family and co-villagers at the back table of a Yemeni-owned restaurant, one Yemeni worker told of this experience. He was walking along Sixth Avenue in Brooklyn, and a man approached him offering $10 if he would perform oral sex. The worker told him to get lost. The Yemenis listening to this experience found the whole thing quite funny. The worker continued with another incident that happened to him. He swore it was true. He was working on a cleaning crew, and he had been sweeping with a broom. He wanted to use a vacuum, so he went up to a woman who worked in the office and asked her, "Where is the *fakyum?*" The woman was shocked at the question, but the worker didn't know what was the matter. The woman told him to ask the other women in the office. He went from one woman to the next, asking "Where is the *fakyum? Fakyum? Fakyum?*" The worker's perfectly natural exchange of the /v/ sound, not present in Arabic, to the /f/ innocently transformed his request for an innocuous household object into a sexual proposition. The embarrassment to the cleaning crew member provided great delight to the Yemeni restaurant workers hearing the story.

CONSTRUCTING AN "EMIGRANT" IDENTITY

The economic necessity for emigration from Yemen creates a shared social identity recognized as characteristic of the people for decades, if not centuries. This "emigrant" identity structures the lives of these Yemenis: motivations and strategies for earning money, subsistence on a bare minimum, and remittance of wages to support families and to achieve economic security and social prestige in home villages. Emigration is an economic strategy in their lives, yet as a shared social identity it becomes the basis for folkloric performance.

The Yemeni's folklore of emigration encompasses a historical sense of mission, starting from the collapse of the Marib dam and the role of Yemenis in the Islamic expansion. Personal narratives express the worker's motivations and justification for his prolonged absence from the family in order to support it. They joke about the absurdity of it all and listen appreciatively to musical performances of poetry expressing their longing for return.

Yemeni emigration to the United States engenders a cultural disorientation as workers face an unfamiliar language and cultural experience. Their shared folklore of emigration allows the workers symbolically to express their trials and social *faux pas*. The tales and jokes represent the collective experience, permitting the Yemenis to laugh at each other without the danger of offense. Moreover, this folklore repertoire is instructive, guiding the newly arrived Yemeni worker away from the pitfalls his compatriots have found.

As emigrant, the Yemeni worker maintains an Old World orientation, adapting his traditional social identities to the New World setting. These traditional social boundaries are not simply transposed from Yemen to New York City; rather, they are reconstituted as the workers adapt them to meet new needs.

FAMILY AND VILLAGE IDENTITIES

The family and village associations are primary identities not only in Yemen but in the emigrant's experience as well. In fact, with large portions of earned money remitted to support family in Yemen and build new houses in the village, one could say that family and village identities provide the *raison d'être* for emigration. The emigrant works hard to be able to return to the village with wealth and social prestige.

Communication with family members in Yemen remains a chief concern and shared interest among the emigrants. Yemenis mobilize their family resources at the points of transition: the departure of veterans for a visit home or the arrival of new emigrant workers. Upon arrival, the emigrant's introduction and transition to American life is buffered by contacts with family and co-villagers who provide the newcomer with lodging and help him find a job. Interaction among family members can help to provide a transition between traditional Yemeni customs and the unfamiliar experience of the emigrant's environment. For example, I observed the activities of three male family members who entered one of the Yemeni-owned restaurants. One of the men had just met his father and brother upon their arrival from

Yemen. The veteran was treating them to a special dinner. When they started eating their Middle Eastern, though not specifically Yemeni dinner, the newly arrived brother had difficulty using the cutlery. The veteran brother instructed the newcomer how to use his knife and fork efficiently, since the newcomer was still accustomed to traditional foodways—using his fingers and eating from a communal dish.

The Yemeni restaurant owners provide an example of family and village ties as emigration resources in action. In 1967, Mohammad Almontaser opened the Atlantic House restaurant, initiating a formula for success emulated by family members and co-villagers alike. Mohammad came from al-Maᶜayana, a small agricultural village with approximately 300 residents, one of six villages of ath-Thuman district of Riyashiyah, near Ridaᶜ in the Yemeni southern highlands.

Mohammad Almontaser's Atlantic House eventually was passed on to an affinal kinsman when he returned to Yemen to open a factory and import-export business in Taᶜizz. His agnatic kinsmen from al-Maᶜayana followed in line, opening new restaurants or purchasing existing Lebanese-owned Middle Eastern restaurants. Kaid Almontaser bought the Near East restaurant in 1971. Mosad Almontaser, with Kaid, opened the Mareb restaurant across from the Near East in 1982, later renaming it the New Near East. Nasser Almontaser opened the Almontaser restaurant. Musᶜid Almontaser opened the Adnan restaurant. Ahmad Almontaser bought the Eastern Star, renaming it Moroccan Star. Qa'id Almontaser, from nearby Talab, opened the Bilqis restaurant. Other Talab villagers tried Mohammad's restaurant formula, opening the Sanaa, Taiz Yemen, Arabia Felix, and Mocha Middle East restaurants. One man from nearby Bayt as-Sraymi who had worked as a waiter in the Near East for several years opened the Middle East restaurant.

The degree to which social interaction among emigrants is rooted in family and village relationships is reflected in the ubiquitous presence of nicknames. Throughout the Muslim Middle East, there is a frequent repetition of common names due to the custom of naming after the attributes of God, the variations on the name of the Prophet Muhammad, and in honor of close relatives (Antoun 1968:159–60). The nickname (*laqab*) is an invaluable way to distinguish among numerous people with common names. Yemeni workers in New York frequently used nicknames as strategies to differentiate among the many Muhammads, Ahmads, ᶜAbdallahs, Qa'ids, and Musᶜids. If a worker is the only one, or one of a few, of his patrilineal descent group, that name may become a term of address, such as when co-workers call out "ya Muraysi" or "ya as-Subai." Nicknames can demonstrate respect. One worker is called shaikh, not because he is related to a tribal leader, but because he is liked and respected. Another man is called imam, not because he is literally a religious leader, but because as a veteran in New York City he gives good advice to many kinsmen and co-villagers. Nicknames can play on physical characteristics or personal attributes. In some cases, nicknames given years ago in Yemen are still actively used as terms of address and reference in New York. Just as in Yemen, the use of nicknames in the emigrants' environment signals the presence of the close network of kinsmen and villagers.

Foodways offer another expression of village identity and introduce certain values of tribal identity. On a regular basis, the cooks of the Near East restaurant prepare shurba or silta, thick meat soups made from the bones of the beef and lamb served to customers. Asit, a thick porridge used for dipping in the soup, hilba, a condiment with fenugreek and hot pepper, and sihuga, a tomato sauce hotly spiced with peppers and garlic, are often prepared with the soups. This food is served and consumed in a traditional manner. The workers gather around a central platter of food, squatting if the platter is propped up on the floor or seated around the restaurant's back table if no customers are present. The thick soup is served in a large communal bowl, with the asit placed in the center. Small dishes of hilba and sihuga are placed by the side, and workers spill these spicy condiments into the communal bowl. Workers reach for the asit, or in its absence commercially baked pita bread, which they refer to as khubz, taking it in their hand and scooping up some soup. When the entire bowl of shurba and asit is finished, one of the workers brings out a pot of soup bones, pouring them into the communal bowl. Each worker then takes some of the meat bones in his hands to complete his meal.

The Yemeni workers emphasize that their use of a single communal dish does not reflect poverty or a lack of available dishes for each person. They consider it an honor and a sign of respect to share food from the same plate. They recount stories of people in the village who will not eat if they are alone; instead, they will go outside to find others to invite to join their meal. Perhaps less extreme but certainly typical, workers make it clear that if they see someone passing by at mealtime, they will invite that person to share their food. These values of generosity and honor are central tribal concepts, but workers also view this

behavior as particular to the villages. The cities of Yemen have gotten too big, they say. People are anonymous to one another, and they don't go out of their way to help one another in the cities. A Yemeni worker in New York who sits down with a plate of food, whether shurba and asit or a slice of pizza, will invariably offer that food to the other people present. Not to do so would be a violation of basic principles of social interaction among villagers and tribesmen.

TRIBAL IDENTITY

The emigrant strategies of these kin and co-villagers can be understood in the context of tribal affiliation. Yemeni social organization, whether urban or rural, revolves around the qabaʿil, the Yemeni tribesmen. The qabaʿil, descendants of Qahtan, the ancestor of all South Arabians, epitomize the traditional Arab virtues: courage, strength, aggressiveness, virility, pride, self-reliance, autonomy, hard work, hospitality, and generosity (Gerholm 1977:115; Adra 1982:146). The qabaʿil are the ultimate power holders of Yemen, to whom nontribesmen, both the religious elite and the various low-status groups, must turn for safety. As warriors, the qabaʿil need the sada as elite and respected outsiders to mediate tribal conflicts. As farmers, the qabaʿil need the services of those who have low-status occupations, but generally consider these activities to be below their own social status.

The Almontasers are qabaʿil. They are descendants of the Bani Hushaysh, a tribe located in northeastern Yemen in the area of Khaulan and Marib. Their immediate ancestors were from the village al-Hindawana, in Khaulan. According to their oral history, when the Turks took power in Yemen hundreds of years ago and extended control to tribal lands in central Yemen, the qabaʿil moved south, founding villages in the southern highlands. The qabaʿil from al-Hindawana, known as al-Muntasir (the victorious), established the village al-Maʿayana. Over generations, they lost a direct connection to their tribal kinsmen in central Yemen as they intermarried with other local tribes and established new local affiliations in the southern highlands.

When the Almontasers refer to each other as cousins (ibn ʿamm), they are invoking relationships across a patrilineal descent group defined by multiple generations. All Almontasers trace their ancestry through two brothers, Saʿid and Ahmad. Those Almontasers in New York City derive primarily from a line through Saʿid al-Muntasir, who had three sons: Ahmad, ʿAli, and ʿAudh.

Although I was not able to obtain full genealogical information for all restaurant owners and workers, there is a clear pattern. The genealogical data suggest that each Yemeni-owned restaurant has a primary link to a particular *usra*, a patrilineal descent group. The various Almontaser restaurants follow this pattern, as do the other (albeit fewer) restaurants of the al-Jahmis from neighboring Talab and the Manhattan grocery stores along Eighth and Ninth avenues of the ash-Shami *usra* from the southern highlands.

Agnatic and affinal kinship proximity appears to be an organizing principle of residence and occupational opportunity, as well as general visiting patterns; however, there is another aspect of Yemeni tribal organization that relates to this Brooklyn Yemeni community. The al-Muntasirs of al-Ma^cayana represent a small village of approximately 300 persons. As mentioned above, they originally derive from a tribal group from further north, but after they settled in Riyashiyah, they abandoned that northern affiliation. The al-Muntasir *usra* joined with several others, as-Subai, al-Ahwas, and al-Qa^catabi, numbering approximately 400, all of neighboring Talab, to form a coalition known as *ahl Talab* (people of Talab). *Ahl Talab*, totaling approximately 700 in number, structurally opposes (or complements) the dominant al-Jahmi *usra* of Talab, also known as al-Jahimiyya. As members of *ahl Talab*, al-Muntasirs have intermarried with the other patrilineal lineages of the same coalition, so that even if co-villagers and *qaba^cil* from neighboring villages are not agnatic kinsmen, sharing membership in the al-Muntasir *usra*, they are likely to be affinal kinsmen or at the very least members of the same *ahl*. These relationships create meaningful and instrumental linkages among emigrant workers as they seek jobs and residences.

Not all elements of tribal identity that are meaningful in Yemen are also actively expressed among emigrants in New York City. Principal markers of the *qaba^cil* in Yemen include weapons, dress, dance, and poetry (Gerholm 1977:115; Adra 1982:56–60). *Qaba^cil* invariably wear the *janbiyya*, a curved dagger with an inlaid handle and decorated sheath and belt, and in addition now commonly carry rifles. Tribesmen and nontribesmen now wear similar clothing, a *futa* (skirt), a Western-style shirt, and imported Western suit coats; however, the turban and the manner of its wrapping indicate tribal affiliation (Adra 1982:58). *Qaba^cil* are known for the *bar^ca* dance, each tribe having its own particular variations (Adra 1982:238–55, 274–88). Additionally, *qaba^cil* are distinguished by their use of the *zamil* poetic form.

Most of these tribal markers are not available to *qaba^cil* who have emigrated to New York City. Only a few Yemenis are reported to have brought a *janbiyya*; but even in these cases, it is not for public display. Emigrants may bring a *futa* to wear privately, but no one reported bringing or wearing a turban. Men recall the *bar^ca* dance, but opportunities for its performance are limited to the rare wedding or nationalistic party.

Of all the distinctive tribal markers, the poetic form *zamil* (pl. *zawamil*) is particularly meaningful among emigrants. Workers not only actively remember these poetic compositions, but they also receive an ongoing infusion of new *zawamil* brought or sent from Yemen on cassette tapes. These cassettes are regularly played in the kitchens of the Yemeni-owned restaurants. The *zamil* is a brief, rhymed composition, generally two lines long, created on a particular occasion and then chanted by a group of men. These brief *zamil* texts, which are easily memorized and recalled years later, encapsulate specific key events in poetic form.

Zamil poetry is the most persistent expression of tribal identity in New York City, but it is not the only one. Workers seek those among them who recall narrative and poetic forms of tribal experience. Ahmad Qa'id is one worker well known for his narrative and poetic performance. He had been a religious leader in Talab, following his father before him and was the imam, the leader of the local mosque. Now in the New York area, he is greeted enthusiastically by other workers who immediately request such narratives as the story of Joseph or tales of Solomon, or epic poems about tribal exploits.

REGIONAL IDENTITY

Dialect—along with physical characteristics, clothing, religious sect, and other markers—identifies regional boundaries in Yemen. Riyashiyah lies right at the border of the north-south division of cultural regions in the Yemeni highlands. These tribesmen are Zaidis, though their fellow emigrants from the areas further to the south, such as Ibb, ash-Shi^cir, and Ba^cadan, are Shafi^ci, two sects of Islam that are subdivisions of the major Muslim sectarian rift between Shi^ca and Sunni. The Yemeni workers in New York City belittled any significant distinction between Zaidis and Shafi^cis, saying that the differences are nothing more than a matter of varying postures during prayer.

Although Yemeni workers generally deny differential regional identity as a significant boundary in favor of the more encompassing Yemeni national identity, regional boundaries are still significant among the emigrants. Among tribesmen from Riyashiyah who share a common regional identity, the regional boundary is rarely articulated; however, when a first-time emigrant fresh from Ibb province met the workers of one of the Yemeni-owned restaurants, the regional boundary was evident. During their interaction, this Ibb emigrant told a joke about a Saudi who is outsmarted by his Sanᶜani worker. The Saudi asks the Sanᶜani if he wants grapes or coffee for his break. The Sanᶜani replies, "First coffee, then lunch, and after lunch, grapes." In this context, this joke invokes a shared national identity as Yemenis who resent their rich neighbors. Significantly, the Ibb emigrant chose a Sanᶜani to represent all Yemenis in his joke. Sanᶜa, besides being the capital, is also a northern city, much closer socially to his Riyashiyah audience than to himself. When I spoke privately to this Ibb emigrant, he commented that he had only recently met these restaurant workers, and he would never have met them in Yemen. He stressed their commonality, saying, "We are all Yemenis"; nevertheless, he was generally reluctant to enter the restaurant.

YEMENI - ARAB - MUSLIM IDENTITY

The multiple social identities discussed thus far are those of greatest social proximity: as family member, villager, *qabili*, Zaidi, and "northerner." They are categories that stress the local and the particular aspects of cultural interaction. In the American context, the categories Yemeni, Arab, and Muslim are cultural identities with potential for a shared identity on a much greater scale.

The workers' sense of their "Yemeni" identity stems from two primary sources: a strong historical consciousness and pride in the glories of ancient Yemen and the emergence of the contemporary state. In the emigrant setting, the workers' primary opportunity to interact with other Yemenis outside their immediate village and tribal network is in *al-jamᶜiya al-khabriya al-yamaniya* (the Yemen American Benevolent Association), located in the vicinity of "Arab Atlantic Avenue" in Brooklyn.

Yemeni workers also closely identify themselves as Arabs, citing general values of honor and generosity, and more particularly their pride in maintenance of the Arabic language. Nevertheless, this self-identification has not led to strong mutual identification or interaction between Yemenis and other Arabs along Atlantic Avenue. Most Yemeni workers report that

they rarely have direct contact with the Syrians and Lebanese who frequent the area; among the Lebanese and Syrian merchants, the Yemenis have a reputation of keeping to themselves.

While the Arab identity is not often the basis of broadly inclusive social interaction, the workers' identity as Muslims forms the basis for self-identification and contact with non-Yemenis. Many of the emigrant workers maintain some level of Islamic observance, whether performing *salat*, the five times per day prayer ritual; attending *jumᶜa*, communal prayer on Fridays at noon in the mosque; abstaining from alcohol and pork; or fasting during Ramadan. Even those who rarely perform any of these activities generally profess a strong identity as Muslim. Among other local Muslims, the Yemenis have a reputation for religious observance and for being tradition-oriented.

AMRIKI IDENTITY

Despite the emigrants' orientation toward eventual return to Yemen, many workers desire to obtain American citizenship. Their motives are principally to enable more family members to come to the United States as emigrant workers and to facilitate easier travel by using a U.S. passport. Yemenis may jokingly refer to those workers who have obtained citizenship as *amriki*, though their primary national self-identification remains Yemeni.

Children of Yemeni emigrant families growing up in New York and attending public schools experience cultural dissonance, not only as Muslims in a Christian society but also as Yemenis in America. They may be expected to be fully competent in traditional cultural patterns to which they have only partial access. When asked his nationality by a group of Yemeni restaurant workers, one youngster responded, "American." Feigning horror at the youngster's answer, the workers insisted, "No, no, you're a Yemeni," but the workers' insistence may have done little to clarify the issue for the boy.

The experience of this distance from a culture of origin and the encounter with a foreign language and culture leads to the development of a multilingual, multicultural repertoire. This is the "folklore of ethnicity," the ability to switch among a variety of cultural codes (Kirshenblatt-Gimblett 1983). The characteristics of a multicultural repertoire and cultural code-switching are present in everyday verbal interaction. Lexical intrusion from English to Arabic and from Arabic to English is common, as when a Yemeni offers another a cigarette, saying, *Inta batsmuk?* Some workers choose English replacements

123. Yemeni restaurant, Court Street, Brooklyn. *Shalom Staub*.

124. Farmworker in muddy asparagus fields, Delano, California. *Ron Kelley.*

125. The Palestine issue and Lebanese conflict involve the Yemeni community in the broader spectrum of Arab political causes. Their concerns are expressed individually (top) or collectively (bottom), as exemplified by a 1983 street demonstration in Dearborn, Michigan. *Tony Maine.*

126. Although Yemeni workers often resolve their grievances among themselves, they marched with their local union in a show of solidarity at the 1984 Democratic National Convention held in San Francisco. *Ron Kelley*.

for their Arabic names. Salih is called Sam by the customers in his Manhattan grocery store; the lineage name al-Muraysi forms the basis for a new "American" identity as Al Marisi. Nevertheless, most Yemeni workers deliberately attempt to minimize this American experience, rarely using "American" as a term of self-identification. Their ideology of return and their economic strategies as emigrants keep them rooted in multiple social identities derived from the Old World but redefined in the American setting.

CONCLUSION

Yemeni workers in New York are first and foremost "emigrants." This emigrant identity places the worker in relation to family in the Yemeni village who depend on his remittances and to other workers in the emigrant environment who share his concerns and pursue similar economic strategies. Through a "folklore of emigration" — the historical legends, jokes, and poetry — the Yemeni worker locates himself among others who face the same harsh experience and bitter separation from family.

The worker's constant awareness of his emigrant status and the desire for eventual return to his home contribute to the focus on the interrelated social iden-

tities as kinsman, villager, and tribesman. Despite the absence of most of the tangible expressions of these social identities, Yemeni workers continue to structure their daily lives within this framework. Their intangible, symbolic cultural resources — language, foodways, folk narrative, poetry, and other traditional forms of Yemeni folklore — emerge as the vehicles for social and cultural identification.

NOTES

1. This study is based on ethnographic fieldwork among Yemeni emigrants in New York City from May 1980 through November 1981 for my 1985 Ph.D. dissertation, "A Folkloristic Study of Ethnic Boundaries: The Case of Yemeni Muslims in New York City" (Philadelphia: Balch Institute Press, forthcoming). My research was supported by a Foreign Language and Area Studies Fellowship administered by the Middle East Center of the University of Pennsylvania.

2. Not all of these restaurants have remained in business. The Sanaa restaurant closed. The Bilqis became a Pakistani restaurant, renamed Noorjahan. The Arabia Felix, Mareb, Middle East, and Mocha Middle East opened in Brooklyn Heights, Cobble Hill, Jersey City, and Manhattan, respectively. The Mareb was later renamed the New Near East. The Middle East and Mocha Middle East closed within a year. Since my fieldwork ended, the Taiz-Yemen and New Near East have closed, leaving the number of stable Yemeni-owned restaurants at six: Adnan, Almontaser, Arabia Felix, Atlantic House, Moroccan Star, and

127, 128. Dance, music, poetry, and decorative arts are an integral part of Yemeni culture. Above, Yemenis wearing traditional tribal dress celebrate a wedding in the village of ʿAmran, Yemen. Below, Yemeni dancers in Delano, California, perform at the festivities commemorating the twenty-fifth anniversary of the 1962 revolution that established the Yemen Arab Republic. *Thomas Stevenson. Ron Kelley.*

129. Saluting the flag, Yemen's independence day celebration, Delano, California. *Ron Kelley.*

Near East. For a detailed analysis of a Yemeni-owned restaurant as ethnic performance, see Staub 1981.

3. Cited in Swanson (1979:47). Swanson also provides a useful review of various theories to explain the persistent emigration from this region (1979:48–50).

4. Stookey provides a more detailed account of the relationship between Yemenis and the emergent power of Muhammad in Medina, tracing the early importance of the Yemeni tribes in Islamic politics and their later marginality (1978:25–33). He notes the critical role played by Yemenis in the Islamic expansion: "The most populous region of the [Arabian] peninsula, it [Yemen] furnished a large proportion of the manpower, and some of the distinguished commanders, of the armies which carried the Muslim conquests westward to Spain and eastward to China; it also supplied many of the colonists who settled in their wake" (1978:32).

5. I have left this and other quoted folklore texts unattributed at the preference of my informants. Although such stories and jokes with negative or critical or even scatological elements are commonly told and enjoyed by Yemenis, the narrators prefer not to draw public attention to themselves. In contrast, poets and narrators of religious tales and folktales are identified because they are honored and respected men in the community.

6. A slightly different version of this joke appears in Ron Kelley's account.

SELECTED BIBLIOGRAPHY

Adra, Najwa
    1982   *"Qabyala*: The Tribal Concept in the Central Highlands of the Yemen Arab Republic." Ph.D. dissertation. Philadelphia: Temple University.

Antoun, Richard
    1968   "On the Significance of Names in an Arab Village." *Ethnology* 7:158–70.

Gerholm, Tomas
    1977   *Market, Mosque, and Mafraj: Social Inequality in a Yemeni Town.* Stockholm: Department of Social Anthropology, Stockholm University.

Kirshenblatt-Gimblett, Barbara
    1983   "Studying Immigrant and Ethnic Folklore." In *The Handbook of American Folklore*, ed. Richard M. Dorson, 39–47. Bloomington: Indiana University Press.

Staub, Shalom (Steven D.)
    1981   "The Near East Restaurant: A Study of the Spatial Manifestation of the Folklore of Ethnicity." *New York Folklore* 7(1–2):113–27.
    1985   "A Folkloristic Study of Ethnic Boundaries: The Case of Yemeni Muslims in New York City." Ph.D. dissertation. Philadelphia: University of Pennsylvania.

Stookey, Robert W.
    1978   *Yemen: The Politics of the Yemen Arab Republic.* Boulder: Westview Press.

Swanson, Jon
    1979   *Emigration and Economic Development: The Case of the Yemen Arab Republic.* Boulder: Westview Press.

130. Snapshot taken in Yemeni Central Highlands.

On the Photographs

JOHN BRUMFIELD
The Art Center College of Design
Pasadena, California

In photographic circles the term "documentary photography" is generally used in reference to a body of images more or less systematically produced by a professionally trained photographer with the intention of depicting persons, places, or events in an editorially cohesive manner. As one might imagine, this kind of imagery is clearly allied to the photography of the popular press, but there are differences. Documentary photography is much less committed to the pretense of objective reportage and it is only occasionally news. Of course, insofar as it records an event, every genuine news photograph may be said to be documentary. But as a genre, documentary photography usually implies something more: the patently selective presentation of a number of thematically related images, organized, more often than not, on the structural model of the photo essay, to which, indeed, such photographers as Eugene Smith have made their definitive contributions.

The key word here is "essay," a word denoting, as it has since Cicero, the practice of an extended examination. Less obviously, it is the expression of an intensely personal interpretation, the participation of the essayist *engagé*: the always stylized, sometimes tendentious, and often frankly partisan point of view. Of course, to anyone who cares to look it will quickly become clear that all photographs are subjective and necessarily so, for the things presented within the photographic frame are the only things that are there. The rest of the world is not there. At least apparently not. Yet surely all kinds of visual references not in the picture may be there in the landscape, a part of the event. For although it is true that the camera appears to represent the raw materials presumably there before it, this must not be taken to mean that the relationships shared by those materials are fully represented, nor accurately represented, nor that this representation is, in any sense, the whole picture.

But remember, when Jacob Riis shot his now famous Mulberry Street photographs he really wasn't guided by the spirit of philosophically disinterested objectivity. He had a point to make. And as with the work of Lewis Hine and Walker Evans and Paul Strand and Robert Frank, the issue had to do with bringing his audience to see things his way.

On the other hand, any historical object may also be read as a culturally iconographic artifact. The politically pointed adventures of Colonel Steve Canyon, the homiletic Mary Worth, Krazy Kat, and Pogo are not simply the inspired personifications of their creators' philosophical fancy; they are value-laden reflections of their era and their audience. Rich with the prints and tracks of every day, they have the look, feel, and smell of their intersections with the world.

They offer us, as little else can, the texture of their time.

The photographs in this collection are of the same kind, for, regardless of the intentions of their maker, each may be read as an image of the *event* of picture making. Thus, even the most apparently innocent of Yemeni snapshots must be understood to be, after all, the product of a series of more-or-less informed choices, for those who make portraits and those who pose for them usually have intentions, and other pictures, in mind. It is also to be remarked that when the image is in any sense a portrait there are always at least two participants: the photographer and the subject, and *both* make the picture. Both are usually operating in terms of some degree of shared conventions and both usually have something to communicate. Moreover, whether neatly within the chronologies of the family album or stuffed into a traveler's wallet, the domestic photograph is, more than occasionally, a visual commemoration of some kind of ceremonial event. Weddings, birthdays, moments of departure or return, the soldier in the boom boom house, the child with his first caught trout — all are the subjects of hallowed photographic convention tempered of course by the mesh of one's idiosyncratic intentions and the proprieties of the occasion.

But given the historic Islamic prohibition against image-making and the abiding circle of taboos impinging upon the public appearance of women, it is remarkable that the present collection has any Yemen snapshots at all. Yet it does. And it is perversely true that on the whole, they're a lot like snapshots taken anywhere, by almost anybody. But not quite. They *are* Yemen snapshots and of a piece with the collective sensibilities of their makers. And whether shivering through a seemingly interminable winter in Buffalo or sweltering in the somewhat more familiar heat of the otherwise impenetrable San Joaquin Valley, the men who carry these snapshots in their wallets are often sojourners in a land as different from their own as possible. They didn't come to assimilate or as tourists. They came to work, to try to live frugally, to send as much money home as possible, and, that done, to return. Thus, partly by choice, partly by virtue of the economics of their situation, partly as a result of the gulf between cultures, and, finally, partly by the nature of the available jobs, they're isolated. Segregated into a corner of the economy from which, even in the best of times, there is virtually no emergence, speaking a language that shares hardly a cognate with American English, and here, abruptly, from what must seem indeed to be another moral universe, they are men transposed to the periphery of a profoundly

distant world, and these snapshots are their touchstones. These images are their connection to the only reality they can possibly grasp, and by that I mean *hold on to*.

The photographs from home, almost without exception, are portraits of the immediate family and, not surprisingly, they are in color. Sometimes images of the house appear, completed or in various stages of construction; it's where much of the money has gone and the house is an object of pride and a testament to the migrants' collective achievement. It may even have been a major stimulus for their journey. Sometimes the snapshots show us something of the neighborhood or, more rarely, the surrounding landscape; but more commonly the house is presented as a setting for a portrait. The men of the family, holding their youngest sons in their arms, line up before an exterior wall; an eldest son poses on the roof, proudly, his *janbiyya* at his belt, the stepped terraces of the village dropping away into the valley below him. The migrant's wife and perhaps his daughters pose together in the main room, or perhaps the entire family, dressed for the occasion, arrange themselves formally against a patterned wall. What we learn of the house, its design and furnishing, comes to us usually as accidental background information, unintentional and haphazard, random pieces of furniture, a few proudly displayed emblems of prosperity, a TV set, for instance, or a bright new telephone with a long cord; but little in the way of the domestic and humble stuff of daily life, little in the way of decoration. For these are intimately formal images, restrained, portraits after all. Intended for the man's wallet, they are images of his family and his house. Thus, beyond the obvious requirements of representation and identification the images are studiously composed catechisms of decorum. Within the absolute sanctuary of his home (and wallet) the migrant's wife may be unveiled but seated demurely with her children, her formally domestic pose betraying no suggestions of emotion, animation, or individuality, for these photographs explore, reveal, or recall almost nothing of the dailiness of daily life: the maker of the snapshot wants to see his family's face. When he looks at their picture he wants them to be looking back and to be dressed for the occasion, for that asserts that one observes the appropriate civilities, that one can afford to properly clothe and provide for one's children and, along the way, it also asserts that the making of this photograph was an event deserving of a degree of preparation and seriousness, for the photograph was going to America.

With obvious exceptions where women are included, the images made outside the house are often

131. Worker's family, Yemen. *Sojourner snapshot.*

of another kind, because they are most usually photographs of men and they reflect a different set of proprieties and another mode of behavior. In portraits of two or more men, of groups of men and boys or of boys practicing the roles of manhood, the images are usually posed, but the poses are more individually, if not whimsically, stylized. There is more psychological room and the subjects clown, strut, and attempt to interject something, capriciously, of themselves, certainly of their self-image. These groupings are clearly fraternal, remarkably egalitarian considering the variety of ages of the participants, and, as often as not, at a gathering place on the street or in the market, before the house or, even more proudly, with their newly purchased jeeps, their four-wheel-drive pickup trucks, and the ubiquitous Land Cruisers whose all-terrain versatility provides the mechanical wherewithal to move just about anything — tools, equipment, lumber, stone — across the rough and irregular local terrain to the site where the house continues to be built.

But for all of that, the men rarely picture themselves *driving* their expensive imported vehicles. And never do they pose with the tools of their labor; nor do they make snapshots of themselves as they sweat to shape the stones and raise the beams of those proud houses. Their jackhammers are the pride of German industrial design and their hydraulic drills the best

that Japan or Korea can offer; but they pose only occasionally with their prestigious jeeps and trucks, and far more eagerly with their guns, with their ceremonial daggers, and with their sons. They hold their children, especially the boys, like their guns, aloft, proudly, and they dress for their snapshot, often wearing either their military uniform or the mixed costume that bespeaks the sophistication of their travel: the Western suit coat, the tribal *janbiyya*, and, above their European shoes, the *futa* or long skirt.

There are exceptions, but rarely do the Yemeni snapshots depict events; and even when a unique or significant event is the occasion for the photograph, the character and certainly the spontaneity of the occasion is submerged beneath the conventions of the snapshot portrait. A birthday gathering, an anniversary, a meeting of the fraternity is composed with no significant difference from a group portrait of one's children: no matter what the occasion, the gathering before the camera is *for* the camera. The images are emblematic mementos. The possessor of the wallet will be away from home for twelve to twenty-four months at least and in that time the children will grow, another room will be added to the stone house, a younger brother will marry, or perhaps an elder of the family will die. The possessor of the prints will read his mail or listen as his family is mentioned in the letter of a neighbor, and he'll look at his snapshots.

132. Boys showing off. San^{c}a, Yemen. *Sojourner snapshot.*

133. Returned migrant, Yemen. *Sojourner Snapshot.*

134. Studio portrait, San^ca, Yemen. *Sojourner snapshot.*

135. Studio portrait, Delano, California. *Settler snapshot.*

136. Street scene, Old City, San^ca, Yemen. *Nikki Keddie.*

The photographs of Nikki Keddie and Jon Swanson fill in and expand upon the world of activity and events to which the Yemeni snapshots but only obliquely refer. Behavior and, as far as possible, the social context are at the point of their focus. Keddie is a historian and Swanson is an anthropologist. For each the photographic image is intentionally informational.

Nikki Keddie photographs only where a foreign woman is allowed to go with a camera, but her concentration is, by and large, on the women. In the snapshots women are presented categorically: clearly and unequivocally as mother, wife, sister, or daughter, models all of domestic propriety. In Keddie's imagery, they are alive. And it is they in this rigidly stratified culture who are working at every task. It is they on the terraces, in the fields and the villages who are doing the men's work and maintaining the continuity of the community and, more directly, the family, while their men are away. They are taking care of business, repairing dikes, harvesting qat, and, of course, managing the economy of the home. In Keddie's work we see women talking, moving through the streets and byways of the village and across the fields. And because Keddie is a woman they allow themselves to be photographed unveiled and sometimes shyly, sometimes frankly, they look at the cam-

era with a directness that is captivating. Influenced by the compositional glazing of such publications as the *National Geographic*, Keddie's imagery, however, is several steps closer to the texture of actual life. Of children exuberant and shouting, playing in the street; a woman collecting water; people passing and pausing on their various errands, greeting one another beneath the painted walls of their houses or meeting amid the dazzling disorder of wares in the central village market, hers is an imagery that attempts to record and, if possible, communicate the feeling and look of life in the community with its characteristically rich and irrepressibly Yemeni blend of patterns and colors and surfaces. Painted, peeling walls, stone and mud, twisting, climbing streets, the sprawling and labyrinthine jumble of proliferating houses, and everywhere the dust and the mountain backdrop. The place, alive and contradictory, begins to shape and situate itself.

It is here, in a manner of speaking, that anthropologist Jon Swanson begins, for his images of the land move from the grandly general to the deliberately specific, from the panoramic to the close-up, bringing to our attention kinds of information that seem to hover on the periphery of the snapshots and are, more often than not, either scenic or situational in the imagery of Nikki Keddie. Partly because

137. Town suq (market), Hamam Damt, Yemen. *Jon Swanson.*

they're foreigners, partly because they have a professional interest, both Keddie and Swanson emphasize activity within an enveloping environment.

But it is Swanson who establishes the larger stage. Incorporating expansive sweeps of the arid, mountainous landscape, patched and quilted with stepped green terraces and staggered farms, Swanson's imagery moves from the rocky peaks across the trails and sloping plains to the first outlying villages and down into the city streets. His images overlap and repeat incidental details, varying our points of view and indicating relationships, scale, and distance: how long is a terrace, how thick or high is a wall, how deep and how wide is an irrigation ditch; what is the relationship of garden to town; where does the village end, and how far must one walk, up how steep a slope, to work the qat fields? In Swanson's work the enormous influence of the physical environment begins to emerge: We see the fields of coffee and sorghum climbing into the mountains, thinning out and growing farther apart as they go up; we see streets leading into the millet, bustling and crowded in the central areas and then narrowing into steeply attenuated rocky footpaths as they reach out past the villages to the small clusters of farms and to the cluttered and then scattered dwindling of individual houses; and everywhere people are moving, trucks, trailers,

camions, jeeps, jumbled with camels and mules and men walking, carrying everything conceivably necessary to build those tall stone houses. And everywhere young men and old, home from America or Saudi, clamber up and down rickety hand-hewn ladders; plow with hoes unchanged in hundreds of years; break, shape, set, and secure stones as did their ancestors—but now with the aid of hydraulic jackhammers from Korea. And up and down the market streets in glaring counterpoint to the richly muted colors of the shops and stalls are teetering piles of pots and tins and fabrics and goodies and gadgets from everywhere, video cassettes, ghetto blasters, tape recorders and a thousand small digital appliances, stuff of every description stacked like beans in the market place, and everywhere men talking and women moving among the stalls. Yet for all the bustle and apparent energy, whatever passes for municipality seems hardly to be either the focus of much of the activity or the generator of its direction. TV antennas bristle from every dwelling; yet commercial buildings are minimally developed, streets are rarely paved, public services hardly in evidence, and industrial development seems all but completely neglected. In the 120 or more years of Yemeni emigration, thousands of men have lived in spartan self-denial to send home cumulative millions, but hardly more than a

138. Merchants in clothes shop, ᶜAmran, Yemen. *Thomas Stevenson.*

comparative handful have invested in anything that might contribute to the trickle-out of an internal economy. And that too, by implication at least, is what Swanson wants to illustrate.

Although varying in emphasis and, of course, filtered by the individuality of their vision, Kurt Wenner and Thomas Stevenson amplify the themes broadly established by Keddie and Swanson; for like them, their object also is to inform. Thus, for all the photograph functions as a kind of empirical evidence: about the look of the place, about the marks and monuments that a people put upon a land; about their movement upon it within the tangle of past and present. Their images are also about the fact that all of this is behavioral, that it is an implicit declamation of identity.

Thus, Stevenson, an anthropologist, gives us a view of new houses in ᶜAmran and, nearby, the villages of Shalthna and Dha'wan, communities that are, to Western eyes, remarkably beautiful with their austerely modulated geometry and subtle color, so much a harmonic, blended piece with the rich tones of the desert and yet so emphatically architectonic. Systematically, he moves in closer, photographing the immediately surrounding environment, the fields, men plowing and planting, others stacking grain, a grower among his rows of qat; and, within the towns,

traditional street vendors, a man selling sheep at a weekly market, the interior of shops, typical and new, and their owners; an auto parts dealer, a pharmacist, a prosperous grocer, and a group of clothiers; a craftsman in front of his welding shop. The poses are formal, the composition is to the point and matter-of-fact. Like his densely economical photograph of the returned emigrant and his used-car lot, Stevenson's photographs index and catalog the socioeconomic gradations of the culture. They are clear and directed and they say, "this is what's here and this is how it looks."

Kurt Wenner, a political scientist, is sometimes dispassionately factual and sometimes dryly ironic. He photographs along the road to Hajjah to show the terracing and the segregated planting, in Shibam to illustrate the "uniquely Yemeni" decorative work on the minaret; and in Thula he makes images of traditional buildings in order to show the characteristic height of the mountain residence, the "typical" stonework, and, at the top of the buildings, those additions he believes to have been funded by remittance income. In Sanᶜa he makes a photograph of an example of the official version of modernized architectural detail and, additionally, to document the foreign labor imported to replace Yemeni workers who are themselves working abroad. It's a short step, then, from this kind of image to those photographs in or near Rida^c, where, for instance, Wenner carefully juxtaposes new modern buildings "constructed almost solely as a result of remittances" against the clutter of contemporary trash, for before the pattern of emigration reached its present proportions, what Wenner now describes as fields of junk were then green fields of crops — community-grown food over which the men of the town labored and upon which the entire town depended. In another Rida^c image he contrasts the stately old fortress, the newer buildings, the dirt street, and, as he puts it, "the fact that the roofs have all sprouted TV antennas, and become a disposal area for other modern junk." His point may be missed by the uninitiated viewer, especially one for whom television antennas are a commonplace, for the contrast is subtle and unless the photograph is much enlarged such detail is likely to go unnoticed. It's an arresting photograph, however, nicely composed with a delicate balance of graduated color and shape, a quality, by the way, that also tends to obscure the photographer's understated irony. On the other hand, it's hard to imagine that anyone will misunderstand Wenner's photograph of the area around Hajjah, because the beauty of the landscape, the isolation and inaccessibility of the villages, separated by such torturous distances and perched each upon its own craggy mountain top, is awesome and breathtaking (see photo 1).

In Detroit Tony Maine photographed Yemeni migrants at work in the automobile assembly plants and on the neighborhood streets, in Yemeni-owned shops and cafes, and in their apartments. A professional photographer, trained in the canons of the American photo essay with strong alliances to the tradition of street photography, Maine, like his colleagues Milton Rogovin and Ron Kelley, is as much concerned with the visual structure and compositional articulation of his imagery as with its "objective" information. That, of course, can be about impact, but it has its aesthetic dimension as well, for Kelley, Rogovin, and Maine have each a carefully developed style, consistently enunciated and, no doubt, meticulously edited; so much so, in fact, that one can fairly guess each photographer's age by the manner in which he frames and organizes his material. But while exhibition photographers must always be understood to have one eye on the circuit, it is equally true that for all of them a major function of their compositional strategy — their aesthetic, if you will — is articulation. Like Hine and Riis before them, they have a point to make.

Professors Keddie, Stevenson, Swanson, and Wenner have their points to make too; but their primary means of making those points is expository prose. Writers by training and preference, they are disposed to the logic of systematic elucidation and the critical explication of data. Visual elaboration is illustrative. And therefore secondary. For Rogovin, Maine, and Kelley, the visual image is primary. The well-made photograph has its own authenticity, its own autonomy. Although it must necessarily always be referential, it is compositionally closed, an apparently self-supporting system of visual interactions, and it gives the impression of functioning as a fact, a dense and persuasive *copy* of reality.

So Tony Maine shows us what's going on: men working on the line, men hanging out on the weekend, passing time in the local coffeehouse, playing cards, trading news from home, visiting with the Yemeni owner of the neighborhood grocery, and, in the spare shared privacy of their apartment, praying. Shown, implicitly: an attempt to maintain the fragile balance of one's identity while accommodating oneself, however superficially, to the exigencies of survival in an alien, indifferent, and potentially seductive environment. It's important, too, that Tony Maine shows us the men at work, for even though it's work done by all kinds of other people also, black, yellow, white, and brown, the images fill out the matrix and push home the actuality of the grind. Tank pit, welding station, spray booth are all real, day after draining day, and dangerous, demanding constant attention: one slip and the conveyor takes away a finger or something else. The line can't stop. The assembly plant is a machine for bringing together parts and turning out cars; and if your concentration flags or your coordination falters or you simply move in the wrong way at the wrong time, chances are you're going to get hurt, for the line keeps moving. The residue of paint builds up like a crust on your skin, seeps into your pores, cakes your hair, your eyebrows, dries the lining of your nostrils — even with a respirator — and coats your teeth; a car every thirty-five seconds every working day of the year; and if the market slumps, if the season lags, during austerity cutbacks, slowdowns, and strikes, the Yemeni migrant is low on the ladder of privilege and the first one off. But even so he has to meet his rent, eat, clothe himself, and send home what he can. And while here, in or out, he must make something of being alive in this strange land.

Yet Tony Maine gives us more than a one-dimensional polemic, for, deepening what might be called the sense of the place that begins to emerge in his imagery of the neighborhood, Maine's color work makes another kind of statement: the visual surprise

139. Steel foundry, Coldwater, Michigan. *Tony Maine.*

of a Yemeni mother shyly veiling her face from the camera as, like countless other mothers in countless other urban American neighborhoods, she walks her small son down the street to school; a teenaged boy, dressed in an amazingly mixed combination of Middle Eastern and Western clothing, poses quizzically against the rich springtime green of a neighborhood lot; or, interrupting her play for a very serious moment, a little girl composes herself with undiluted charm. These are images whose lyricism and understated ambiguity bespeak an optimism that transcends, without contradicting, his more rigorous imagery of the work place.

As almost everyone knows, color in photography contributes another system of nuances to one's visual vocabulary, affecting our perception of a place or our interpretation of an event. And it's his use of color that makes Jonathan Friedlander's factories as intriguingly ambiguous as Maine's neighborhoods, for these huge, dominating structures, so commonly associated with drudgery and so connotative of oppression, are also presented as monumentally arresting sculpture, carefully integrated into a tightly composed landscape. Drawing on a muted and often richly dark photographic palette, Friedlander's industrial imagery moves between the more alienated world of Antonioni's *Red Desert* and, in such images as his *View*

of South Dearborn, for instance, the delicate subtlety of a Dutch landscape.

It is almost a commonplace that the mainstream of photographic tradition, especially since the 1930s, has been to present such industrial structures as monumental at least, implicitly dominating and tacitly oppressive — as an overwhelming presence in the landscape. Friedlander's factories *are* a presence. They dwarf their surroundings. But scale here is not all; for his are among the most artfully composed photographs in the collection and, tempered by his articulation of color, his imagery slips over into the tradition of the pastoral landscape. True, there are no shepherds piping bucolic ditties in the vacant lots of Dearborn, but, as his photographs of children should suggest, there's the irrepressible tug of a romantic's vision here — the desire for a harmonic integration that, of course, blurs and complicates the easy and more usual categories of presentation.

Neighborhoods are the subject of much of the imagery of Shalom Staub, a folklorist who concentrates here on the ethnic restaurants of the Yemeni community in New York. Focusing on the look of the place, Staub records that mix of traditional and metropolitan styles that becomes, at street level, the architectural clash and clutter so typical of emigrant neighborhoods. At its best, this is what "atmosphere" and "community" are all about; and, at his best, Staub gives us a Brooklyn sidewalk transformed into a Yemeni bazaar and, of course, another apparently endless variation on that manner of making a living that has sustained so many entrepreneurial emigrants throughout the history of metropolitan America.

In Buffalo the Yemeni emigrant's desire to make, indeed, a good and substantially comfortable life has resulted in the development of a genuine community. Families are established, children attend school, and, albeit tentatively, small businesses are purchased and the Yemenis, like so many others before them, settle into the often reluctant and always difficult process of assimilation. Thus, in a number of ways, the photographs of Milton Rogovin speak both to the images of Nikki Keddie and Jon Swanson and to the Yemeni snapshots, for his is essentially an imagery of a people at home. The important thing here is that "home" is now Buffalo, New York, and Rogovin has made one quietly understated photograph in which the bleak sky, bare trees, and the block-long mounds of newly cleared snow remind us that the dreary file of frugally functional dwellings marching stolidly left and right down the street to infinity represents a new world indeed. It's clearly a working-class neighborhood and, seen from the street, it could be almost anywhere in the rust belt of smokestack America. But each household presents the photographer, once inside, with a complex and uniquely contradictory synthesis of the exigencies of cultural accommodation. Because similar as they are—and they are similar in many ways—each household inevitably expresses its individual version of the conflicting pressures with which it contends: the tenacity of religion, Arab music, menus and family mores, traditional modes of dress and the decorative iconography of one's roots, all in tension with the ever-present seductions of enveloping urban America. So, posed with what seems sometimes to be an impenetrable decorum, Rogovin's portraits emerge a densely expressive mix of influences, crosscurrents, and accommodations: school kids dressed in a thoroughly occidental mishmash of bargain basement styles, but put together in an irrepressibly Yemeni assemblage of colors, textures, and patterns; meals prepared with a veritable phalanx of contemporary appliances, but served and eaten in the traditional manner; and the family, still a Mozarabic nucleus, gathered together as for a snapshot portrait, the subtleties of their grouping a visual elaboration of Yemeni propriety.

Three thousand miles away on the other side of the continent, Ron Kelley photographed Yemeni migratory laborers in the Delano area of California's San Joaquin Valley. Remarkable for its cohesiveness, Kelley's visual range is especially rich and informative for, having lived with the workers and by traveling from camp to camp, following the seasons, Kelley was able to make images that represent both daily life and the agricultural cycle of the worker's year. This imagery may be seen to fall into three loosely overlapping groups: informal portraits of single individuals and occasional groups of two or three men together; men working in the fields, singly or more generally, in small groups; and men at leisure either in camp or at places of recreation in town—usually Delano or a neighboring area. Composed impeccably, with an eye for incisive juxtaposition and contrast, Kelley's photographs are both objective description and commentary. In this sense, the economy of his imagery is syntactic, excluding irrelevant detail, compressing essential information, bearing down as Riis would have it, to make a point: the stuff of irony, of tension, humor, and humane pathos. And, while he seems, to my mind, to be absolutely true to the integrity of the Yemeni experience, in this respect his photographs are as much about the psychological reality of that experience as its time and place: a single man posed against a stark blank sky, his coat pulled up above his head like a protective hood, stares intensely at the camera; another, sitting impassively in a sparsely furnished workers' barracks, stares across the room into a TV set; and a third, alone in a doorway, sunlight and shadow dividing his face, stares out as if shocked or stunned; men sleeping, pacing, passing time, reading the Koran, or, in their spare moments, praying—in one image, before an almost spectral light and on a carpeted floor carefully delineated to indicate the proper borders of a prayer rug. Men trying to hold on to their way of life and the fabric of their identity. Yet there are ironies Kelley cannot ignore. On a city street, framed by towering date palms, a Yemeni immigrant of twenty-two or -three turns skeptically to examine a middle-aged American Shriner got up theatrically in the Muslim costume of his fraternity, while behind them local Arabs-on-parade prepare to strut their ceremonial stuff. In another image a migrant poses in a T-shirt on whose front appears the motto: "Thank God I'm a Country Boy from Porterville, California."

Time and place are important, of course, for the scene is the San Joaquin Valley: one of the largest, richest agricultural valleys in the world, where, over three hundred years ago, the first large-scale production farms were established by Spanish missionaries in order to provide a continuing flow of food for the attenuating line of military advance. Those farms,

140. Family portrait, Lackawanna, New York.
Milton Rogovin.

too, were worked by disenfranchised labor, slaves herded up in chains from Sonora or dragged from the surrounding hills. The discovery of gold accelerated the awareness that this, indeed, was promising real estate. California was forcibly annexed to the union and, by the treaty of Guadalupe Hidalgo, hundreds of thousands of acres of range and agricultural land were summarily transferred, thereafter to be worked by foreign and native labor, first Mexican, then Chinese, Dust Bowl whites in the 1930s, Japanese, and more recently Filipinos. It's the San Joaquin Valley of Carey McWilliams and John Steinbeck and Dorothea Lange, of Cesar Chavez; of the Chinese exclusionary laws and Okie persecutions; of Filipino antimiscegenation legislation; of anyone whose race or class or economy is enunciated in the language of servitude. It is also the San Joaquin Valley of the Harris Ranch, Rio Bravo, Chateau Fresno, and, those most ubiquitous of landlords, the brothers Giannini. The Valley is one of the major oil centers of the United States and, increasingly, the location for the corporate offices of the service and satellite industries of agribusiness, land development, transportation, and information processing. It is one of the fastest-growing population centers in the nation and it is developing a managerial middle-class whose shops and malls and restaurants and manicured tract homes are daily layering the veneer of civility and

well-mannered and manured presentability over the more existentially raw continuum of labor from which this wealth derives.

The migrant comes to the San Joaquin Valley to work on farms that can only be profitable if they are organized as efficiently and impersonally as the assembly lines of Detroit and Freemont. Like his brethren in the northeastern factory, the migrant becomes little more than a cipher in a process, isolated beyond the fringe of an utterly oblivious community, separated by the gulf of language and culture, and lonely. He is a sojourner, and the extremity of his condition underlines our own.

But for all of that, it should be remembered, especially in a work such as this, the whole is often far greater than the sum of its parts, for the peculiar power of photographic imagery lies to a very large extent in the cumulative import of what might be called its connotative domain: how, perhaps, an image *feels* and what *that* adds up to. Wenner's irony, Rogovin's dignity, Maine's street-smart humanity — these are communicated not by the denotative or reproductive accuracy of the image, but by its effective content, that peculiar mix of elements — cultural, philosophical, moral — that gives significance to meaning. In this regard, photographic reproductions are almost always more than merely empirical, because representation is almost inevitably value-

141. Winter pruning, Delano vineyards, California. *Ron Kelley.*

laden, heavy with the weight of tradition, convention, association, and suggestion.

Among the photographs he made in the San Joaquin Valley, Ron Kelley has one that I like to use in my classes. It was shot in the vineyards north of Delano early one foggy fall morning down a long channel between the vines. In the misty distance, maybe thirty yards down the row, is the small gray silhouette of a Yemeni fieldworker. He's moving down the row with a pair of long-handled lopping shears, too far away for us to see clearly, and he's pruning the vines. Between us the earth is littered with fallen canes, for the vines are to be cut back to three or four primary branches so that in the spring, with the sun's warmth and the rains, after a winter of root growth and storage, the vine will burst into fruition.

So I show this photograph to my students, asking if that's what it's about, if they agree that this is indeed an accurate representation of that crucial step in the vinicultural process, and, not surprisingly, their answer is almost always no; they tell me that it's really something else: that with its lopped limbs and twisted writhing shapes, black in that eerie morning gray, this is an image of crucifixion, and I ask myself, given the diversity of this collection, what do you know when you know that?

About the Contributors

Mehdi Bozorgmehr is a doctoral candidate in sociology at the University of California, Los Angeles. His main interests are immigration and ethnicity, with an emphasis on Middle Easterners in the United States. With Georges Sabagh, he has co-authored articles on the characteristics and adaptation of Iranians in Los Angeles. Sabagh and Bozorgmehr are principal investigator and project director, respectively, of a study of Iranians in Los Angeles funded by the National Science Foundation.

John Brumfield serves on the faculty of the Art Center College of Design in Pasadena, California. He is the recipient of NEA grants for photography and writing and the author of numerous articles on social signification and visual meaning in photography and the arts, several of which have been translated into Spanish, French, German, and Japanese. Brumfield's photographic works have been widely reproduced and are in the permanent collections of various museums, including the Museum of Modern Art in New York, the San Francisco Museum of Modern Art, and the Los Angeles County Museum of Art.

Jonathan Friedlander directs the outreach program for the G. E. von Grunebaum Center for Near Eastern Studies and is associated with the Office of International Studies and Overseas Programs at UCLA, where he coordinates university-based projects which promote professional training, media development, and public education. In addition to his research on Yemeni workers and the Iranian exilic experience, he is the writer-producer of a documentary on Arab immigration. Friedlander's academic interests encompass social history, popular culture, and the visual realm — the subject of his doctoral studies at the University of California, Los Angeles.

Nikki Keddie, professor of history at UCLA, has exhibited her photographs in Paris, Los Angeles, and Seattle. A past president of the Middle East Studies Association of North America, Keddie has authored many books and articles on the Middle East and the Islamic world, most recently *Roots of Revolution: An Interpretive History of Modern Iran* and, as co-editor, *Shi^cism and Social Protest*, both published by Yale University Press.

Ron Kelley is a photographer and writer residing in Santa Monica, California. He holds a B.A. degree in anthropology from Michigan State University and an M.F.A. in photography from UCLA. Kelley's interests span a wide range of issues relating to socialization, self-expression and public identity, mass media, and personal/cultural meaning as transmitted in photographs. He is the principal photographer of the on-going studies of the Yemeni and Iranian emigrant experiences and is a contributor to the *Los Angeles Weekly*.

Tony Maine is best known for his striking classical style, avant-garde perspective and incisive visual statements which combine balanced content with compositional experimentation. His diverse portfolio ranges from ritualistic tribal funerary ceremonies in the Philippines to the powerful images of Yemeni autoworkers and their families in Detroit. Maine's principal photographic work, focusing on the habits and life-styles of Americans, has been the subject of exhibitions and publications.

Sheila Pinkel is on the faculty of Pomona College in Claremont, California, and is chairperson of the photography program. She has exhibited widely throughout the United States and is the recipient of two NEA individual artist grants in 1979 and 1982 and a Sloan Foundation Grant in 1987 for development of an interdisciplinary course in the humanities, sciences, and photography. Currently, she is an international editor of *Leonardo*, a quarterly magazine dedicated to the arts, sciences, and technology, and a national board member of the Society for Photographic Education.

Milton Rogovin, for the past thirty years, has chronicled life in Appalachia, urban industrial America (including a study of Yemeni steelworkers in his native Buffalo), and in the communities of miners in France, Scotland, Spain, Germany, and China. These and other photographs from travels to Cuba and Chile are in the permanent collections of the Metropolitan Museum of Art and the Museum of Modern Art in New York, the Philadelphia Museum of Art, the Museum of Fine Arts (Houston), George Eastman House, Library of Congress, Bibliothèque Nationale (Paris), Fotograkiska Museet (Stockholm), and the Preus Fotomuseum in Norway. In 1983 he received the coveted W. Eugene Smith International Award for outstanding humanitarian and artistic contributions to the field of photography. His most recent publication is titled *Milton Rogovin: The Forgotten Ones*, published jointly by the Albright-Knox Art Gallery and the University of Washington Press.

Georges Sabagh is professor of sociology and director of the G. E. von Grunebaum Center for Near Eastern Studies at the University of California, Los Angeles. He has published numerous scholarly articles on the demography and sociology of the Middle East, fertility of Mexican Americans, and residential mobility in the United States. Sabagh's current research focuses on Iranians in Los Angeles, demographic and socioeconomic characteristics of Middle Easterners in the United States, and labor migration in the Arab world.

Shalom Staub conducted fieldwork among New York Yemeni workers from 1980 to 1981 prior to his completing a Ph.D. degree in folklore/folklife at the University of Pennsylvania. His doctoral work will be published as *Workers and Traditions: Negotiated Ethnic Boundaries among Yemenis in New York City* by the Balch Institute. Articles based on this research appear in *New York Folklore* and in *Between Two Worlds: Essays on the Ethnography of American Jewry*, Jack Kugelmass, editor (Cornell University Press, forthcoming). Staub currently serves as executive director of the Pennsylvania Heritage Affairs Commission, a state agency dealing with cultural conservation and ethnic awareness issues.

Thomas B. Stevenson received a Ph.D. degree in anthropology from Wayne State University. His experience in Yemen includes two research projects in the highland town of ʿAmran: in 1978–79, an 18-month study of changing patterns of social organization conducted under a grant from the Social Science Research Council and the American Council of Learned Societies and, in 1986–87, a 6-month investigation of the impact of factory employment on social structure and migration supported by a Fulbright Islamic Civilizations grant. He is the author of *Social Change in a Yemeni Highlands Town* (University of Utah Press, 1985). Dr. Stevenson is an associate of the Middle East Studies Program at Ohio State University and teaches throughout central Ohio.

Jon Swanson received his Ph.D. degree in anthropology from Wayne State University. He lived for five years in the Yemen Arab Republic and a total of ten years in the Arab Muslim community of Dearborn, Michigan. Dr. Swanson has written extensively on the subject of Yemeni migration, rural economy, and society. He is currently at the School of Social Work, the University of Michigan, Ann Arbor.

Manfred Wenner received his doctorate from Johns Hopkins University in 1965. He has taught at the Universities of Washington, California, and Wisconsin, at Salzburg College, and is presently in the Political Science Department at Northern Illinois University. A native of Switzerland, he has published numerous articles dealing with Yemeni history, politics, economics, and culture. Wenner is the author of *Modern Yemen* (Johns Hopkins University Press, 1967), and *North Yemen* (Westview Press, forthcoming).